Postcolonial Agency

Plateaus – New Directions in Deleuze Studies

'It's not a matter of bringing all sorts of things together under a single concept but rather of relating each concept to variables that explain its mutations.'
Gilles Deleuze, *Negotiations*

Series Editors

Ian Buchanan, Cardiff University
Claire Colebrook, Penn State University

Editorial Advisory Board

Keith Ansell Pearson
Ronald Bogue
Constantin V. Boundas
Rosi Braidotti
Eugene Holland
Gregg Lambert
Dorothea Olkowski
Paul Patton
Daniel Smith
James Williams

Titles available in the series

Dorothea Olkowski, *The Universal (In the Realm of the Sensible): Beyond Continental Philosophy*
Christian Kerslake, *Immanence and the Vertigo of Philosophy: From Kant to Deleuze*
Simone Bignall, *Postcolonial Agency: Critique and Constructivism*
Jean-Clet Martin, *Variations: The Philosophy of Gilles Deleuze* (translated by Constantin V. Boundas and Susan Dyrkton)

Forthcoming Titles in the Series

Miguel de Beistegui, *Immanence – Deleuze and Philosophy*
Jean-Jacques Lecercle, *Badiou and Deleuze Read Literature*

Visit the Plateaus website at www.euppublishing.com/series/plat

POSTCOLONIAL AGENCY

CRITIQUE AND CONSTRUCTIVISM

Simone Bignall

EDINBURGH UNIVERSITY PRESS

For Katija, and in memory of Jim, Doris, Pat and Norm

© Simone Bignall, 2010, 2011

First published in hardback in 2010 by Edinburgh University Press

Edinburgh University Press Ltd
22 George Square, Edinburgh

www.euppublishing.com

Typeset in Sabon
by Servis Filmsetting Ltd, Stockport, Cheshire

A CIP record for this book is available from the British Library

ISBN 978 0 7486 3943 4 (hardback)
ISBN 978 0 7486 4383 7 (paperback)

The right of Simone Bignall
to be identified as author of this work
has been asserted in accordance with
the Copyright, Designs and Patents Act 1988.

Contents

Acknowledgements	vi
Introduction	1
I *Critique*	
Chapter 1 The Problem of the Negative	29
Chapter 2 Postcolonial Appropriations	60
Chapter 3 The Problem of the Actual	100
II *Constructivism*	
Chapter 4 Power/Desire	131
Chapter 5 Subjectivity	155
Chapter 6 What is 'Postcolonial'?	192
Conclusion: Postcolonial Agency	231
Bibliography	238
Index	253

Acknowledgements

Many people have assisted me in the production of this work, and to each I extend my gratitude. In particular I thank Moira Gatens, who gave wonderful support, encouragement and criticism on the whole draft at various stages of production. I am extremely grateful for her attempts to save me from my worst naiveties and for sustaining me with her sense of humour and her timely help. Paul Patton, Diana Coole and Leela Gandhi also gave invaluable advice on the manuscript in its entirety, and while I have no doubt that many weaknesses remain, I hope that I have accommodated their sternest criticisms. In any case, their advice has immeasurably improved the work, and for this I thank them.

I have greatly benefited from my long associations with Paul Patton and with Duncan Ivison, both dating from a very early time in the writing process when I took courses of study under their respective instruction. I appreciate their comments on parts of the work written early on, and their assistance in helping me arrive at useful ways of conceptualising the material. Kay Schaffer also gave early advice on how to approach postcolonial theory as a problem, and Carol Bacchi taught me how to 'think the problem' in the first place. I am most grateful to Victor Wilson for taking the time to talk with me about 'listening respect', and the Ngarrindjeri community from whom I have learnt so much about micropolitical practice. I also owe thanks to Mark Galliford, Anna Hickey-Moody, Peta Malins and other anonymous readers who offered collaboration, helpful criticism and input on the sections of chapters submitted for publication in various journals and books along the way. With respect to these, I gratefully acknowledge the permission given to include material drawn from prior publications. Chapters 1, 2 and 3 develop aspects of the work previously appearing in 'Indigenous Peoples and a Deleuzian Theory of Practice' in A. Hickey-Moody and P. Malins (eds), *Deleuzian Encounters: Studies in Contemporary Social Issues*, Sydney: Palgrave MacMillan, 2007: 197–212. An expanded version of Chapter 4 appears as 'Postcolonial Agency and Poststructuralist

Acknowledgements

Thought: Deleuze and Foucault on Desire and Power', *Angelaki* 13(1), 2008: 127–49. The first section of Chapter 5 initially appeared as 'A Superior Empiricism: The Subject and Experimentation', *Pli* 18, 2007: 204–21, while the last sections of Chapter 5 and the third section of Chapter 6 contain material also considered in 'Affect and Assemblage: Ethics beyond Enjoyment', in S. Bignall and P. Patton (eds), *Deleuze and the Postcolonial*, Edinburgh: Edinburgh University Press, 2010: 78–102. Chapter 6 develops ideas that were first presented in an article co-authored with Mark Galliford: 'Reconciling Replicas: The Second Coming of the *Duyfken*', *Cultural Studies Review* 9(2), 2003: 37–68. The benefit of an Australian Postgraduate Award gave invaluable financial support in the crucial early stages of writing. I was finally privileged to welcome the assistance given by Máiréad McElligott, Carol MacDonald, Claire Colebrook, Nicola Wood, Eliza Wright, Ian Buchanan and others at EUP.

I acknowledge, with love and thanks, the supportive roles played by my friends and family. I am particularly thankful for early talks with Mike Pulsford and Sarah Fairhead, and the support given by my parents Kathy and Robert. Special thanks are also owing to Maxine Daly and Stan Woods, for helping in many ways. Finally, I am grateful for my most joyful relationships: I give thanks to Greg Dayman for sustaining me with love, faith and encouragement; to Lydia and Oliver; and to Katija, who inspires me and makes me proud. This work is dedicated to her. My hope is that she will inherit, and create with others, a society that strives to develop its capacity for experiencing joy.

Introduction

Ours is a birth-time and a period of transition to a new era. (Hegel 1977: ¶11)

Twilight of the Idols – in plain words: the old truth is coming to an end. (Nietzsche 1992: 86)

Critiques of colonialism and of associated forms of imperialism – territorial, cultural, epistemological and so forth – are well established and provide ongoing fuel for the deconstructive task of decolonisation. However, certainly in the former imperial centres, conceptual tools for imagining modes of constructive agency suited to the reconstruction of post-imperial forms of society remain woefully underdeveloped. For example, in their collaborative work on *Empire*, Antonio Negri and Michael Hardt argue that 'the multitude' must 'confront directly and with an adequate consciousness the central repressive operations of Empire. It is a matter of recognising and engaging the imperial initiatives and not allowing them continually to re-establish order.' However, when they ask what 'specific and concrete practices will animate this political project?' they admit: 'We cannot say at this point' (Hardt and Negri 2000: 399–400). Without an alternative conceptualisation of agency and ethical practices of social construction, attempts to transform cultures infused with the legacy of colonialism often remain in hiatus, structured by a form of agency that has been complicit with practices of Empire, and which postcolonial society must surely reject.

In later work, Hardt and Negri (2004) return to the crucial problem of the practical political organisation of the 'multitude' in resistance to Empire. However, in truth, their notions of Empire and resistance signify something quite different from the familiar political practices of European imperialism and national processes of decolonisation, which have indelibly shaped the modern world. For them, Empire describes a new form of global social control, which does not function primarily through binary class hierarchies prompting dialectical struggle, nor through a sovereign imposition of power, but is rather more diffuse, pervasive, subtle, sinister and hegemonic. Accordingly, they also reject the notion of the postcolonial, especially as it is described in the work of Homi Bhabha, seeing this as critical of, yet caught up in, an old model of power defined by binary opposition and sovereign domination, which the contemporary political world has largely outgrown (Hardt and Negri 2000: 143–5).

While it is clear that power now takes a different form in the new global Empire and is increasingly diffuse and slippery, necessitating new forms of resistance and political organisation, I argue here that it is important to create and maintain a place for the postcolonial in national practices of political and cultural engagement. By 'postcolonial' I do not intend to convey a temporal distance we already inhabit, historically 'after-colonisation', as if the colonial period is something we have left behind, now subsumed by new political forms, as Hardt and Negri seem to suggest. Rather, I see the postcolonial as usefully describing a qualitative difference, yet to come, in practices defining social construction, self-concept and attitudes of being, relating and belonging. While power most certainly takes new forms today, we also continue to act within, against and according to a lasting legacy of colonial sociality. Globally, the continuing 'internal colonisation' of indigenous peoples upon their own territories attests to this legacy. In order to address adequately and transform the global historical legacy of European imperialism, we require a political concept of the postcolonial. This should make conscientious use of a power to disrupt the diverse effects of historical colonisation, through envisaging and instituting alternative postcolonial forms of society and enabling the careful practice of non-imperial modes of action and relation. In certain respects this concept of the postcolonial as the introduction of a social tendency and a future effect, within the concrete conditions of the present, echoes aspects of Negri and Hardt's conception of the multitude as a force for inventing that which is 'not yet' (2004: esp.220–2). It may also be the case that a concept of postcolonial practice could significantly assist in the creation of new assemblages of 'the multitude', actively involved in the resistance to contemporary forms of globalisation and Empire. However, in this work, I consider the postcolonial in relation to the continuing effects of colonisation – and particularly in relation to contemporary efforts towards reconciliation between indigenous and non-indigenous peoples in Western post-colonial nations – rather than in the context of the emerging political forms of global Empire.

Guiding this work is a conviction that ontology shapes agency,

Introduction

while practice provokes thought. That is, understandings about the nature of selfhood and worldly reality inflect theories of action and capacity and in turn, these theories have corresponding effects upon the material and communal practices they inform. Recursively, problems or difficulties associated with the performance of a practice provoke new concepts and understandings about the practice in question, the problems and goals that shape it, and the forms of agency, selfhood and co-operative enterprise that might more successfully underwrite its performance. In this case, the provocative practice motivating my thought is the global phenomenon of postcolonisation in formerly colonised societies, which occurs in piecemeal and locally distinct ways through various processes of reconciliation between indigenous and non-indigenous communities. Throughout this work, the unhyphenated term 'postcolonial' is used to convey a sense distinct from the term 'post-colonial', which at times problematically suggests premature claims to an already lived temporal and moral distance from the process of colonisation, but usually and more carefully indicates the need for ongoing critical attention to the continuing legacy of colonisation in national life. While acknowledging the need to retain a critically engaged notion of 'post-colonialism', I will generally use the term 'postcolonial' in a more future-oriented and constructive sense, to indicate a qualitative historical difference *yet to come* in the relationships and material conditions that constitute the various instantiations of the postcolony, and particularly in relationships between indigenous and non-indigenous peoples. Here, 'postcolonisation' implies a critique and rejection of colonial forms of sociality; it also, however, gestures beyond critique and moves towards constructivism in so far as it properly emphasises a positive task barely begun: the conceptual creation of 'a new horizon' describing new forms of non-imperial mutuality, and thus genuinely *post*colonial society (cf. Bhabha 1994: 1; Hall 1996; Attwood 2000). The ultimate aim of this project is to suggest some positive content for this notion of the postcolonial.

Describing a movement towards genuinely postcolonial forms of society, postcolonisation should introduce a discontinuity or a difference into colonial histories. This historical discontinuity is required if post-colonial societies are to 'exit' from habitually imperial assumptions and practices of relation, and take the opportunity to reconstruct modes of social existence upon an alternative, non-imperial political and ethical basis. The process of postcolonisation therefore requires not only an appropriate philosophy of transformation encompassing a general theory of historical discontinuity, such as that developed by Michel Foucault, but also a particular concept of transformative agency that enables one consciously to enact a postcolonial ethic of relation to others, and to engage a collaborative politics of material transformation in order to construct postcolonial institutions and communities of practice with others.

Just as the experience of colonisation was divergent for colonisers and the colonised, it is appropriate that contemporary responses to histories of colonisation also differ across the colonial divide. Formerly colonising cultures must grapple with the legacy and responsibility associated with the repugnant history of their colonial domination of others; formerly colonised peoples must seek to reaffirm their identities, communities and cultures and so reconstruct their broken societies. Ideally, national processes of postcolonisation witness both responses occurring simultaneously as diverse peoples thrown together by colonisation struggle to find friendly ways to co-exist. Because postcolonial theory most commonly addresses the revitalisation and recognition of the agency of colonised peoples through their acts of resistance and decolonisation, it often reinforces a colonised/colonising dichotomy, which positions the colonised class as the active or resisting force chiefly responsible for postcolonisation and neglects to attribute an equal responsibility and transformative capacity to formerly colonising subjects. This work seeks to balance this tendency. It is primarily addressed to non-indigenous, Western readers like myself, who have inherited the legacy of our colonis*ing* settler forebears and who now ought to help transform this historical injustice by acknowledging and redressing the continuing privileges that we have accrued and institutionalised through colonial history and which still significantly define many facets of contemporary social life. Proper redress involves not only making reparation for past injustice and instituting formal political equality in the present, but also the effort to begin a new ethos of intercultural relationship.

Globally, relations between indigenous and non-indigenous peoples remain fraught with hurt, resentment, suspicion and guilt, tempered by relatively rare moments of intercultural harmony and mutual affirmation. Marked by formally entrenched inequalities, cultural disagreement and frustrated acts of reconciliation, postcolonial nations demonstrate a prevailing tendency towards the mutual disaffection of uneasily co-existing indigenous and non-indigenous societies (see Altman and Hinkson 2007). Intercultural engagements are commonly stunted, curtailed and paralysed by

Introduction

conflicting imaginaries, representations and understandings, extending the mutual apprehension and incomprehension begun with colonisation (see Gatens 2008). While to some extent this situation might be blamed upon the reluctance of settler classes to forfeit the privileges they have accrued though colonisation and their associated failure to recognise the calls by indigenous people for just treatment, fair belonging and social inclusion, I believe this is not the full story behind the persistent faltering of national processes of postcolonisation. Indeed, the tendency towards mutual disaffection in many cases co-exists with general public support for a better relationship between indigenous and non-indigenous peoples, which continuously and insistently resurfaces throughout history in various guises. Particular events in national histories, such as the signing of treaties, the proclamation of 'sorry days', or the recognition of native title, repeatedly attest to moments of public acknowledgement that until this historic problem of unhappy relationship is resolved, all within the postcolony will be diminished, for it is a problem of injustice that is congenital and inhabits the deepest heart of nations, sullying vital aspects of national self-concept and international poise. In this work, I suggest that existing models of transformation embedded within Western postcolonial theory have given inadequate support for peoples actively engaged in the effort of postcolonisation. If ontology shapes agency, we might accordingly and fruitfully ask: what view of selfhood, of agency, lies at the heart of the transformative theories we currently draw upon to bring about just social change? And how might we usefully change these self-concepts, in order better to perform new postcolonial practices of society?

Over recent decades the former question has also provided a point of departure for the latest versions of the debate between liberals and communitarians (Rawls 1971; Sandel 1984; Taylor 1985a, 1989; see Frazer and Lacey 1993). On the one hand, a tradition extending from Kant to Rawls asserts a theory of fair justice framed by the notion that a rational and deliberative subject exists prior to and independent of experience. According to liberalism, guiding principles of justice *must* be developed from a transcendental *a priori* position, unencumbered and untainted by particular selfish desires, which arise from embodied experience and concrete situation. On the other hand, communitarian thinkers draw from a tradition of Hegelian thought to insist that this liberal ontology of the atomist self and its procedural politics give a false and impossible abstraction of selfhood, which some also point out is insensitive to the group identities and affiliations that call for recognition in postcolonial constituencies (I.M. Young 1990).[1] Communitarians argue that subjectivity, or being, is in fact always already intrinsically bound up with our connections to others; fair justice requires us to acknowledge this embeddedness and our determination by others within the communities of cultural practice that give our lives meaning. Accordingly, communitarian philosophy counters the ontological presumption of the *a priori* liberal subject, by insisting that subjects are produced through their social situations and experiences, in a process of subjective becoming mediated by their social others. Not wanting to continue this debate here, I will simply affirm my agreement with communitarian thinkers (and those liberals who have accommodated a communitarian perspective) that subjectivity is constructed in concrete social and cultural conditions. This, then, is the first ontological commitment I have made: to view the self as embedded and embodied, socially constructed and in significant respects constituted by cultural context. However, the dominance of Hegelian philosophy in communitarian thought has deflected critical attention away from the nature of the constructive process from which selves are understood to emerge. It is generally assumed by the participants in the liberal/communitarian debate that if a self does not already exist transcendent to social circumstance, then selfhood in fact comes into being more or less in the way Hegel first described in his *Phenomenology of Spirit*. Furthermore, the convergence between the production of the dialectical self and the progress of social history in the *Phenomenology* commits many contemporary constructivist philosophers to a dialectical view of historical process, and so also to dialectical theories of transformative action.

On this view, history represents a gradual unfolding of the rational organisation of society; social agency consists in the collective effort to describe and realise this rational end. Transformative action can be evaluated as progressive when it moves society towards an ideal state of perfect and rational consensus, reflected in social organisation. The ideal functions as a transcendent, final cause of social action, which draws history inexorably towards completion, and society towards agreement and unity. Hegel's marriage of ontology and history insists upon the incidental development of self and society towards final perfection or completion. Accordingly, elements of the social theory that draws from Hegelian thought connect a notion of social progress to ideas about the full expression of selfhood, affirming a certain convergence between subjective agency concerned with

Introduction

the development of being and collective agency directed towards the progress of society. On this view, subjective agency involves striving for the ultimate elimination of the conflictive divide between self and other, in pursuit of the mutual recognition that affirms each in being. As in the case of social progress, a predetermined, ideal state of wholeness or unity functions as a transcendent, final cause of subjective development.

According to this trans/formative process of self and society, difference or multiplicity has a critical function since it signifies where and how the ideal of perfect unity is failing. It describes a certain lack of coherence, which makes it the critical force of transformation; difference compels the processes of social progress and subject-formation, by negating the perfection of the present form. However, the desired final goal is realised only when the contesting or negating difference is itself fully negated, or else assimilated and internalised within an expanded unity. The ontological negativity of desire and difference motivates and underscores this process of transformation: history is compelled by the negativity of lack, need, absence or difference that signals disunity, and by the desire to 'negate the negative', by assimilating or internalising negativity within a greater and more representative unity. This ambiguous, and arguably imperial, attitude of desire aimed at ameliorating the ontological negativity of difference is problematic for postcolonial theories of transformation and transformative agency.

To a certain extent, critical theory, psychoanalysis and deconstructive poststructuralism have challenged the conventional concept of dialectical process by insisting upon the permanence of ontological negativity, such that the processes of subject-formation and history are seen to have no finite teleology. Thus, while Hegel's dialectic (and Marx's too) is propelled by a productive tension between conflicting classes, but is eventually resolved through negation and the ultimate elimination of conflicting differences with the reaching of a final harmonious unity or identity, most poststructuralist and critical theories of subjectivity and society retain a permanent, transforming role for difference in processes of ontological construction. Difference and desire are seen to reside at the heart of being, propelling the construction of subject and world ever onwards. However, while denying teleology, such perspectives remain committed to the underlying motivating force of the negative. That is, the process of ontological construction (the history of being, or the being of history) is still seen as a movement compelled by negativity and by the 'negation of the negative'. Historical action is still considered to be motivated by desire, which signals ontological lack; and it still projects satisfaction – though this is now understood to be impossible, a futile pursuit – in terms of the desire for the ideal elimination of difference and the resulting achievement of a stable and consistent self, reconciled with the material world. Satisfaction is impossible, either because the desired elimination of difference can be only temporarily enjoyed until desire moves on to a new object and the productive tension is renewed, or because the subject is irreducibly multiple and fragmented, and desire itself is not unified. For philosophies of this sort, difference and multiplicity thus signify the permanent incompleteness, the persistent lack of being, of the subject. However, as in dialectical thought, difference is the negativity that prompts desire and so causes the ontological *striving* for self-sufficiency, even though the permanence of the negative – the resilience of difference – means that the project of desire in subjectivity and material construction is always ill-fated, since the projected final unity is only ever illusory, and one can never reach the ideal fullness of replete being. As Diana Coole (2000) explains, because it is the ontological force of critique and transgression that propels the constant transformation and the improvement of the given material world, negativity is a core concept in critical and transformative political theories from Kantian liberalism and Hegelian communitarianism to most versions of critical Marxism and poststructuralism. In this work, while my discussion is relevant to the other philosophical perspectives that celebrate the generative force of negativity, my critical focus is mainly centred on dialectical philosophy as a privileged site of generative negativity and of the activity of negation that responds to this ontological condition. The seduction and persuasive hold of dialectical philosophy in Western political theory stems initially from the transformative potential of the ontological negativity it emphasises, and secondly because of the collective unity it idealises.

This is no doubt why, despite the ambiguous and arguably imperial attitude towards difference that results from the causal force of ontological negativity and the movement of desire it provokes, much postcolonial theory operates within the assumptions of this dominant mode of critical thought. Postcolonial transformation is usually understood to be the effect of a negating class action; responsibility for such transformation is perceived to rest with the negating class. The transformative action itself is successful to the extent that the negating class can assert the authority of its action by claiming

Introduction

a unity of expression through class identification (itself achieved through the suppression of differences internal to the class), and by demonstrating a broadly disruptive presence in the face of a spurious and exclusive national unity. Policies and practices of transformative action informed by this body of theory have often been constrained by these assumptions about difference and desire, identity, critique, negation and causation. For example, in post-colonial 'settler' nations including Australia, New Zealand, South Africa and Canada, policy towards reconciliation has been particularly constrained by discourses of disadvantaged identity and desire for national unity. These support the connections between indigeneity, difference, lack and negation, and so problematically reinforce the representations that supported the emergence of colonial power relations in the first place. My guiding question accordingly takes form: what qualities might describe a *postcolonial* transformative practice, one that does not perversely slip into a repetition of sameness, or a sly recuperation of the imperial concepts, practices and techniques it seeks to supplant?

I seek an answer by taking an alternative approach to history and rethinking the movement of postcolonial reconciliation, not as progressive unification, but as the collective enactment of a historical *dis*continuity, such as that theorised by Foucault (see 1984a, 1984b, 1972: 3–17). The ontological grounding for this view of history is found in the work of Gilles Deleuze, who takes part in a minor tradition of Western philosophy including Spinoza, Bergson and Nietzsche. Deleuze employs a wholly positive conceptualisation of ontological becoming, grounded in the concept of positive desiring-production and resulting in an alternative view of the self and a non-dialectical view of history. Since I agree with Charles Taylor (1985a, 1989), Michael Sandel (1984) and others that ontology shapes agency, I will argue that this alternative view of ontological desire, becoming and selfhood also corresponds to a different conceptualisation of transformative action, and in turn, to alternative theories about historical processes of social change. Here, history does not realise a given ideal order, which operates as a transcendent final cause. Rather, social organisation is the result of an open-ended process of actualisation that has an immanent cause: social forms emerge and transform as an effect of the shifting relations of power into which bodies enter. Social agency involves an effort to understand and organise one's relations, in ways that cause the actualisation of preferred forms of collective society, such as those that might be characterised as postcolonial. Contra Peter Hallward (2006), I will argue that Deleuze's philosophy supports both a critical and a constructive agency, which is materially engaged and has a creative, positive and ethical relation to difference. These qualities suggest how this philosophy of transformation can usefully inform practical critiques of colonialism and the reconstruction of postcolonial societies. In particular, the notion of agency carried within this tradition of philosophy describes a form of reflexive subjectivity that can be receptive to the kinds of possibilities and ethical responsibilities faced by agents in creating and sustaining multicultural, postcolonial societies. In this work, I argue that this quality of agency and of historical process, derived here from this alternative and wholly positive ontology and description of the becoming of being, is necessary for genuinely postcolonial practices of transformation.

On this view, there will be no culmination of history in a grand narrative or a final moment of national unity. Postcolonisation is an ongoing practice of social construction that requires the permanent cultivation of a postcolonial ethos of relation, which acknowledges and affirms difference, positively conceived. The process of social transformation is not drawn towards a climax that functions as its transcendent cause. Instead, it has an immanent causation. It is compelled from within, according to the actions of the participants who produce postcoloniality as an effect of their interrelationships. Postcolonisation takes place only to the extent that it is performed within a community's practices of relationship and protected by the constitutional and institutional forms of agreement that formalise these practices. The fundamental aim of this work is to explain this notion of the immanent causation of social transformation, with particular respect to global processes of postcolonial reconciliation, and with special attention to my home society: post-colonial Australia.

Several thinkers that I associate with a positive variant of poststructuralism because their philosophies do not rest upon a notion of generative negativity – Deleuze, Guattari and Foucault – have also thought about the immanent causation of history, and their collected works provide a point of departure for my argument. While the ontological basis for my argument is found in the philosophy of Deleuze and Guattari, the formal basis is found in Foucault's work on ethos. He explains how at its most general level, history – the formation and transformation of society – is caused by a human disposition to be sociable, to form relations of force or power. This somewhat unremarkable claim becomes interesting when Foucault highlights Kant's

Introduction

comments on Enlightenment and maturity, suggesting that sociability takes a historically particular form when individuals identify with a certain 'attitude', which he defines as

> a mode of relating to contemporary reality; a voluntary choice made by certain people; in the end a way of thinking and feeling; a way too of acting and behaving that at one and the same time marks a relation of belonging and presents itself as a task. A bit, no doubt, like what the Greeks called an *ethos*. (Foucault 1984a: 39)

When individuals identify with a particular attitude, they position themselves in readiness for a particular kind of social relation. The universal disposition to be sociable, along with the historically and culturally particular dispositions described by individuals' chosen attitudes towards others in their concrete social relationships, may be thought to exist as permanent, virtual, immanent causes of historical transformation. These causal dispositions are not overtly recognised or acknowledged as such in social discourse, but rather tend to exist as the unthought conditions of the emergence of historically particular epistemes and forms of sociability. However, Foucault points to Kant's discussion of the Enlightenment and maturity as a way of suggesting that historical events such as the Enlightenment, or in our case postcolonial reconciliation, are significant precisely because they offer a moment of transparency, in which individuals are able to access this virtual foundation of their actual social forms, and subsequently to subject their most profound and constituting attitudes to criticism and redefinition. Historical discontinuities signal epochal attitude shifts, marked by events such as reconciliation, in which societies are able to modify their structures of relationship according to novel modes of social disposition. Conscientious individual practices of new and alternative attitudes, broadly conceptualised in relation to ideas of preferred forms of community, compel an accompanying shift in the actual social forms and structures that materialise these virtual dispositions. According to Foucault, Kant describes the Enlightenment as an exemplary event of this sort, compelling widespread shifts in the self-conscious 'modification of the pre-existing relation linking will, authority and the use of reason' (Foucault 1984a: 35). In other words, historical discontinuities mark shifts in public modes of *agency*, which in this work is a term which will be used to describe the relation, through practice, of desire (will), power (authority) and subjectivity (use of reason).

Foucault's work on Kant and Enlightenment suggests the useful idea that a public shift in 'attitude' provokes a redefinition of agency in terms appropriate to the problem posed by the present society at the moment of critique. In our case, the problem globally posed by society is the legacy of colonisation. As a solution, reconciliation is at once a release, a responsibility and the actualisation of a disposition towards postcolonial sociability, which is brought about in local contexts through individual performances of an appropriate attitude or ethos of engagement. This attitude is materialised in a community of practice with others, producing collective actions, behaviours and modes of feeling, thought and belonging, which embody alternative ways of being in the world. The new postcolonial attitude and the new mode of agency it introduces may, with consistent effort of practice, eventually become entrenched in the institutional structures of a postcolonial society. If the first aim of this project is to explain the notion of the immanent causation of social transformation, my second aim in this work is to describe a mode of agency suited to a historical performance of postcolonisation. My final aim is to describe a postcolonial attitude of 'listening respect'.

Method of approach

I began with the guiding idea that ontology shapes agency. It will therefore be helpful to outline, in a general way, what I mean by this essentially contested term 'agency', and which of its aspects will remain beyond the scope of my concern. I will be using the term 'agency' primarily to refer to action that is both causal and purposefully directed, although never free from constraints. Agency differs from action, in that the latter 'is not essentially or originally conscious, that to make it so is an achievement, and this achievement transforms action [into agency]'(Taylor 1985b: 84).

Like Diana Coole (2005: 124), I maintain a certain 'ontological agnosticism regarding who or what exercises agency'. As will become clear in Chapters 3 and 5, this corresponds to my Spinozan/Deleuzian understanding of corporeality, which holds that a body is *any* form of meta-stable organisation, in which composing elements maintain an enduring consistency of relationship. In this sense, a body may be an individual or a collective; in fact on this view, *every* body is at one and the same time a singularity and a multiplicity. However, not all bodies are agents. I will argue that bodies must exercise three essential attributes in order to have agency: they must be *desiring* (the condition of causality), they must be *potent* (the condition of

Introduction

capacity), and they must be *reflexive* (the condition of directedness). Accordingly, agency refers to a bodily coincidence of desire/power/subjectivity. Since this triadic relationship might be expressed in various ways, according to the variable and context-specific nature of one's experience of desire, of power and of subjective being, I consider that agency is a flexible attribute of a body, which shifts and comes into play in different ways, according to the concrete specificity of actual situations, actual relations, actual desires and powers, and actual reflexive abilities. I will detail this theory of agency in Chapter 5.

An adequate philosophy of active social transformation requires an element of critical agency (aimed at the existing, problematic structure) and an element of constructive agency (aimed at producing a preferred structure, which does not yet actually exist). However, one's capacity for critique, for thinking about various desired outcomes, for deliberation, and for chosen action is never unconstrained. I consider that agents experience their subjectivity as embodied in particular ways and embedded in the particular cultural contexts in which they live. I also take the view that an agent's tools of criticism and evaluation are developed within a cultural context, and that the agent therefore cannot 'step outside' of culture to find a truly transcendent, uncontaminated ground from which to criticise his social structures and evaluate his desires. Even so, while discussions about agency often focus upon the relationship between an agent's free will and the determining structure, meaning or 'power' that shapes and limits this will, it is not my purpose to tease out this relationship or to carve out a position within this debate by giving a particular emphasis to either freedom or determinism. In Chapter 5 I will argue that there is always a capacity for critical and constructive agency, but that agency is always performed under constraints, within a determining structure. I will argue that agency involves a necessary attendance to, and negotiation of, the forces of desire and power that constitute the agent, but may simultaneously be partially constituted by the agent, through complex practices and expressions of subjectivity.

While this gives a loose defining form to the concept of agency, which will be added to in later chapters, in the discussion that ensues my primary intention is not to argue for the validity of this definition of agency as a coincidence of desire/power/subjectivity, nor to argue for the inalienable freedom or the fundamental determinism of the agent. In fact, beyond the basic description and position I have just given, my guiding question is not 'What is agency?' or 'When is agency possible?', but 'Which one? Which form of agency towards history-making, towards others, might enable postcolonial relations and social structures?' Furthermore, attending to this potential multiplicity and variation in modes of agency raises other qualitative questions about the constituting concepts of desire, power and subjectivity: *which* concept of 'desire' is useful for motivating and causing processes of postcolonisation? How can 'power' be adequately thought in relation to this notion of desire? Which notion of 'subjectivity' might enable practices of postcolonial sociability?

Concept creation

At its most general level, this work is intended as a contribution to global processes of reconciliation and a support for locally effected postcolonial practice. Central to the task of postcolonisation is the revision of ways of thinking about social cultures, identities and modes of intercultural relationship. There is a need to cultivate a critical awareness of prevailing modes of acting and relating, and a need to develop ways of evaluating the postcoloniality of social behaviours. We need to be able to decide when our actions contribute to the perpetuation of colonial modes of relation, and when they support postcolonial sociabilities. The first two chapters will show that the discourses of critical transformation that currently inform reconciliation, postcolonial theory and approaches to transformative resistance in general, are drawn from particular concepts of desire, power and subjectivity embedded in a concept of generative ontological negativity. I will argue that this generative negativity supports an imperial mode of agency, which finally perpetuates the sorts of social relations that postcolonialism seeks to disrupt. However, this book is not simply a critique of colonial forms and their legacy in contemporary practice. Indeed, in the second half of this work my focus is primarily on a constructive task, which is to provide a new concept of social transformation and the practical reconstruction of a postcolonial present. This *creates* a postcolonial concept of agency. As such, this work is firmly situated within 'the practice turn in theory',[2] and is an exercise in practical philosophy, in Deleuze and Guattari's (1994) precise sense of philosophy as a constructivist discipline involving the creation of concepts.

Their definition of a concept as an event of assemblage can assist in describing this endeavour. On their view, a concept is a point of coincidence of the components that make it up (1994: 23). In addition, a concept relates to neighbouring concepts, which inflect its consistency and its sense: 'Every concept relates back to other concepts, not only in its history, but in its becoming or its present connections. Every concept has components that may, in turn, be grasped as concepts' (1994: 19). For Deleuze and Guattari, then, the questions of philosophical method are: '"what to put in a concept?" and "what to put with it?" What concept should be put alongside a former concept, and what components should be put in each?' (1994: 90). I will present a concept of agency as an assemblage of the component concepts of desire, power and subjectivity. I will also argue that agency is modal: asking 'Which agency?' means asking 'Which concept of desire? Which concept of power? Which notion of the subject?' Whereas the component concepts of desire, power and subjectivity have usually been defined and assembled in ways that produce a concept of *imperial* or *colonising* agency, I will redefine these component concepts in a way that enables an assemblage of *postcolonial* agency. This redefinition of the component concepts, and their assemblage into an emergent concept of agency, will create the possibility of a further association with an entirely new concept of postcolonial practice. By the conclusion of this work, I hope to have drawn out the identity of this new understanding of 'postcolonial' that emerges with the assemblage of 'postcolonial agency'.

In describing philosophy as the creation of concepts, Deleuze and Guattari employ a particular image of thought. On their view, concepts are formed and transformed by a complex process of actualisation (1994: 35–61; Deleuze 1994: 168–222; see also Patton 1996b, 2010). A concept is an 'event', a becoming actual, which occurs when thought imposes a regular set of connections, or a consistency, upon previously unconnected ideas (Deleuze and Guattari 1994: 133). For example, a general concept of agency exists because its constituent elements of desire, power and subjectivity are associated in a regular relation. This consistency gives the concept 'agency' a recognisable identification. The imposition of actual conceptual form through repetition of association is an event, which thought brings about when it draws together certain virtual relations between elements and thereby creates the concept as an actual entity. According to Deleuze and Guattari, even when they exist as actual or established forms, concepts and their constituting components continue to share a set of virtual relations with other concepts and components, which ensure that they are always open to modification or alteration by being brought into alternative relations and compositions (Patton 1996b: 318). Concepts thereby always exist in a state of becoming. In the first instance, their becoming is described through their formative process: the association of fragments, their assemblage in formal relations, and their consolidation as consistent. However, concepts can also always be modified or recast by a new proximity to a different problem or a new neighbourhood of related concepts (Patton 1996b: 318). In our case, the old concept of agency is recast by its new proximity to the problem of post-colonialism.

A created concept might always also be subjected to a critical decomposition of its given form, back into constituent elements (Deleuze and Guattari 1994: 67–8). This alternative movement of 'counter-actualisation' or 'deterritorialisation' traces a path from the given form, back to the constituting conditions of its determination. This movement is critical because it frees the concept from the limits imposed by its actualised form by returning it to a virtual, and therefore indeterminate state, in which it is able to be re-assembled with alternative configurations: 'to the extent that the pure event is imprisoned forever in its actualisation, counter-actualisation liberates it, always for other times' (Deleuze 1990: 161). This work describes a movement between actual and virtual concepts of agency. The existing concept of agency is problematised in terms of its imperialism and counter-actualised into its constituting concepts of desire, power and subjectivity. These concepts are then redefined, before being recomposed or 'reterritorialised' as an alternative assemblage of *postcolonial* agency.

The conceptualisation of agency developed here corresponds with an underlying view of worldly transformation described by Deleuze (e.g. 1991b: 91–115, 1994: 185–222), which similarly envisions history as a movement between a virtual and an actual, as will be described in Chapter 3. History is seen as a process of bringing into being, or a making actual, of a virtual reality. The role of philosophy in this movement is to invent concepts to enable the exploration, through thought, of this virtual reality. This work is intended, therefore, as an intervention in an actual state of social relations, identified here as the problematic present in which indigenous peoples continue to be colonised upon their traditional territories by the cultural forms of non-indigenous political society. The transformative power of philosophy begins with its denial of the inevitability, or 'self evidence', of actual forms. The permanent existence of the virtual within the actual denies the self-evident authority of the actual, and opens up

Introduction

the possibility of thinking alternative, virtual modes of existence and actualising them in practice. By thinking through the virtual, philosophy opens up other possibilities for thinking about the organisation of society. This can help to bring about the actual performance of postcoloniality, which exists even now, as a virtual reality, or as a reality that is yet to be made actual.

In creating a concept of postcolonial agency, this work contributes to this effectuation in two ways. Creating a concept of *postcolonial* agency as a mode of practice or performance outlines a alternative and currently virtual mode of social existence. However, in creating a concept of postcolonial *agency*, I hope this work will help to effect the actualisation of this virtuality that is postcoloniality. The concept of agency is intended to provide a means of thinking how to make the virtual postcolonial, actual. In a real sense, then, this work is intended as a practical tool for postcolonisation. The concept of postcolonial agency 'is the contour, the configuration, the constellation of an event to come' (Deleuze and Guattari 1994: 32–3) and also, simultaneously, it is a configuration of a type of practical approach that will be necessary to make the event of postcoloniality come about.

Conceptual personae: constitution of the problem

According to Deleuze and Guattari, the creation of a locally organised collection of concepts – the development of a philosophy – involves the invention of particular philosophical agencies in the form of 'conceptual personae'. As the 'agents of enunciation' of a philosophy, the role of conceptual personae is to organise the assembly of concepts, to synthesise thought and make it articulate concepts as events (1994: 65). A conceptual persona constitutes a point of view, according to which concepts will be created, with specific intents and purposes in mind (1994: 75). Concepts are created in response to particular problems, which they intervene in and exist to solve: 'All concepts are connected to problems without which they would have no meaning and which can themselves only be isolated or understood as their solution emerges' (1994: 16). However, 'problems are not ready-made but must be constituted and invested in their proper symbolic fields' (Deleuze 1994: 158–9). The original role of the conceptual persona is to constitute a philosophical problem as such, thereby creating the conditions for the creation of a concept as solution (Deleuze 1994: 162; Deleuze and Guattari 1994: 73).

This work is 'enunciated' through the agency of an invented

postcolonial character. Thinking through this character, I imagine what it takes to exist in actual postcolonial relations with others, and which conceptual tools are required to help forge this mode of sociability. This character shares certain features with established postcolonial philosophers including Frantz Fanon, Gayatri Spivak, Homi Bhabha, Edward Said, Benita Parry and Aijaz Ahmad, and indeed draws from their work in various ways. I have also learned from, and share some particular concerns with, indigenous activists and social justice advocates including Mick Dodson, Irene Watson, Victor Wilson and Taiaiake Alfred. Non-indigenous activists, writers, philosophers and historians concerned with issues of colonisation and postcolonisation – including among many others Henry Reynolds, Robert Young, James Tully, Duncan Ivison, Kate Grenville and Paul Patton – have also influenced my understanding of the problems constituting the 'symbolic field' of postcolonial theory and practice. By selectively drawing from these areas of work, as well as from my own practical engagements with the process of postcolonisation in Australia, the conceptual persona I put to work here carves out a definitive position in critical response to the existing field of postcolonial theory and practice by constituting the field itself – its established problems and engagements – as problematic, in four main respects.

The first of these is the notion, pervasive within Western thought, that generative ontological negativity plays *the* sole causal role in the constructive processes of subjective and social becoming. This view of causation is not isolated to postcolonial theory; much Western constructivist social and political philosophy – including dialectics, transformative critical theory, psychoanalysis and some strains of poststructuralism – assumes that reality is productively driven by the desire to plug an original lack or absence. However, this notion of causation raises a problem that relates particularly to postcolonial theory, because ontological negativity drives the constructive process in terms of the desire to eliminate or assimilate difference, where difference is the critical negativity that is at once the cause of transformation and the trouble to be resolved. The ontological negativity of this causal desire results in an imperial agency of construction, aimed at the management of difference. In thinking through this problem, this work contributes to recent work on desire in philosophy (e.g. Butler 1987) and postcolonial theory (e.g. Bhabha 1994; Young 1995), and to Diana Coole's (2000) important work on negativity and politics. I agree with these thinkers that desire and negativity are principal organising concepts in Western political thought and practice,

Introduction

particularly bearing upon concepts of agency and critique. However, unlike Coole I will adopt a postcolonial perspective critical of the imperial character of Western philosophy and will consequently take a less celebratory approach to negativity; and unlike Butler and others, I will foreground the alternative concept of desire described by Deleuze as a positive force of causation, generating an alternative concept of constructive agency.

The second cluster of problems identified here concern the uncritical emphasis postcolonial theory and practice places upon the politics of negation and opposition, which are widely assumed to be both appropriate and necessary in critical and transformative perspectives, but which foreclose the necessary mutualism and positivity associated with the co-operative production of 'the new horizon' that is arguably necessary for a genuinely postcolonial practice. One problem here is that agency is understood to rest with the oppositional negating class, which accordingly bears the brunt of responsibility for postcolonial transformation. This elides the transformative capacity and responsibility of the dominant political class – in this case, the settler society. While an indigenous agency of social construction and transformation is, of course, essential to the success of postcolonisation, in this work I aim to create a concept of postcolonial agency that also responds to the transformative capacity of non-indigenous peoples responsibly seeking to participate in the creation of postcolonial forms of sociability, and it is to non-indigenous peoples that my account is primarily addressed. Accordingly, while I have critically attended to the ways in which both indigenous and 'mainstream' actions towards decolonisation and reconciliation have been constrained by the use of dominant Western political categories and frameworks, I draw mainly from a minor tradition *within* Western political philosophy – including Spinoza, Nietzsche, Foucault and Deleuze – to propose an alternative philosophy of transformation, grounding a new concept of postcolonial agency. In formulating this concept and striving to construct a model of agency that is adequate to the needs of mutual engagement and hybrid perspectives of sociality, I have also listened to indigenous philosophers and learned from indigenous perspectives. Indigenous peoples may therefore also find this concept of postcolonial agency and the practices it augurs relevant and useful in rethinking and enacting the postcolonial world, possibly by developing the ideas of self, agency and common practice presented here in conjunction with other concepts drawn from non-Western traditions: this, however, is the subject of other works, perhaps best authored by those who, unlike myself, write from the subject positions of the formerly colonised. Thus, while I hope this work will be broadly useful for all peoples involved with the task of postcolonisation, I take the view that indigenous and non-indigenous traditions are conceptually diverse, and one need not be privileged over the other when a variety of approaches can combine to reach an agreeable outcome.

A third problem, also specifically bearing upon postcolonial theory, is the problem of postcolonial temporality and historical change. Postcolonial theory generally proposes solutions to colonialism that are unable to break free from a fundamentally imperial outlook and attitude, because it assumes an underlying concept of agency that remains grounded in negativity. Rather than effectuating a genuinely postcolonial sociability, then, postcolonial theory remains fettered to a mode of imperial agency, which ultimately perpetuates the problematic structure of existing social practices. This problem bears upon currently inadequate notions of postcolonial temporality, quality and novelty, signalled by the continuing and pervasive practice of colonial agency and its effects, which include the production of actual social relations, actual social structures and standards, and actual theories of transformation. Failing to attend to this problem, reconciliation currently means introducing a different degree of indigenous participation in existing structures, without necessarily subjecting the nature or quality of these to scrutiny. This movement fails to depart properly from the policies of assimilation that have problematically characterised culture and race relations in previously colonised locations. The solution to this problem is proposed here as the construction of an alternative concept of postcolonial agency, as a form of micropolitical scaffolding capable of materialising novel institutions and codes of hybrid social practice based on mutual agreement, which operate according to an alternative, postcolonial ethos of relation. Conceived thus, postcolonial reconciliation is not simply a formal obligation and a responsibility of State; neither is it solely an 'indigenous issue' that is primarily the responsibility of indigenous peoples to pursue. Rather, it involves the practice of an ethics and a 'politics of friendship' that is everyone's responsibility. My aim is therefore to describe postcolonisation as the introduction of a *qualitative* difference, an altogether different quality of sociability, which supports different kinds of social structures and is in turn sustained by them, and which definitively breaks with colonialism and post-colonialism, to begin a postcolonial history. This call for

Introduction

a 'future form, for a new earth and people that do not yet exist' (Deleuze and Guattari 1994: 108) is facilitated by the creation of a new concept of postcolonial agency.

A fourth problem explored here is the lack of sustained engagement between postcolonial thought and Deleuzian philosophy, and the quick tendency of many postcolonial thinkers to dismiss Deleuze as irrelevant or inconsequential, or even hostile, to postcolonial concerns and commitments. It is true that Deleuze seldom references the thinkers and writers of the postcolony, and furthermore, certain Deleuzian concepts – nomadology in particular – are seen to appropriate, romanticise and intellectualise indigenous experience and ways of life, extracting these from their concrete formulations and disregarding the devastating impact of colonialism on actually existing nomadic peoples (Miller 1993; Wuthnow 2002; Kaplan 1996). This apparently imperial indifference on Deleuze's part is often thought to be compounded by his failure to provide concepts of resistance, critique and political society that address the collective concerns of 'peoples'. Worse, rather than enabling the authentic expression of the subjective agency of formerly colonised peoples, his concepts are often perceived to contribute to the postmodern demolition of consistent expressions of selfhood and collective ideals – including human rights – widely understood as necessary platforms for co-ordinating strategies of resistance. In her early essay, 'Can the Subaltern Speak?' Gayatri Spivak (1985) famously criticises Deleuze and Foucault for their disinclination to 'speak for' the subaltern other, and renders problematic their rather facile assumption that the other can 'speak for' herself. Spivak insists that Deleuze and Foucault are guilty of a Eurocentrism that fails to acknowledge how subaltern critique must be presented within the privileged structures of Western epistemology and representation in order to be comprehended or perceived as sensible. Accordingly, she points to the troubling forms of exclusion that arise when resistance to domination is forced to adopt the same terms of subjective representation that have historically been the cause of imperial oppression; and furthermore, that as formally 'other' in this system of representation, the authentic speech of the subaltern remains always already outside the bounds of 'what can be heard'. Spivak's early postcolonial criticism of Deleuze's relation to the political has recently been supplemented by Peter Hallward (2006, 2001). While Hallward's work brings Deleuze's thought within the contemporary ambit of postcolonial theory, he argues that Deleuze is less interested in cultivating an involvement with the material world in order to transform it, than in escaping it through pure contemplation. Deleuze's perceived penchant for philosophical and historical abstractions – his preference for virtual creativity over the analysis of actually existing political situations – disables scope for concrete acts of engagement with the world, and therefore with the actual scars that continue to mark societies in the post-colonial world. Consequently, like Spivak and others, Hallward insists Deleuze has little to offer with respect to political organisation and concrete transformation.

By foregrounding the important materialist concept of desiring-production in Deleuze's thought, which Hallward does not fully investigate, I explain how desire operates as the qualitative causal force of material creation and transformation, which mediates virtual creation and actual creatures. In describing a postcolonial attitude of 'listening respect', practised by cultivating that which Deleuze refers to as an 'impossible ear' (2007: 160), I offer a partial response to Spivak's concerns about the audibility of 'subaltern speech'. Accordingly I seek to offer an alternative and postcolonial reading of Deleuzian political philosophy, which I argue allows for agency, ethics, strategic organisation and concrete engagement with a problematic material existence. I hope that this reading will contribute to emerging work interested in forging connections between Deleuze and the postcolonial (see Bignall and Patton 2010), offering fruitful resources for postcolonial political theory and new insights into the vexed and complicated relationship between postcolonial theory and poststructuralism (Ahluwalia 2010).

Assemblage

This book is comprised of two main sections. The first deals mainly with the task of critique. My initial targets are the particular reading of the ontological negativity of dialectical desire, given by Kojève in his seminar on Hegel in the 1930s and assimilated by thinkers including Lacan, Sartre and Fanon in the mid-twentieth century, as well as the hugely influential concept of agency generated by this view of self and process. My ultimate targets are the body of postcolonial theory (*pace* Fanon) and associated transformative practices that are grounded in this model. My aim in the first section is to criticise the kind of agency suggested by the dominant Western understanding of desire, subjectivity and history-making and to suggest that, in the postcolonial world, there is a need for an alternative method of

Introduction

critical and formative practice. The second section of the book then shifts focus from the task of critique to the labour of construction. My attention is here focused on constructing a concept of postcolonial agency, which in turn enables the conceptualisation of postcolonial practices of sociability. I argue that, because it is grounded in a positive notion of productive desire, Deleuze's 'philosophy of becoming' supports concepts of agency, difference and ethics of relationship between self and other, which better inform thinking about postcolonial processes of transformation.

In Chapter 1, I describe the view of history (the philosophy of process) which has assumed great currency in Western political theory over the past centuries, and which has its origins in Hegel's dialectic. I explain how, in twentieth-century philosophies following Kojève's interpretation of Hegel in the 1930s, the active cause of history is understood to be desire, but particularly conceptualised in terms of a void or a lack. Furthermore, this negative form of desire directs the process of history in a particular way. Thus, I argue that politics informed by this particular concept of desire take a particular form and move in a particular fashion *because* they are caused by an underlying negativity, absence or lack. This form of desire positions the desiring subject in certain ways with respect to the objective difference that negates the unity and consistency of the subject, and which the subject simultaneously yearns for and fears. Difference is then the negativity that drives the dialectic of desire and satisfaction; but simultaneously it is the problematic absence or lack, which desire seeks to eliminate, or the disturbing excess, which desire seeks to assimilate. In this way, the component concepts of desire, power and subjectivity are defined in ways that produce a concept of *imperial* or *colonising* agency, which makes history or transforms society through a negating action directed towards difference.

In the second chapter, I suggest that postcolonial theory remains seduced by this view of history, which foregrounds social transformation as a progressive process driven on the one hand by the generative negativity of desire for a missing unity, and on the other hand by the critical opposition between classes. In so doing, such postcolonial theory remains tied to an imperial philosophy of difference, which is implicit in the central role played by difference, conceptualised as 'the negative' and by action, conceptualised as the 'negation of the negative'. The association of difference and negativity reinforces a problematic slippage in representations of indigenous peoples, who are commonly perceived to embody difference or 'disadvantage' in both non-indigenous and indigenous discourses about society and postcolonial reconciliation. Indigenous difference is thereby the driving mechanism of postcolonial reconciliation or unification, but simultaneously the problematic negativity that must itself eventually be negated. In practice, this has meant that indigenous peoples have usually borne the responsibility for prompting postcolonial transformation, often by identifying as disadvantaged and by pitching their claims for amelioration of their systemic disadvantage to recalcitrant States and dismissive non-indigenous communities, which invariably respond only by instituting policy underscored by new forms of assimilation. It has also meant that the transformative capacity and responsibility of non-indigenous peoples has been devalued and dismissed in much postcolonial political thought. In the main, Western postcolonial theorists and activists have not managed to escape from the post-Hegelian legacy of thought about the nature of social transformation, which continues to inform platforms for resistance, reconciliation and social construction. While such action has been instrumental in decolonisation struggles, it finally remains complicit with the structures of agency it opposes, and so has limited application in reconstructive processes aimed at creating genuinely alternative types of postcolonial society.

In Chapter 3 I seek the basis for a new resolution to the problem of post-colonial agency, not by drawing attention to alternative readings of Hegel resulting in more nuanced positions within the tradition of dialectical philosophy, nor by drawing on non-Western concepts and traditions of thought and transformative practice, but by contrasting the problematic conception of agency grounded in causal ontological negativity, together with the process of social trans/formation it generates, with Deleuze's non-dialectical concept of different/ciation. In this chapter, I show how Deleuze offers an alternative philosophy of becoming, which is grounded in a positive model of desire and insists upon a positive and creative role for difference. On this view, history is not produced by the negation of difference, but by affirming and multiplying it. This chapter will outline the kind of critical practice enabled by this philosophy of transformation, thereby addressing the concern that a purely positive philosophy of transformation and difference is unable to sustain a critical politics.

Taken together, desire and power define the conditions and impetus for action; in Chapter 4 I consider these as the constructive forces in the actualisation of being. As in theories of generative ontological negativity, desire is here considered as the primary causal force of production. However, unlike these philosophical traditions, desire is not here conceptualised in relation to lack. Rather, desire is the constructive force bringing association, relation or assemblage, and its aim is not the negation of difference, but the production of connections between bodies, resulting in the creation of new complex bodies through the novel combination of their constituting parts. Similarly, power is conceptualised in terms of constitutive force relations between bodies: the type of force shapes the nature of the relationship and the kind of complex body that is formed.

Subsequently, I describe the kind of subject who desires in this positive and creative fashion, who is enmeshed in relations of power or force with other bodies, and who is in fact produced by these relationships of desire/power, which compel a process of actualisation. The focus of this fifth chapter is the problem of strategy: when the subject emerges as an effect of a productive process, how can the subject strategically and causally shape this process? I will argue that the subject is an event, a situation, a performance, an assemblage and an expression of strategy. This chapter finally considers the relationship between subjective style, desire/power and ethics/politics, with respect to the underlying ontology of bodies, forces and relations and the two types of satisfaction described by 'enjoyment' and 'joy'.

In Chapter 6, I consider the content of the notion of the 'postcolonial' in more detail. My intention here is to describe postcolonialism as a mode of social performance involving the actualisation of complex social relationships structured by a practised ethical orientation towards others, which materialises as the institutions, discourses and structures of postcolonial society. More precisely, postcolonial society results from a chosen practice of desire, here described in terms of a particular attitude of 'listening respect' resulting in a certain 'politics of friendship' variously described elsewhere by Jacques Derrida (2005) and by Leela Gandhi (2006), that positions individuals in relations of postcolonial sociability. I describe this postcolonial attitude, and consider how it potentially operates as an immanent cause of the actualisation of postcolonial society. The final part of this chapter considers some material and institutional implications of the notion of the postcolonial that has been developed here.

My concluding remarks consider the nature of the relationship between philosophy and practice, with respect to the problem of public commitment and faith to the social process of transformation. The future-oriented practice of postcolonisation might be enabled by the alternative conceptualisation of agency presented here, and indeed, the success of this work might best be judged by its 'untimeliness', by the events that its concepts invent, express and call forth. However, the concept of postcolonial agency I have described achieves actual saliency only in the practices that materialise it. Concepts of sociability remain virtual until they are acted through responsible, collective practice; the postcolonial exists even now, but as a virtual we must labour to make actual through carefully chosen practices of desire.

Notes

1. For examples of liberal attempts to accommodate cultural difference, see Ivison (2002), Raz (2009), Kukathas (2003) and Kymlicka (1995).
2. Notable theories of practice include Bourdieu (1977, 1990) and de Certeau (2002). These theories of practice enjoy an increasing favour: see the volume edited by Schatzki, Cetina and von Savigny (2001).

I
Critique

1

The Problem of the Negative

> Far from being concerned with solutions, truth and falsehood primarily affect problems. A solution always has the truth it deserves according to the problem to which it is a response, and the problem has the solution it deserves in proportion to its *own* truth or falsity. (Deleuze 1994: 159)

In the first two chapters, I will critique the way postcolonial theory usually presents the problem of postcolonisation.[1] My main objective is to consider how postcolonial theory utilises two of the most influential organising concepts in modern and contemporary political theory. These are firstly negation, which privileges the possibility of critique and the potential for transformation in social analysis; and secondly recognition, which underlies various forms of 'identity politics' and claims for equality. I will trace the influence of these two concepts from their early expression in Hegel's philosophy, through Sartre and Fanon, to much current postcolonial theory. The discussion will particularly attend to the ways in which both recognition and negation are informed by the dialectical category of desire. In (post-)Hegelian philosophy, desire is negatively conceived: it signals a lack and a longing, which is understood to be the constitutive or constructive force of identity-formation occasioning recognition, but also and simultaneously the deconstructive or negating force that compels the transformation of existing reality. I will argue that this ambiguity results in conceptualisations of subjectivity, agency and process that are problematic, and finally unsuitable, as supports for postcolonial theory and for practical efforts at postcolonisation.

In this first chapter, I present a dialectical view of reality and historical process. I will consider the centrality of the concepts of recognition and negation within this ontology, and in particular, I will critique their respective associations with the dialectical category of desire. In the course of this discussion, I will describe the particular notion of agency that emerges from the understanding of causation in dialectical processes, which as we will see, is intimately bound up with negative notions of desire and difference. In so doing, my discussion touches upon the works of Alexandre Kojève and Jean-Paul Sartre. I will also briefly consider the criticisms of dialectics argued by poststructuralists and others, but will argue that such thinkers nonetheless usually remain committed to the generative force of negativity, and indeed that their criticisms of the dialectic are often made because they worry that the teleological movement of dialectical reconciliation betrays negativity, which they seek to preserve and extend as a critical force that contests the given.

In the following Chapter 2, I will consider how postcolonial theory has drawn from dialectical philosophy, especially through the influential formative writings of Frantz Fanon. I will argue that most postcolonial theory remains complicit with an imperial philosophy of difference when it tacitly accepts that negation is the motive force of construction and change, and that recognition of identity is the basis of equality. This continues to position difference ambiguously: as the critical force of social transformation, but simultaneously as that which must be negated, expelled or assimilated as society progresses towards equality and harmony. This relationship between difference and transformative action results in a problematic, imperious conceptualisation of agency. Subsequently, looking at reconciliation in the concrete historical context of contemporary Australia, we will see how attempts made at postcolonisation have been compromised when the conceptual apparatus of dialectical philosophy has informed transformative action. Finally, the problem of postcolonial social transformation will be defined for our purposes as a problem of agency. If it is to avoid reinforcing the kinds of power relations and modes of being that it seeks to contest, a postcolonial theory of practice must escape the limits set by generative negativity and associated concepts of existence, process, agency and causation. The transition to postcolonial practice requires an alternative conceptualisation of ontological generation and change, and thus of social and critical agency, to that which has informed colonialism.

Dialectical negativity

At least since the Enlightenment and until the advent of postmodernity, Western social philosophy has claimed to be critical and progressive, guided by principles of rational evaluation and moral betterment. While recent versions of postmodern theory (including some versions of postcolonialism) have effectively debunked some of our most deep-seated assumptions about rationality and progress,

The Problem of the Negative

this new kind of Western theory nevertheless usually continues to uphold the importance that traditionally attaches to the idea of critical negativity and the role of negation in socio-political practice. The 'negative' is an absence or lack that disturbs the claimed perfection, unity or completeness of a given arrangement of reality or social life. 'Negation' refers to the moment of critique, to resistance and the transgression of 'that which is'. Diana Coole writes: 'To invoke negativity is thus to exhort political intervention while already performing a political act: it destabilizes illusions of perfection, presence and permanence by associating the positive with petrified and illegitimate structures of power' (2000: 11). In addressing the negative, we are forced to confront 'that which is not', and implicitly, *why* it is not, and perhaps also how it might become. The negative is therefore characterised by its critical opposition to the positive, to the given, to the identity or form of being which has presence or facticity. The negative is alterity, difference itself. The privileging of negativity is therefore also a privileging of difference, and negation is an act that celebrates and affirms difference.

At face value, this strategy of negation does not seem problematic for postcolonial theory and the politics of reconciliation. However, the association of negativity and difference results in an ambiguous theory of practice. Difference is reified as the compelling or causal force of critical transformation, but simultaneously treated as the problematic absence, lack or disadvantage that must be eventually resolved or dissolved, as society reconciles its differences and forges greater unity through mutual recognition. The association of negativity and difference is complicated by slippage in the signification of the terms. In particular, 'difference' signifies not only 'critical, creative potential' but also 'otherness'. In contemporary discourses of postcolonial reconciliation, 'otherness' then also aligns with 'indigeneity' and 'inequality'. The subsequent associations of negativity and difference, and of difference and indigeneity, tend to reinforce negative representations of indigenous peoples, as 'lacking', 'disadvantaged', 'victims', 'absent', or even 'disruptive' and 'divisive'. I will return to this problem in the final section of Chapter 2.

According to Diana Coole:

> It is Hegel's dialectic that introduces negativity explicitly into modern thought and it is to his work that its provocateurs must always return, either to lament his failure to remain faithful to the negativity he discerned, or to read him against the grain in order to retrieve it. (2000: 43)[2]

Hegel is fundamentally a philosopher of process. As he understands it, the philosopher's task involves 'grasping and expressing the True not only as *Substance*, but equally as *Subject*' (Hegel 1977: ¶17). For Hegel, it is not enough to grasp being in its substantive immediacy, its objective essence or its simple 'is-ness'; the real or the true can only be properly comprehended as the 'process of its own becoming' (Hegel 1977: ¶18). Hegel's ambition is therefore to comprehend and describe reality, by expressing the process of development according to which it has come to be. By cultivating an awareness of how reality becomes, the philosopher in turn becomes the self-conscious subject of that process. The subject emerges at the point where the philosopher, reflecting upon the history of that which has come to be, recognises how this historical process has shaped his or her eventual being in the world. Finally, in coming to understand the mechanism of this process, the philosopher becomes an active subject able to take charge of the process, and can begin self-consciously shaping reality through reasoned purposive action (Hegel 1977: ¶21–2).

According to Hegel, reality develops in a dialectical fashion, and it is this proposed dialectical structure of reality that foregrounds the negative and negation in contemporary philosophy and transformative practice. At once ontological and phenomenological, the dialectic describes a universal structure of development, which explains how a given being, structure of reality or thought arises and transforms over time.[3] The dialectic is thus a description of productive process (or life) and of transformation (or history) in general. It is a 'movement of negativity whose labour lends a common choreography, and indeed a single itinerary, to both thought and being, thereby rendering speculative philosophy, ontology, logic and epistemology more or less equivalent' (Coole 2000: 45–6). This generality enables us to use a dialectical model to conceptualise not only the emergence of the self-conscious, human subjectivity that we understand to be necessary for the coherent, moral agency of individuals, but also the schematic development of social evolution, or a world history of human existence *per se*. According to Hegel, everything that can be thought of as 'being' comes into existence via a dialectical process of production.

In his reading of Hegel, Alexandre Kojève explains that 'reality is dialectical only because it implies a negative or negating element: namely, the active negation of the given' (Kojève 1980: 185–6). According to dialectical reason, every concept of being is determined as such in relation to that which it is not, and to which it is logically

The Problem of the Negative

opposed. The positivity of being is discernible as such because of its logical opposition to the negativity that confronts it. A given identity is thus established by its opposition to all that is different or is 'not'; however this determining relation to difference means that identity cannot be thought without difference, or as separate from the difference that negates it. Thesis and antithesis – being and nothing, identity and difference, self and other, master and slave – are thus bound together into an ambiguous and unstable relationship, in which the two categories are at once opposed and united.

The moment of contradictory unification introduces the notion of dialectical becoming as the negation or transformation of being. Thought together, being and nothingness – identity and difference – become fluid, as they pass over and dissolve into each other in the process of dialectical unification. With the synthesis of opposing terms, the difference between them is at once transcended and preserved, as the process of the transformation of being is driven by the struggle to resolve difference while retaining its determining form. For Hegel, the instability of the contradictory relationship between opposing yet mutually determining categories of existence yields a productive tension, which propels the transformation of being as it seeks to bring about a more adequate unity with the difference that determines it.

The dialectical production of being is thus characterised by the successive transcendence of given oppositions and the repeated synthesis of ever more expansive degrees of unification. However, negativity – difference in the form of opposition or contradiction – is always preserved in this process, since it is always required for the renewed determination of being. The dialectic progresses only by reinstating new oppositions, which are in turn transcended. As a result, being unfolds by its progressive unification with all that is different to it. In embracing and overcoming the negativity or difference with which it is confronted, the Hegelian subject ultimately expands to recognise itself reflected in the world at large, and simultaneously perceives that it carries difference within, as its own condition of possibility (see Butler 1987: 8–9). The subject finds its metaphysical place only by finally recognising that external difference is simply an immanent feature of its being. The reasoned, 'purposive activity' of the Hegelian subject is therefore communitarian, directed towards bringing about a more adequate unity with the external world, which is the otherness that determines its existence as such.

In conceptualising ontology as a dialectical process, Hegelian philosophy assumes several things. Firstly, the trajectory is driven by negativity, which establishes a primary contradiction or opposition between elements. Secondly, the process incrementally eliminates this element of contradiction with the gradual and progressive unification of the elements. Thus, thirdly, difference is conceptualised as contradiction, which is the driving force of the process, but simultaneously is that which is to be eventually eliminated by the final achievement of unification. And fourthly, reality is not 'created' but 'realised' in this process, in the sense that everything that comes to be always already exists, or is pre-given, and is simply 'made real' or established in fact by the elimination or surpassing of the difference that contests it. Being is here produced as a movement from possibility to reality, by a process in which alternative possibilities for being are eliminated (Deleuze 1994: 211–12, 1991b: 96–9). Therefore in reading the *Phenomenology*, we understand retrospectively that Hegel's subject was 'there all along', although not immediately or substantially present. The absence of the subject is a void pregnant with promise, and we find ourselves 'poised for his arrival', discerning the subject in the 'wings' and 'margins' of Hegel's text. In fact, the subject appears at the exact point where the reader identifies with the narrative, at the instant where we recognise that *we are the subject*, and that Hegel is describing our own mode of becoming (Butler 1987: 20).

While the dialectic of realisation is most certainly a plausible and instructive ontological model, the dialectical version of productive and transformative process is not the only possible conceptualisation available. Indeed, in the third chapter I will compare the dialectic with an alternative model of ontological process, and I will suggest that this alternative model is better suited to a postcolonial understanding of the role of difference in the processes of life and history, of self and social construction and transformation. However, at this point my aim is to consider how the conceptual linkage between dialectical negation and difference lends itself to constructive and transformative practices that are imperious in character. The concept of 'desire' perhaps best illustrates this linkage. The category of desire in the *Phenomenology* is significant to this work for two main reasons. Firstly, desire is conceptualised as the privileged site of negativity; desire is a longing defined by a condition of lack, and it compels the transforming actions (negations) that would alleviate that lack. As the compelling force of dialectical transformation, desire is a *cause* of history. Secondly, the fact of desire raises questions about its

The Problem of the Negative

satisfaction. What kinds of actions can satisfy desire? And at what point is desire/history fulfilled?

Debates over the possible solutions to these questions have revived interest in Hegel and dominated interpretations of his thought, especially by early twentieth-century philosophers like Kojève and Hyppolite. Indeed, Kojève's seminar in the 1930s, which focused upon Hegel's section on desire and recognition in the *Phenomenology*, strongly influenced the French reception of Hegel and the critical revision and appropriation of his thought by subsequent generations of scholars, including Sartre, Lacan and Adorno. Their conclusions about the co-implication of desire, negativity and action have in turn shaped the way much contemporary philosophy, including postcolonial theory, thinks about agency and social transformation.

In thinking desire, Hegel draws from a long tradition in Western philosophy, stemming from Plato's *Symposium*, that associates desire with a feeling of emptiness, a void or a lack in the subject (see Silverman 2000). The subject desires the fulfilment he lacks, and desire thereby signifies the incompletion or imperfection of the subject. The void attested to by the existence of desire in the subject compels the subject to act to alleviate the feeling of emptiness or dissatisfaction. Kojève describes how action satisfies desire only through the negation of the desired object: '[T]he I of Desire is an emptiness that receives a real positive content only by negating action that satisfies Desire in destroying, transforming and "assimilating" the desired non-I' (1980: 5). This passage indicates the pervasive, yet variable and finally ambiguous, role of the negative by drawing our attention to its operation at several moments in the process of dialectical transformation. Firstly, *desire* itself is associated with negativity, evident in the feeling of emptiness or lack. Secondly, the object of desire is *difference*, and this too is defined negatively, as non-identity, or as all that 'is not'. Difference is the 'negative in general' that is lacking in the subject (Hegel 1977: ¶37). Finally, *action* and the transformations it brings about are both conceptualised as negation. And the nexus becomes even more complicated when we consider that the object of this negation, or desire's intention, is the negative, or difference, itself. Action is intended to eliminate the emptiness within the subject by negating that difference which it lacks; action negates the negative, with the aim of forging a more expansive unity.

Thus, the negative is the 'void as the principle of motion' that causes dialectical transformation and the movement caused is itself a mode of negativity (Hegel 1977: ¶37). Negativity is the generative force of dialectical processes, and it is also the nature of the movement itself: the dialectic is the 'labour of the negative' (Hegel 1977: ¶37). Accordingly, dialectical transformation is supported by a somewhat ambiguous notion of negativity, or difference, which is understood to be simultaneously the '*defect* of both [subject and object], though it is their soul, or that which moves them' (Hegel 1977: ¶37). The negative is at once cause and action; moving principle and process; an object/other coveted only to be destroyed, if possible. Negation is the elimination of difference by its assimilation into a greater unity, but it is also the creation of difference by the transformation of the given.

In order to consider how this ambiguity might be played out on the terrain of postcolonial history, social transformation and cultural difference, it is useful to identify the nature of dialectical desire in more detail. What does such desire intend? What is the mode of action or type of agency that occasions the satisfaction of dialectical desire? At what point is desire finally satisfied? In considering these questions, I will focus upon Kojève's interpretation of Hegel, as this reading has been most influential in the critical and poststructuralist revision of dialectical philosophies of transformative action, including Marxism, throughout the twentieth century. My aim here is not to assess the overall correctness of Kojève's reading of Hegel, but to trace the emergence of the hugely influential conceptualisation of agency from Kojève's seminar, through Sartre, Lacan and Fanon, to many current postcolonial philosophies of transformative action.

Dialectical desire: Kojève

Kojève's reading of Hegel's account of desire in the *Phenomenology* presents desire as the constitutive movement of self-conscious being:

> It is in and by – or better still, as – his Desire that man is formed and is revealed – to himself and to others – as an I, as the I that is essentially different from, and radically opposed to, the non-I. The (human) I is the I of a Desire or of Desire. (Kojève 1980:4)

By recasting the *Phenomenology* as a philosophy of historical action, Kojève extends Hegel's notion that desire both forms and reveals subjectivity. For Kojève, 'all human Desire is finally a function of the desire for recognition' (1980: 7), and the struggle for recognition is the dynamic principle of all historical progress. As Judith Butler comments in her reading of Kojève: '[D]esire's transformation into action,

The Problem of the Negative

and action's aim of universal recognition, become the salient features of all historical agency' (Butler 1987: 64). Like Hegel, Kojève sees that desire *causes* history in general since it is the compelling force of the transformation of the given, but he further emphasises that it is the nature of desire's intention that *gives shape* to history, making it particular by qualifying the types of actions that will lead to the satisfaction of desire (1980: 134). Accordingly, he agrees with Hegel that desire constitutes subjectivity, however, he insists that the intended object of a desire will constitute the desiring subject as a particular kind of being.[4]

In the *Phenomenology of Spirit*, the ultimate aim of desire is understood to be the expression of substance as subject. According to Kojève, as the narrative develops we come to understand that for Hegel, desire has a more immediate, twofold intention. In the first place, it is linked with recognition: the subject desires the affirming recognition of the other. Secondly, desire is linked with the effort to transform the external world into a creation of human action and will (Hegel 1977: ¶196; see Butler 1987: 57). Butler writes that this implies:

> Self-consciousness is mediated not only through another self-consciousness, but each recognizes the other in virtue of the form each gives to the world. Hence, we are recognized not merely for the form we inhabit in the world (our various embodiments), but for the forms we create of the world (our works). (1987: 57–8)

For Hegel, self-consciousness involves the revelation and the expression of the ontological unity of the subject and the external world. Kojève, however, rejects Hegel's harmonious ontology of expansive unification, and insists that the proper aim of desire is the transcendence of the givenness of the natural world through its transformation into a product of human activity and will. 'Rather than *revealing* the mutually constitutive dimensions of subject and substance as ontological presuppositions of their encounter, Kojève asserts consciousness as *creating* its relation to the world through its transformative action' (Butler 1987: 69–70).

For Kojève, this 'proper' intention makes desire the principle of comparison between self-conscious humanity and natural beings. Consciousness becomes reflexive and truly 'human' when it intentionally and actively transcends the given or natural world through the work of negation. The subject is affirmed as such when this negating and transforming activity is recognised by others. Thus, the universal aim of desire is recognition. However, the subject does not simply seek the recognition and affirmation by others of her inert being, but rather the recognition her agency in the transformation of the given world. The subject desires acknowledgement of her creative authority, and this is felt to be satisfied when others recognise that the world has been transformed by the actions of the subject. 'Work that exemplifies human being as transcending the natural and which occasions the recognition of Others is termed *historical action* . . . the mode through which the world of substance is recast as the world of the subject' (Butler 1987: 68). Negation (of the material world) is the mode of action that occasions recognition and hence the satisfaction of dialectical desire.

Transposed to the terrain of history, the dialectic produces a process of historical totalisation, driven by the struggle for recognition manifest at the ontological level (see McCarney 2000). The struggle for recognition is presented here as a contest over the authorship of history. Only those subjects who have asserted and acted out their power to transform the world will be recognised by others as agents of material creation and transformation. 'Man' acts upon the world in order 'to make the other recognize his superiority over the other' (Kojève 1996: 50). The type of agency capable of negation is active and creative, but also authoritative and dominating, controlling the direction of history by manipulating its production and interpretation, perhaps even by suppressing the constructive agency of others. The desire for recognition is the driving force of history, but the struggle for recognition gives shape to history, as the participants engage each other in the contest for authority, each reifying his own material and cultural achievements while defaming or denying the significance of the contributions made by others. The next chapter will consider the ways in which the type of agency associated with the dialectical production of history shows many of the fundamental characteristics of imperial dominance. For now, it is sufficient to note that the text of universal history emerges as the story of the victorious agents in this eminently political struggle for recognition, accompanied always by the subtext of the many alternative histories of the Others – the stories of resistance and oppression, of silenced cultural values and meanings, of difference and its suppression through refusal and non-recognition.

We might therefore understand imperial world history as the practical experience of dialectical social evolution. On this interpretation, Hegel's dialectic accurately describes the process of human

The Problem of the Negative

social becoming, and imperialism is an inevitable aspect of the development of a universal human Spirit from the dynamic of conflict and struggle (Kojève 1996: 51). However, Hegel's commitment to ontological harmony ultimately resolves the struggle for mastery, ideally promising a final moment to the dialectic, in which desire is satisfied and mutual recognition is possible. Thus, dialectical philosophy traces social evolution from the lower forms of domination and empire, towards the expansive unity manifest in the universal recognition of human interdependence. On this view, Hegel's philosophy proffers a perfect end to our imperfect, imperial history. Armed with the understanding that the dialectical view of reality allows us, we can begin self-consciously to work towards the creation of social forms that make reciprocal recognition possible. Upon reaching this ideal, we will have satisfied desire, and because it then lacks the compelling, causal force that is desire, the dialectic of human conflict and resolution will cease.

However, as Diana Coole (2000) and others (e.g. Kojève 1980; Adorno 1973; Butler 1987: 14) point out, in positing this final unity Hegel (and Marx, following him) 'betrays' the permanent possibility of critical negation. If, as Judith Butler suggests, mutual recognition of each agent's transformative power is only possible in the context of a 'shared orientation toward the material world' (1987: 57), how are we to reconcile the significant differences in our various cultural approaches to and beliefs about this world? How, for example, might a corporate mining company and an indigenous community understand such a 'shared orientation' to the land? The danger is that a 'shared orientation' might only be possible if it is orchestrated through ideology which forces or persuades the surrender of one community's beliefs and mode of existence to another's. In such a situation, each recognises the other's self-conscious, transformative action upon the world; however one mode of action is 'recognised' to be more 'valuable'. Experience shows us that the value of capital, rather than the value of, say, cultural heritage, tends to dominate when such conflicts of value arise. The final resolution of differences is here simply a final silencing or elimination of minoritarian values, which in many important instances arguably ought to remain significant and irreducible, in a postcolonial society. The potential threat posed by this kind of final 'unity' suggests that a dialectical end, in which critical negation no longer compels the challenge and transformation of dominant or majoritarian social values, can never be a valid option for postcolonial theory or practice.

By rejecting the principle of ontological resolution or harmony espoused in the *Phenomenology* and elsewhere, Kojève is able to extend Hegel's commitment to the principle of negation (Kojève 1980: 5; 1996: 52ff. see Butler 1987: 63). Whereas for Hegel, desire is the cause of a negating activity that culminates in a given *telos* – the recognised interdependence of self-consciousness and the external world – Kojève posits desire as a permanent cause of negation, without a pre-established end. On this interpretation of Hegel, desire is necessarily a permanent feature of human existence, since it is the ground for human agency, self-consciousness and historical being. Desire can never be *ultimately* satisfied, since satisfaction implies the recognition of the subject as a *desiring subject*. Desire is thus the permanent pre-condition for subjectivity (cf. Hegel 1977: ¶167). Furthermore, this (re)formulation of the ontological negativity of desire as the cause of a permanent activity of negation, unfettered by a predestined outcome, aligns desire with freedom. As the ground for human agency, desire compels the perpetual transformation of the natural world into a product of human creation. Consciousness creates reality through the negating action compelled by desire, and this open-ended process of creation is essentially an expression of human freedom (Kojève 1980: 5; Butler 1987: 70).

Sartrean desire

Kojève's interpretation of Hegel at this point clearly prefigures early Sartrean existentialism,[5] which in turn had considerable influence upon contemporary anti-imperial theorists and activists, such as Frantz Fanon. Sartre's 'postcolonial' influence is perhaps best attested to by Fanon's invitation for him to write the Preface to *Les damnés de la terre* (1961; see Sartre 1967). In addition, Sartre's many popular writings on colonialism and neo-colonialism (2001) and his work on anti-Semitism (1948) provided a prominent explanation and moral critique of the psychology of racism and empire (see Young 2001). More generally, the Sartrean existentialism figured in *L'Être et le néant* (1943), with its rejection of teleology and its emphasis on lived experience and responsibility attached to existential choice, helped to shape the theoretical base that postcolonialism was to draw from and develop in future decades.

The primary purpose of my discussion of Sartre is to trace the effects of his influence on Fanon and the subsequent development of anti-colonial and postcolonial thought. In the ensuing discussion, I

The Problem of the Negative

will focus upon Sartre's relatively early work, rather than the more mature position represented by his *Critique de la raison dialectique* (1960). While both Sartre and Fanon more or less independently arrived at more definitively Marxist conclusions in their later works (Sartre 1960; Fanon 1961), and while this Marxism clearly influenced the subsequent emergence of some strains of postcolonial theory, Sartre's early focus on subjectivity, desire and being in *L'Être et le néant* (1943) provoked and informed Fanon's initial analysis of racial/racist identification and subject-formation in *Peau noire, masques blancs* (1952), and it is this analysis of self/other sociability and its subsequent trajectory across the field of postcolonial theory that I firstly wish to interrogate.

Following Kojève, Sartre identifies desire as the defining characteristic of human being when he makes the claim that 'fundamentally man is *the desire to be*' (1996: 565). Underscoring this conception of essential human striving is the '*a priori* description of the being of the for-itself, since desire is a lack and since the for-itself is the being which is to itself its own lack of being' (1996: 565). Being-for-itself desires what it lacks, which is the ontological status of being-in-itself. As Judith Butler explains in her commentary, the object of the fundamental human 'desire to be' is 'to overcome externality and difference, in order that the self might finally coincide with itself and hence have a completed self-understanding' (Butler 1987: 124).

However, for Sartre, this movement of the for-itself towards that which it lacks and desires is marked by a final impossibility, since being-for-itself does not desire simply to become a *thing* in-itself. It wants to become a self-conscious being-in-itself-for-itself, which would entail that it simultaneously lack and possess what it lacks. For Sartre, in desiring to be its own foundation, the *pour-soi* desires to be God, and so is directed by its fundamental desire for an impossible outcome (see Howells 2000; Butler 1987: 124–5; R. Young 1990: 28–48). The paradoxical nature of being-for-itself entails that it is perpetually caught between attraction for and repulsion from being-in-itself. Being-for-itself is a 'pursued-pursuing' (Sartre 1996: 361–2). It strives towards being-in-itself; however because the fixture or completeness of being-in-itself would negate this fundamental striving, it simultaneously flees from being-in-itself as it seeks to persevere in its own nature.

Like Hegel, Sartre associates subjectivity with desire, which is a primary and constitutive negativity and simultaneously the mode through which this ontological lack is to be overcome. But unlike

Hegel's ever-expanding subject, which is finally revealed and comes to understand itself as it discovers its encompassing unity with the world, Sartre's subject will never overcome its primary ontological disjunction. For Sartre, as for Kojève, a permanent structure of ontological lack is a necessary feature of human being. Characterised by negativity and a resultant striving for fulfilment, being is 'condemned to be free': 'Freedom is the concrete mode of being of the lack of being' (Sartre 1996: 565). While Hegel's subject completes its teleological journey by self-*realisation*, Sartre's subject endlessly *creates* itself by choosing the actions and modes of comportment that will define its particular character. Throughout this process of free self-creation, a being suffers its freedom, permanently and anxiously aware of the responsibility that accompanies existential choice.

According to Sartre, the fundamental desire to exist is a negativity that compels the becoming of being, but desire also has a more complicated existential role and structure, since it operates on several levels of human action. The generalised 'desire to be' indicates an unspecified intention towards life and participation in the world. However, within this broad ambit, desire also structures a more particular 'fundamental choice' in the mode of living or attitude towards others an individual decides to practise, which indicates *how* the subject intends to be (Sartre 1996: 563). Finally, the choice to desire becomes even more particular when it is directed towards specific others or objects of attraction. Sartre argues that both the fundamental desire to exist and the desire to live in the particular way indicated by the subject's chosen orientation towards the world are discernible in the subject's choice of concrete desires toward particular objects or others (Sartre 1996: 567; Butler 1987: 123–7). In selectively constituting particular others/objects as desirable, and in choosing how to act upon these concrete desires, the subject constitutes her desired mode of existence, which in turn evinces her broad desire to be: 'desire is consent to desire' (Sartre 1996: 388).

While the fundamental desire to be and the desire to exist in a particular mode of being are not immediately and transparently revealed by one's concrete desires and actions, Sartre insists these existential aspects of desire can be known through reflection. Indeed, the task of the subject is precisely to reflect upon one's concrete desires in order to discern how these immediate choices have contributed to the emergence of a particular chosen way of life. More particularly, the task of the existential subject is to evaluate one's concrete choices by reflecting upon how these bear upon the existential project of self-

The Problem of the Negative

creation. As Judith Butler comments: 'Reflection upon desire is, then, a reflection upon myself as a choice of being: *to reflect upon desire is to acknowledge choices one has already made*' (Butler 1987: 130). Living 'responsibly' therefore requires that one select one's desires with respect to how these fit in with the broader picture of one's chosen way of being, and that critical self-reflection is an essential aspect of desiring, evaluative choice-making and action.

As will become clear in the second part of this work, I am basically in agreement with this understanding of desire's function in the processes of subjective and social construction. I will argue that it is essential for individuals to evaluate their desires, their relations and their actions towards others with respect to how these contribute to the chosen practice of a 'postcolonial' way of life. However, I also believe it is necessary to extend the scope of Sartre's argument about the relation between desire and existential choice. For Sartre, one's choice of objects desired and one's attitude of response to these chosen objects of desire constitutes one's desired way of life. However, he fails to extend the scope of choice to *desire* itself.

Because he conceives desire as an ontological given, Sartre confers only one nature on desire. For Sartre, desire is *always* a lack, a mode of negativity that compels human striving and action. His analysis of the possible attitudes of response to desire is limited by this definition of the nature of desire. Accordingly, one can only choose modes of comportment towards the objects of one's desire that respond to this negative conception of desire. As we shall see, such responses are fundamentally limited to actions of appropriation, assimilation and elimination. In Sartre, there is little scope for the practice of a post-imperial attitude of relation with desired others. In coming chapters, I will draw attention to an alternative conception of desire, not associated with negativity, and I will argue that the creation of postcolonial existence will require us to *choose* this positive mode of desire in the act of transforming our colonial history and renegotiating our social relations. Thus, I will develop Sartre's suggestion that it is not only the objects and relations chosen as desirable, but also *how* one chooses to desire these things that is significant in the construction of subjective and social life. This is so because the nature of one's desire conditions the types of satisfaction – appropriation, submission, alliance and so on – one is liable to take. Therefore, in reflecting upon one's existential choices, one needs to consider both desire's intention and desire's nature. I can begin to explain my reasoning by taking a closer look at Sartre's analysis of inter-subjective desire and recognition. Sartre's analysis of inter-subjective relations is particularly important here because of its influence upon Fanon's analysis of inter-subjective race relations,[6] which in turn has been highly influential in the development of comparatively recent postcolonial analyses, such as Edward Said's and Homi Bhabha's.

In considering inter-subjective desire, Sartre focuses particularly upon sexual desire: 'My original attempt to get hold of the Other's free subjectivity through his objectivity-for-me is sexual desire' (Sartre 1996: 382). This privileging of sexual desire is particularly evident in the chapter in *Being and Nothingness* on 'concrete relations with others', which focuses solely upon sexual desire; however Sartre's literary works also generally consider sexual desire as the primary dimension of intersubjective relations. Sexual desire accordingly becomes his privileged example of a concrete desire directed towards a particular other. However, sexuality does not exhaust the ambit of desire, which more broadly signifies the necessary social orientation one has towards others. Thus *Anti-Semite and Jew* (1948) also considers inter-subjective desire, but focuses particularly upon the dimension of race and one's desire for/fear of the racial Other. Fanon (1952) also privileges the dimension of race when he shifts the focus of Sartre's analysis to inter-subjective race relations and the desire/fear of the racial other in the situation of colonialism. We have seen that, for Sartre, the fact of desire constitutes the object as desirable, and thus in this sense, desire chooses its object. The choice of the object desired will also implicitly constitute an existential choice, which will contribute to the subject's creation of a certain mode of being, and attest to his fundamental desire to create the self-identity that he essentially lacks: 'consciousness chooses itself as desire' (Sartre 1996: 388). Sartre's interrogation of the various concrete forms taken by sexual desire reveals how a desiring body negotiates this creative freedom in relation to the difference represented by the body of the Other.

In facing the Other, the self confronts the fact of difference and experiences the essential negativity of being in the world with others. The self perceives that it is estranged from others and distanced from ideal ontological unity with the material world. The desire to unite with the Other is the impulse to overcome negativity and difference, to render one's being-in-the-world-with-others immediate, positive and present (Sartre 1996: 221–303). In other words, desire is a project of self-determination, in which the primary role of the Other is to mediate the relation of the subjective being-for-itself with objective being-in-itself. The Other is the 'foundation of my being', since I experience myself as I appear to the Other; 'the Other is the indispensable mediator between myself and me' (Sartre 1996: 222, 365). The Other 'reveals' me to myself, and as such is the condition of my self-consciousness, just as my gaze is the condition of the self-consciousness of that other. Desire therefore concerns the way in which we situate ourselves in relation to others, and how we define ourselves in situation. Desire is the 'building of ourselves that we perform daily' (Butler 1987: 97), as situated beings defined by our relations with the other beings in our situation.

Our mutual being-for-others is thus, for Sartre as for Kojève and Hegel, a necessary fact of human existence, and the desire for the recognition of the Other is the driving force behind the development of human subjectivity. However, Sartre expands upon Kojève's interpretation of the Hegelian desire for recognition in order to spell out how this desire prompts certain kinds of actions that characterise the existential subject, the self-conscious being-for-itself striving to be in-itself. Although Sartre does not develop this train of thought, this in turn suggests the possibility of other kinds of desire corresponding with other kinds of action and subjectivity, and so leads towards the genealogy presented here, in the chapters to come.

For Sartre, 'concrete relations with the Other . . . are wholly governed by my attitudes with respect to the object which I am for the Other' (1996: 363). The Other objectifies me when he looks at me. This look defines me by conferring meaning upon me from without. In this sense my being is 'stolen' by the Other, and my being-for-others is experienced as possession (1996: 364). However, my goal is to be the foundation of my own being. I want to grasp this defining look of the Other and make it my own: 'I am – at the very root of my being – the project of assimilating and making an object of the Other' (1996: 363). Accordingly, for Sartre, being-for-others creates a 'circular' movement of desire, in which the subject oscillates between a desire to be identified by being objectified 'for the Other', and the desire to 'recover' oneself by 'absorbing the Other' (1996: 364). Described by Sartre as a movement between sadism and masochism, while the desire for recognition represents an abstract need for connection with others, it is always also embodied in particular modes of affecting and being affected. Sadism and masochism are then the two alternative 'fundamental' postures, attitudes or modes of comportment that we can choose to adopt when soliciting the recognition of the Other who we desire to 'bring us into being' (1996: 363; see Butler 1987: 138–56).

The first way in which I can 'recover' myself or 'absorb' the Other is by making the Other an object-for-me, by returning the Other's look with my own gaze (1996: 382). According to Sartre, sexual desire is the original experience of this attempt to objectify the Other. Sexual desire is then conceptualised as a project of subject-formation in which 'consciousness makes itself body' (1996: 389). In desire, my aim is to ensnare the Other's freedom within the facticity of her body, compelling her free recognition of my subjectivity through her awareness of the effect I have upon her body. However, this project of desire is bound to fail, since in reducing the Other to flesh, I also make myself flesh: my body is the instrument by which her body is made flesh. I am therefore at some point during the sexual encounter made sensible of my own object facticity, and of my consciousness as a 'consciousness swooning in its flesh beneath the Other's look' (1996: 398).

The initial failure of desire as a project of subjectivity can then prompt a sadistic approach towards the Other, which extends the original project of desire by using alternative means. Like sexual desire, sadism is an attempt to reduce the Other to flesh, but the sadist refuses to use his own flesh as a means to objectify the Other. Instead instruments are used to force the Other to submit to an identification in which he becomes nothing more than flesh. However, sadism too, is bound to fail as a project of subjectivity, since the sadistic self inevitably becomes identified as an instrument for giving pain. This instrumentality or utility returns the sadist to an objectified existence as for-the-other, and with this moment of objectification, his subjectivity immediately crumbles. Alternatively, the sadist may become aware of his own pleasure, and thus return abruptly to a sensibility of the corporeality he attempts to deny. In any case, if it were possible for the sadist to succeed in objectifying the Other, this too would subvert the aim of subjectivity, which is to possess the free subjectivity of the victim. As object, the victim loses this free subjectivity, and so loses his purpose for the sadist, and the process once again fails.

However, for Sartre, the 'failure of one [strategy] motivates the adoption of the other' (1996: 363). The second way in which I can attempt to recover myself or absorb the Other is by adopting a masochistic attitude towards that Other. This attitude enables me to 'make myself be by acquiring the possibility of taking the Other's point of view on myself' (1996: 363). I freely and subjectively choose to remain an object for the Other, which enables me to assimilate the Other as other-looking-at-me, and hence also enables me to identify myself as a subject being-looked-at. However, in so doing, I am making use of the Other, who is thus really an instrument, an object, of my project of self-recovery. This objectification of the Other signifies the inevitable failure of this second strategy, for once made object, the Other ceases to exist as a free for-itself. The free subjectivity of the Other was that which I sought to absorb, since it is this quality that enables the Other to define me by looking at me and recognising me as a particular being. My masochistic attitude towards the Other thus inadvertently subverts my goal and so this particular strategy of self-recovery likewise fails.

For Sartre, our 'complex patterns of conduct toward one another are only enrichments of these two original attitudes' (1996: 407). Consequently, on his view at this point, human relations are essentially about conflict, rather than community.[7] Furthermore, intersubjectivity is fundamentally a dynamic of objectification, driven by ambivalent desire for the Other. I seek the Other, who has the power to recognise me and bring me into the fullness of being, yet also threatens my experience of self, objectifying me and causing me to flee into self-objectification.

In *Being and Nothingness*, this fundamental dynamic of desire, recognition and objectification is described as a reciprocal struggle between 'two freedoms confronted as freedoms' (1996: 379). Accordingly, Sartre insists:

> Everything which may be said of me in my relations with the Other applies to him as well. While I attempt to free myself from the hold of the Other, the Other is trying to free himself from mine; while I seek to enslave the Other, the Other seeks to enslave me. We are by no means dealing with unilateral relations with an object-in-itself, but with reciprocal and moving relations. (1996: 364)

However, Sartre is, of course, acutely aware that social relations are seldom 'reciprocal and moving', but often rigid and oppressive forms of systemic objectification, in which one class of people 'unilaterally' objectifies another class. *Anti-Semite and Jew* (1948) is perhaps his first systematic attempt to deal with this problem of non-mutuality in subject relations. Here, Sartre gives his classic account of oppression as non-recognition, and urges the oppressed to engage in authentic affirmations of their identity.

In *Being and Nothingness*, Sartre defines being in terms of situation. One, in fact, *is* one's situation in relation to others. Similarly in *Anti-Semite and Jew*, he begins by identifying Jews, not in terms of essentialist Jewish characteristics, but by the 'identity of their situations' (1948: 145). The situation of 'being-Jewish' is not freely chosen by the Jew, but largely constructed by the anti-Semite. The Jew is 'over-determined' from without: 'not free not to be a Jew' (1948: 77). According to Sartre, the oppressed class has two varieties of response to this over-determination. The first is a flight into 'inauthenticity', which involves the kind of self-deception elsewhere described in terms of 'bad faith'. The 'inauthentic' Jew seeks to deny his situation, for example by appealing to human universals that can hide the particularity of being a Jewish human.

By contrast, an 'authentic' response is to claim the identity thrust upon one by the recognising Other, and to attempt to invest this identity with appropriate and positive meaning. This strategy involves actively and proudly 'repossessing' the being that the Other has 'stolen' in the process of identification. However, Sonia Kruks emphasises: '[A]lthough authenticity might permit the affirmation of existential freedom in the face of oppression, it does not in itself address the social situation of the Jew'(1996: 126). The choice of the Jew to respond authentically is a moral or ethical choice that influences self-conduct, but which does not clearly challenge or alter the social and political fact of oppression.

In struggling with this lacuna, Sartre ends *Anti-Semite and Jew* with the somewhat sketchy solution of a 'classless society'. Presumably, in such a society, mutuality would be restored to relations of objectification, which would then be fluid and reciprocal bases of recognition, rather than systemic and rigid structures of oppression. While Kruks (1996: 127) rightly takes issue with the 'de-situated and schematic vision of history' Sartre falls back upon, a further concern is posed for postcolonialism. Sartre's 'classless society', in which each might exercise an equal right and capacity to objectify others and to be objectified, does not challenge the fundamental mode of comportment one has towards others in this process of identity construction. The goal is mutual recognition, but through mutual objectification. And for Sartre this involves assuming the fundamental postures of sadism or masochism in the attempt to absorb and assimilate the Other. The problem here signalled is that a genuinely postcolonial relation with the Other is inconceivable in terms of these attitudes.

In the first sections of this chapter we have found, in Hegel, a model of subject-formation in which being is produced through negation. In Sartre's early existentialism (strongly influenced by Kojève's revision of Hegel), this process is elaborated: he considers subject-formation to be partly reflexive, involving the considered actions of the self upon its own self, but primarily argues that the process takes place as reciprocal negation involving others. We recognise each other as we transform each other through the subjective act of objectification. Through this process of reciprocal negation, we bring each other into the fullness of identity we each originally lack, but simultaneously we are rendered as objects under each other's subjective gaze. I am brought into being as I make the other be-for-me, but I am also made object by and for the Other, who is similarly engaged in her own project of soliciting *my* recognition. The desire for recognition by the Other thus becomes the primary motive for the actions and modes of conduct individuals engage in, as they struggle to define themselves in a social situation. In conceptualising desire as the motive force related to one's essentially negative lack of being, satisfaction is only thinkable in terms of appropriation and possession (of the Other's *subjective* recognition and affirmation of me), and contradictorily, in terms of the *objectification* of the Other as evidence of my own subjective capacity.

Negativity: Sartre, psychoanalysis, poststructuralism

The *Critique de la raison dialectique* (1960) tempers the radically free existential consciousness Sartre describes in *L'Être et le néant* (1943) with a Marxist emphasis on structural determination, thus significantly revising his early philosophy of autonomous self-direction towards a far more encumbered view of selfhood. Whereas subjective freedom was initially privileged with absolute and unfettered choice, in the *Critique* freedom is understood to be materially situated, contextualised and constrained; the individualistic concepts of 'consciousness', 'lack' and 'desire' are refigured in this text as 'praxis', 'scarcity' and 'need', and so are more firmly connected to the material conditions determining identity and social forms.

This new emphasis nonetheless maintains the privileged notion of causal negativity in Sartrean social philosophy. Just as lack (and the negative form of desire it entails) was presented as an ontological given in *Being and Nothingness*, in the *Critique* material scarcity is the assumed given of social existence: 'scarcity . . . exists as a fundamental determination of man' and indeed, 'we are united by the fact that we all live in a world which is determined by scarcity' (1976b: 138, 136). The condition of scarcity defines the material basis of need and so explains how the 'actual state of the world can provide motivation for action' (1976b: 20). Sartre here echoes the more materialist aspects of Kojève's reading of Hegel with the grounding of negation in terms of historical agency conceived as material transformation. 'Everything is [now] to be explained through need; need is the first totalising relation between the material man and the material ensemble of which he is a part' (1976b: 80). Praxis is the purposive human activity directed towards satisfying need, ideally geared towards ending productive alienation and effecting the dialectical reconciliation of 'man', who is simultaneously (and contradictorily) the subjective producer of material reality, and the materially produced object. Accordingly, in the later Sartre, not only is causal negativity retained as a basis of historical determination, the concept of negation is also privileged in the notion of praxis conceptualised as purposive agency and transformative action.

Several commentators (McBride 1991; Aronson 1980; see Fox 2003: 108) have noted the ambiguous implications his emphasis on scarcity provokes for Sartre's political theory. Often in the *Critique*, scarcity is presented as a 'kind of inert material fact, a historical fate which social transformation would not obviate', which threatens to 'plunge human relations into hostility' (Fox 2003: 108,109) because it marks the 'impossibility of co-existence' (Sartre 1976b: 129; Fox 2003: 109). In this way, scarcity provides a material basis for the fundamental condition of ontological conflict earlier described in *Being and Nothingness*. While significant aspects of the *Critique* represent Sartre's attempt to think beyond this natural hostility in terms of the possibility of forging a collective solidarity of materially transformative human activity, group identification is only ever a reactive response to the determining condition of scarcity. As Nik Farrell Fox notes:

> By restricting group identification to a purely reactive status . . . Sartre omits both those concepts (such as love, friendship, kinship) through which we can reach an organicity of communal relations as well as vital, enriching experiences of intersubjectivity that arise from spontaneous gatherings (Fox 2003: 112).

Accordingly, the negative or reactive form of collective sociability arises mainly from the limited way Sartre theorises this as stemming from the determining, negative condition of need, rather than as a positive form of relationality, in which humans are united 'through common experiences of joy, friendship, sacrifice, love, partnership,

The Problem of the Negative

generosity or pleasure'(Fox 2003: 145). For Sartre, because it remains conditioned by determining negativity, group fusion is always haunted by a fundamental individualism, alienation and imminent hostility, as well as by the ossifying tendency towards serialisation; even in this later 'Marxist' work, community remains a problematic concept for Sartre. Regrettably, space restrictions prohibit a more detailed consideration of the implications of negativity in Sartrean political theory, but Chapter 2 will return to the problem signalled here, in order to reconsider the consequences of philosophical negativity in the context of postcolonial theory and political practice.

For now, it is important to note that Sartre is not alone in his privileging of causal negativity and critical negation. As Diana Coole (2000) explains, emphasis on negativity and its linkage with critique and transformation is a persistent and defining feature of modern and postmodern critical political philosophy. Negativity is discernible in Kant and celebrated in Hegel, and continues to be elaborated in the twentieth century through Marxian philosophy and the 'negative thinking' of the Critical Theorists of the Frankfurt School – most notably Adorno and Horkheimer – as well as in more contemporary work in post-Marxism and poststructuralism. Although Nik Farrell Fox (2003) insightfully describes Sartre as a precursor to these most recent movements in philosophical and political thought, the influence of Jacques Lacan is perhaps more palpable: arguably poststructuralism and post-Marxism both remain committed to an underlying concept of generative negativity introduced mainly via the conduit of Lacanian psychoanalysis. While a detailed consideration of Lacan's thought is beyond the scope of our concern, a brief excursus through his theory of the subject will be helpful when, in Chapter 2, I will outline the role played by negativity in postcolonial 'identity politics' and concepts of social transformation.

Lack, delay and psychic fissure are the defining features of the subject according to Lacan, who was a youthful participant in Kojève's seminar on Hegel, desire and recognition in the 1930s. In his commentary on Lacan and the political, Yannis Stavrakakis explains that Lacan's theory of the subject has been so influential because it 'can provide poststructuralism with a new conception of subjectivity compatible with its own theoretical foundations' (1999: 13); and furthermore, Michele Barrett claims it also suggests a way of addressing the 'lack of attention paid to subjectivity by Marxism's theory of ideology' (1991: 118–9; in Stavrakakis 1999: 14). This shared reference point of Lacan's theory of subjectivity thus also suggestively poses a way of bridging the divide between (anti-humanist) poststructuralism and (humanist) Marxism.

Lacan's achievement is to elevate the Freudian idea of 'splitting', which refers to the internal division of the psyche or ego as a result of the existence of the unconscious, into the constitutive force of subject-formation. Lacan begins with the idea that the unity of the ego is only ever ambiguously realised, since identification involves a leap of imagination to capture an illusory sense of wholeness, which is nonetheless destabilised by the fundamental alienation of the self from its image of itself. While the fragile ego emerges in the imaginary, the failure of self-security prompts it to seek an alternative basis for stability in the symbolic realm of language; the subject properly develops in the symbolic order, which binds and renders consistent the constructed self-image of the ego through the common structures of language and signification. The subject comes to exist as it is signified through language, but here too, the unified subject is finally impossible, permanently marked by the fundamental alienation of the signified object from the signifier that represents it and incompletely captures/produces its meaning. For Lacan, the 'kernel of the real' is that which resists symbolisation; the signified subject thus never achieves a full presence constituted outside of language, and its desire (to exist as objectively 'real') is never satisfied. For Lacan, the subject is forever uncertain and split, 'fundamentally biased and incomplete, inexpressible, fragmentary, differentiated and profoundly delusional' (1993: 145).

However, this notion of the 'lacking' subject provides the basis for a politically efficacious theory of subjectivity. In fact, poststructuralist works on subjectivity mainly develop the implications of the notion that certainty of essential identity is impossible, coupled with the idea that this lack constitutes the perpetual *desire* for identity, and hence is also a ground for subjective action:

> A lack is continuously re-emerging where identity should be consolidated. All our attempts to cover over this lack of the subject through identifications that promise to offer us a stable identity fail, this failure brings to the fore the irreducible character of this lack which in turn reinforces our attempts to fill it. This is the circular play between lack and identification which [marks] the human condition; a play that makes possible the emergence of a whole politics of the subject. (Stavrakakis 1999: 35)

Contemporary emphasis on 'identity politics' arises from the idea that (individual and collective) identity is represented and defined

The Problem of the Negative

in relation to others, who are simultaneously the desired source of recognition that affirms or confers identity and the feared or hated source of misrecognition that contests identity. This tension prompts the negation and transformation of given forms of identification, as one labours to create more stable forms of representation via affirmative relationships, leading to more adequate forms of recognition: subjectivity is theorised as situational, relational and always in construction. This conceptualisation resonates with attempts by some postcolonial theorists to think identity in terms of diaspora, hybridity, situation and performative strategy: '[not as] a recovery of a pre-existent state, but a textually invented history, an identity effected through figurative operations and a tropological construction of blackness as a sign of the colonised condition and its refusal' (Parry 1994b: 17; see also Bhabha 1987; Hall 1987).

Beyond the politics of identification and representation, Lacanian psychoanalysis is politically efficacious in another way: Slavoj Žižek (1989, 1993), Ernesto Laclau (1990), Chantal Mouffe (1993), Laclau and Mouffe (1985) and others (see Stavrakakis 1999: 40–71) explain that not only is the Lacanian *subject* impossible; the *object* is also essentially lacking, and this second notion of ontological impossibility similarly constitutes a causal negativity with important implications for critical politics. As was the case with the impossible subject, the impossibility of the Lacanian object derives from his insistence that the real is precisely that which escapes representation. The real is 'pre-symbolic'; it is an excess which cannot be captured by an act of representation and symbolic expression. All our attempts to represent the objective world (in Lacan, 'the Other') accordingly involves an act of linguistic foreclosure, which institutes a gap between the represented fictive 'real' and the true, unrepresentable real. This slit or fissure is, then, the negativity that may be grasped, or at least gestured towards, in order to criticise and contest the adequacy of representations of the objective world. In this way,

> Lacanian theory opens the road to a realist constructionism or a constructionist realism; it does so by accepting the priority of a real, which is however, unrepresentable, but, nevertheless, can be encountered in the failure of every construction. (Stavrakakis 1999: 86)

The political significance of the lacking object thus lies firstly in its critical effect: in denying that representations such as 'the social' or 'the nation' can capture the entirety of the real and adequately express the truth of the social world that is the domain of Other,

Lacanian thought draws attention to the illusory or fictive character of such representations, creating an aperture for their critical deconstruction.

Furthermore, the essential lack of certainty or coherence that is the experienced reality of social existence – the distance between *real* social conflict and *ideal* visions of social harmony in our political representations – generates the collective desire for an adequate, truly representative image of society; here, lack constitutes not only the basis of critique, but also provides the ground for the collective action of social construction in a bid to satisfy this desire. In effect, the Lacanian theory of the lacking subject and the foreclosed, incomplete object suggests that it is possible to 'rediscover a sense of political and personal agency through the unthought within the civic and the psychic realms' (Bhabha 1994: 65), and this 'unthought' forms a new ground for political action, which is no longer discernible in positive representations of authoritative identity or presence and the recognition it occasions, but in the essential *lack* or absence of identity. This lack constitutes an active and permanent desire for satisfaction as the recovery of a lost, 'pre-symbolic' and utopian fullness, which fantastically promises the alleviation of the ontological emptiness of selfhood and configurations of the social, and which accordingly motivates agents to action.

The *motif* of negativity clearly remains influential in the contemporary revision of dialectics in terms of this new 'dialectics of impossibility' that provides the basis of an argument for radical and transformative politics (Laclau and Mouffe 1985: 13). In many ways, Sartre's and Lacan's work can be thought to prefigure current notions of negativity in poststructuralist philosophy, as evidenced by their respective notions of the decentred subject and their rejection of a metaphysics of presence. These themes are echoed, for example, in the critical emphasis Jacques Derrida places on the negativities of deconstruction, deferral, fragmentation, undecideability, aporia and *différance*; or in Julia Kristeva's work on the uncanny (1990, 2000) and the abject (1982) that 'disturbs identity'. However, an alternative vision of a more positive social ontology is also momentarily contained within the same body of thought. For example, in Sartre's late work *Cahiers pour une morale* (1983), conflict is no longer seen as historical necessity, but as a historically contingent consequence of alienation; this contingency entails other forms of sociability are possible, including an 'authentic love' which 'signifies something wholly other than a desire to appropriate' (Sartre 1983: 362; in Fox 2003:

144–5). Lacan's insistence on the excessive quality of the real and *jouissance* is similarly suggestive of an alternative, positive ontology in which 'nothing is lacking' (Lacan 1988a: 313); and the Derridean 'supplement' offers a similar glimpse of the positive. While we might acknowledge that traces of an ontologically creative and transformative positivity are discernible in the work of these thinkers, it is important to note that they more often tend to treat positivity as an object of critique, rather than a critical force of transformation. In this critical tradition characterised by a conceptual privileging of the generative negativity of lack or absence, positivity is most often associated with presence, and hence with petrified and illegitimate structures of established reality.

By comparison, the Nietzschean poststructuralists – including Foucault, Deleuze and Guattari – maintain a significant emphasis on the positive productivity of power and desire. Indeed, unlike most of their contemporaries who insist upon the continuing need for critical negativity in philosophy, Deleuze and Guattari are emphatic about the properly creative and affirmative nature of philosophy, naming 'desiring-production' as a basis for constructive *and transformative* practices. Accordingly, Chapter 3 will turn to Deleuzian philosophy as a fresh resource for thinking the postcolonial. Deleuze's work appears most fitting for our purposes, because of his insistence that a positive conceptualisation of difference is needed in order to explain adequately the causal role it plays in materially constructive processes of desire and creative transformation.

Desire, negativity and politics

We might pause at this point to consider what the discussion so far has accomplished, with respect to the goals of the project. This chapter began with a description of the philosophical view that every form of being that exists (and becomes) is produced and transformed through a dialectical process. Hegel refuses the Cartesian notion of the essential, knowing subject as a first cause of being. Rather, being is defined in terms of its becoming, and this process involves a coming-to-self-knowledge that is ambiguously driven by an immanent cause (negativity, difference, lack) and by a final cause (ideal unity, mutual recognition). Thus, action that directs and produces dialectical becoming is driven by an ontological ideal of the fullness of being (which operates as an ultimate, final cause); by the *a priori* absence that defines lack of fulfilment, evidenced by difference (which operates as a first cause); and by the motive force of desire (which mediates and directs the resolution of the contradiction between the first and final causes). These notions are defined in ways particular to dialectical philosophy, each bound up with a concept of negativity or negation.

In Hegel, the ultimate unity of being is pre-given and is finally realised by the dialectical process in which identity and difference are harmonised. However, with Kojève's revision of Hegel, this ontological harmonisation, which proceeds in accordance with the character of the final cause, gives way to permanent ontological displacement. On this view, there is no final reconciliation of difference and identity. Instead, being endlessly creates itself through the labour of negation. This refusal of teleology significantly revises our understanding of dialectical process, becoming the point of departure for much contemporary poststructuralist and postmodern theories (and their mid-twentieth-century precursors). No longer solely defined as the process by which a predetermined and essential nature is realised through the labour of negation, dialectics becomes a tool of ongoing critique and constructivism, enabling a novel conceptualisation of being in terms of permanent becoming, while also emphasising the permanent possibility of critical negation and the philosophical resilience of a difference which is unable to be entirely eliminated, since it is the permanent precondition and the immanent cause of existence.

Nonetheless, negation remains the *modus operandi* of this revised dialectical process. Therefore, while poststructuralism has often been described as anti-Hegelian, this is correct only in so far as it rejects the *teleology* associated with Hegel's dialectical process, and hence also rejects the principle of final causation and the vision of progress towards a perfect end defined by such a teleology. Poststructuralism rejects the end to the dialectic, but on the whole remains committed to the notion of generative negativity and to the critical and transformative process of negation, which privileges difference both as immanent causation and as the permanent transformation of the given. The theory of the subject produced by lack, as well as the impossibility of 'the social', potentially addresses the conflict dividing poststructuralist and contemporary Marxist theories of social transformation, including Marxist and poststructuralist postcolonial theory. However, that both positions retain an underlying commitment to constitutive negativity causing productive and transformative process bypasses an important problem, which as we shall see in Chapter 2, is also raised by Fanon in his thinking about

The Problem of the Negative

subject-formation and politics. The crux of this problem is not simply the nature of representation *per se*, but the nature of the dialectical process of becoming, which progresses through expansive unification and the exclusion or assimilation of difference, in response to a primary and constitutive lack. While poststructuralism effectively denies the closure of the representations of the subject and society, it most often emphasises how this 'impossibility' is itself a generative negativity, a lack, which constitutes the ground for the desire to act. And this action takes form as the (finally impossible) dialectical struggle to represent identity, by progressively assimilating, or excluding and suppressing, the elements that escape representation and disrupt it. While such constructions of self and society might always contain the possibility of their transformation within them, because it is a movement of negativity and negation, the dialectic is itself problematic for postcolonial theory; this is because of the particularly negative role played by difference in the political process of recognition/misrecognition.

Particularly through Kojève's revision of Hegel, agency has been conceptualised in relation to these quite particular notions of causation and action that depend upon – and are supported by – certain embedded assumptions about the negativity of incomplete subjectivity, the appropriative nature of desire, and the possessive quality of power. A certain understanding about the nature of action and agency emerges from these particular assumptions about subjectivity, desire and power. Firstly, action is indelibly linked with the notion of negation and the transformation of the objects comprising one's external world, since the effects of this kind of action compel the other's recognition. Secondly, while action ultimately aims to bring about being, it is directed at the mediating other who brings the self into being through the act of recognition. Accordingly, action primarily consists in adopting a particular kind of attitude or approach towards the other, which elicits the desired response; namely, the desired bringing into being of the subject. We saw how, according to Sartre, dialectical subject-formation suggests that there are two fundamental attitudes one must take towards the other: sadism or the objectification of the other, and masochism or the objectification of the self for the other. In both cases, the aim of action is to control or manipulate the agency of the other's recognition, in order for the subject to emerge into the fullness of self-determined being. These conceptualisations of action and agency in Western political thought appear deeply problematic from the perspective of postcolonial theory and practice, in so far as they reinforce characteristically imperial attitudes and modes of sociability. With this groundwork in place, I am now able to describe how, through Fanon, much postcolonial theory creatively appropriates Sartre's perspective on identity and recognition, and in so doing, remains fettered to a problematic conceptualisation of agency towards others and the world.

Notes

1. Aspects of my discussion in these chapters appear as Bignall (2007a).
2. We might surmise that Hegel's dialectic is the dominant model of transformation in modern and 'progressive' thought *because* of this emphasis on negativity.
3. Hegel affirms this dual aspect of dialectical logic throughout his various works. For example, in the *Science of Logic*, the dialectic is described as 'the absolute method of knowing and at the same time is the immanent soul of the content itself' (1969: 28); and in the *Phenomenology of Spirit* he states: 'This alone is what is rational, the rhythm of the organic whole: it is as much knowledge of content as that content is notion and essential nature' (1977: 156). In his *Introduction to the Reading of Hegel* (1980), Alexandre Kojève notes that the dialectic is Hegel's description of reality, not his method of philosophy, although philosophy prior to Hegel is dialectical in method. Hegel's achievement is in writing a sort of descriptive meta-philosophy, which reflects upon its own process, and 'grasps and expresses' that process as dialectical. For commentary see Coole (2000: 53).
4. In fact, Kojève claims that he is simply giving an accurate interpretation of Hegel's argument; however many commentators on Kojève have insisted that his interpretation of Hegel significantly revises the text of the *Phenomenology*, and as such, constitutes an independent philosophical text.
5. Sartre was of course influenced by other philosophers, notably Kierkegaard, Heidegger and Husserl. However, the emphasis of *this* discussion is on desire and the negative and how these concepts have defined transformative agency, and for this reason, I will solely be considering the influence of Kojève's/Hegel's work on Sartre. There is some uncertainty about whether Sartre personally attended the Seminar; however there is no doubt that *Being and Nothingness* was heavily influenced by the ideas Kojève introduced into French intellectual society at the time.
6. I have focused on Sartre's analysis in *Being and Nothingness*, and Fanon's analysis in *Black Skin, White Masks*, rather than their later works, as these early texts explicitly consider the dialectical development

of subjectivity through desire and recognition. In fact, both Sartre and Fanon moved towards more explicitly Marxist conclusions and attempted to address the conditions of collective action, rather than subjective action, in their later works. Although beyond the scope of my immediate discussion, this movement between a focus on subjectivity and a focus on collective politics as the 'proper' or significant concern of social philosophy is repeated across many strains of contemporary political thought, including postcolonial theory, which remains riven between a poststructuralist destabilisation of authority and identity, and a (post-)Marxist affirmation of resistance strategy grounded in some authoritative notion of collective identity. I will return to this problem in Chapter 2.

7. See especially 1996: 429: 'The essence of the relations between consciousnesses is not the Mitsein; it is conflict.' As indicated in Note 6, in his later thought, Sartre does try to apply existentialism to the socio-political field in his attempt to forge a Marxist notion of community. However, like much current social theory, this later text is marked by the tension created by his commitment to both permanent negation and a possible community of universal recognition. In Chapter 2 I explore this tension in relation to postcolonial theory.

2

Postcolonial Appropriations

At this point we leave Africa never to mention it again. For it is no historical part of the world; it has no movement of development to exhibit . . . The History of the World travels from East to West, for Europe is absolutely the end of History, Asia is the beginning. (Hegel 1900: 99)

Our sense of critique is too thoroughly determined by Kant, Hegel and Marx for us to be able to reject them as 'motivated imperialists' . . . A deconstructive politics of reading would acknowledge the determination as well as the imperialism and see if the magisterial texts *can now be our servants*, as the new magisterium constructs itself in the name of the Other' (Spivak 1999: 7; emphasis added).

Like other postcolonial theories, this work is concerned with the legacy of colonial dominance in the social relations and institutions of the present. Postcolonial theory has in fact developed in response to this basic problem, and might best be characterised as aiming to find an appropriate solution by conceptualising and evaluating methods for the transformation of societies and cultures shaped by colonialism. An important aspect of this project is the critical destabilisation and deconstruction of the cultural authority of the colonising subject. A second aspect is the conceptualisation of social transformation in terms of the political agency of the 'subaltern' classes, repressed by colonial rule and the imposition of colonial culture. Resistance to colonialism and continuing cultural imperialism is enabled by the identification of a collective, self-conscious and oppositional subjectivity. This political self-consciousness is asserted through counter-discourse and concrete action, working against the discourses that have been mobilised to justify the processes of colonisation and against the exclusive policies and social arrangements that reflect and reinforce the authority of the colonisers.

However, these two strategies – destabilising colonial subjectivity and affirming oppositional subjectivity – uneasily co-exist. In fact, they often conflict and are a source of debate across the fractured terrain of postcolonial theory. The difficulty is that the critical movement of the destabilisation of the colonial subject also applies to any attempt to establish a conception of subjectivity capable of organising resistance. The critique of the authority of the subject is perceived to undermine coincidentally the unity, authority and agency of resisting subaltern subjects. Postcolonial activists, feminists and a whole range of minoritarian critics perceive that their difficult task is to carry out the destabilisation of the dominant subject position by drawing attention to its illusory claim to coherence and unity, while simultaneously forging a collective identity able to sustain and lend political weight to such a critical practice.

Furthermore, for the same reason that it has a complicated relationship with 'subjectivity', postcolonial criticism also has a vexed relationship with 'history'. On the one hand, resistances to colonial rule have most successfully been articulated through liberationist theories of revolutionary process, such as Marxism or culturalist nationalism, which are grounded in the vision and the progressive historicism of the Hegelian dialectic. On the other hand, as was suggested in the previous chapter, commonly conceptualised as a progressive process of enlightenment via dialectical negation and sublation, historicism is itself grounded in an imperial ontology and theory of desire, and a Eurocentric finality (Chakrabarty 2000; R. Young 1990). The political and philosophical commitment to progressive history consequently leads the critic to collude with the forms of colonial thought and practice that 'enabled the European domination of the world in the nineteenth century' (Chakrabarty 2000: 7).

This is why Leela Gandhi (1998: 167) explains postcolonial theory is 'caught between the politics of structure and totality on the one hand, and the politics of the fragment on the other'. She traces this fissure through its formation from the different, often contradictory, theoretical contexts of Marxism and poststructuralism. Accordingly, she identifies 'structure and totality' with Marxism, and 'fragment' with poststructuralism and postmodernism. The conundrum is that the poststructuralist emphasis upon the impossibility of the unified subject and of teleological history remains indispensable for critical postcolonial *theory*, while dialectical philosophies such as Marxism which rely on a concept of unified, collective and oppositional political subjectivity and a vision of historical progress, are seen to supply the most compelling basis for transformative *politics* (Gandhi 1998: viii-ix). Postcolonial theory is complicated by the need for poststructuralist and deconstructionist methodology which serves the purpose of destabilising colonial identity and its historicist underpinnings, but which apparently conflicts with the resisting agents' need to assert a self-defined, collective identity, with a unified set of political aims, as a ground for their political resistances and demands as 'peoples'.

In this chapter, I intend to show how this fissure can be mapped onto the ambiguous role played by 'desire' with respect to the actions of 'recognition' and 'negation' in dialectical philosophy. The purpose of such a mapping is to demonstrate that both 'poststructuralist' and 'Marxist' versions of postcolonial theory remain complicit with a model of agency that relies upon a notion of generative and critical negativity, inherited from dialectical philosophy. The debates *within* postcolonial theory may then be seen to obscure this commonality, and so also obscure the broader problem raised by the imperial character of 'negative agency'. This character was previously suggested in Chapter 1, and will now be elaborated upon. My intention, therefore, is to suggest that theorists working within both versions of postcolonial theory need to reconsider their relationship to philosophical negativity.

Subsequently, this chapter will look at the way these problems, internal to the field of postcolonial theory, are mirrored in the discourses and desires that have shaped action for reconciliation in Australia. The conceptual apparatus of dialectical negativity constrains transformative practice, which implies that there is a pressing need to cultivate alternative concepts of agency, transformation, identity and difference to those embedded in the conceptual model of the dialectic. The following chapter will accordingly consider the difficult possibility of 'thinking outside of the dialectic', in terms of an alternative model of transformation which can facilitate critique without linking difference with negativity.

Fanon: desire, recognition and post-colonial negation

The work of Frantz Fanon, and its appropriation by successive generations of postcolonial theorists, is particularly useful in tracing the image of contemporary postcolonial debate onto the various studies inspired by Hegel's dialectic of formative and transformative process. This is perhaps because Fanon's work has been 'annexed' by postcolonial theorists on both sides of the debate.[1] Arguably, this is possible because aspects of Fanon's work remain deeply ambiguous. For example, as Neil Lazarus comments, 'Fanon's critique of bourgeois nationalist ideology is itself derived from an *alternative nationalist standpoint*' (Lazarus 1999: 162). Or, while Homi Bhabha and Robert Young both make much of Fanon's contention that

Postcolonial Appropriations

'The Negro is not. Any more than the white man' (Fanon 1967a: 231), claiming him for a so-called 'post-humanist' poststructuralism, Fanon's discourse nevertheless remains couched in the liberationist language of existential humanism. Fanon's critique of Eurocentric humanism is therefore conducted through an alternative humanist perspective, which explicitly seeks to 'set afoot a new man' (Fanon 1967b: 246; see Bernasconi 1996). As with other interpretations of Hegel and neo-Hegelian philosophies, a closer look at Fanon's assumptions about, and manipulation of, the tension between dialectical negation and recognition can help to shed light on the ambiguities and limitations of his position, and on subsequent developments in postcolonial theory.

Fanon's early chapters on 'The Fact of Blackness' and 'The Negro and Recognition' (1967a) are perhaps his most condensed treatment of the theme of recognition. He begins by asserting that, in a social world shaped by colonialism and its aftermath, a subjected people will seek to affirm their national presence and political relevance by soliciting recognition from the colonising class. Through this acknowledgement, a colonised people seeks to negate the ways in which it has been effaced by the colonisers. However, influenced by Sartre, Fanon is troubled by the political duplicity threatened by the act of recognition, which not only gives the colonised class form in the eyes of their beholders, thereby rescuing them from 'nothingness', but also simultaneously fixes this class into the form given by the defining gaze of the recognising agent. Furthermore, the fact of blackness and the racism attached to prejudice about skin-colour constrain the possible responses of the colonised African individual. Unlike Sartre's Jew, who might opt for an inauthentic response and 'pass' as a non-Jew, Fanon's Negro is always marked by this blackness. Since there is no escape from blackness and the identification it confers, the native is always 'overdetermined from without . . . the *Negro* teacher, the *Negro* doctor' (1967a: 116–17). According to Fanon, the only response available to the colonised native is to affirm the authenticity of a positive identity derived from the fact of blackness.

However, Fanon rejects the notion that there are essential qualities and characteristics that capture black nature and experience, like those celebrated by Césaire, Senghor and other poets and theorists of negritude: rhythm, physicality, 'emotive sensitivity', ecstatic irrationality, a mystical connection with the natural world (1967a: 122–33). In part, then, Fanon's rejection of the strategy of negritude stems from his understanding that the assertion of an essentially black self-certainty grounded in past traditions can only be achieved by disavowing or devaluing other ways of 'being black' that have greater contemporary relevance, such as those experienced by Fanon himself as a black, French-Martinique intellectual, living in Paris, trained in Western psychoanalysis and a Marxist sympathiser, who finds himself alienated from heartfelt association with the attributes characteristically celebrated by negritude.

The problem, though, is not simply that negritude utilises archaic cultural forms to assert a positive Negro presence in the present. In fact, according to Fanon, negritude makes two fundamental mistakes: it searches for a Negro culture in the past, a glorious culture which might assuage the colonised native's 'anxiety to be present' (1967b: 173) in a history which systematically effaces native cultures through colonialism; and it fails to see that 'every culture is first and foremost national' (1967b: 174). In asserting a universal and essential Negro culture that gives positive form to a Negro subject, negritude responds to colonial discourse in terms derived from that same discourse. Fanon explains that just as 'colonialism's condemnation is continental in its scope' (1967b: 170), so too negritude asserts a pan-national Negro culture which ignores actual heterogeneity in the problems facing colonised peoples in different parts of the African diasporas. The construction of 'black' identity by the white or colonising class is usually a tool of oppression. The construction by blacks of their own quintessential cultural identity grounded in past traditions usually resists this situation, providing an alternative and positive image of blackness. However, in both instances an artificial stereotype is imposed upon an actually diverse collection of peoples. For Fanon, the crux of the problem concerns the colonial imposition of a misrepresentative universality with the colonial construction of 'the Negro' as its object; it follows that only by asserting local cultures which affirm the dynamic particularity of positive, culturally defined black identities, will people oppressed by racism and colonialism break free from the terms of universal misrepresentation that have become the legacy of colonial discourse.

For Fanon, 'a national culture is the whole body of efforts made by a people in the sphere of thought to describe, justify and praise the action through which that people has created itself and keeps itself in existence' (1967b: 188). National culture is thus intimately connected to a people's labour of material and intellectual production, is about self-creation, self-expression and self-determination, and grounds the emergence of collective self-consciousness. For this reason, according to Fanon, this 'self' defined by culture is best represented, not as a universal or global human subject, nor a racialised global subject such as the Negro, but as a national self emerging alongside and through the acts of cultural production that define a nation. In fact, he claims 'culture is the expression of national consciousness' (1967b: 198). Furthermore, the existence of a national culture depends upon the liberation of that nation from external domination: 'to fight for national culture means in the first place to fight for the liberation of the nation' (1967b: 187). However, as Fanon realises, the nation itself is a universalising force: '[T]he building of a nation is necessarily accompanied by the discovery and encouragement of universalising values' (1967b: 199). The important thing for Fanon is that these universals are not imposed from above by a colonising power, but created and identified by the people themselves in the act of building a nation 'which is born of the people's concerted action and which embodies the real aspirations of the people' (1967b: 198).

Here Fanon ends up at approximately the same place as Sartre does in *Anti-Semite and Jew*, with a vision of a 'people', a classless society defined by the boundaries of their nation, in which all might contribute equally to the construction of a national culture and identity that embodies the expression of their 'real aspirations'. Such a vision rests upon an ideal notion of social equality, but obviates the question of actual historical dominance of certain classes and castes prior to the political upheaval of colonisation, and so elides the historically different capacities for cultural expression in groupings internal to a nation. However, as with my analysis of Sartre in the previous chapter, my purpose here is not to assess the viability of Fanon's solution of a classless society of nation builders (of unremarked gender), but rather to draw attention to a constitutive ambiguity in Fanon's work, and to trace its effects on subsequent postcolonial theories. In particular, the ambiguity we find in Fanon concerns his rejection of homogenising universals at the global level, accompanied by his assertion of a universal at the level of the nation. On one hand, Fanon cleaves to the pole of difference and its power to negate a false universality; on the other hand, he cleaves to the pole of identity and its power to solicit recognition of a national cultural unity.

According to Homi Bhabha (1994: 44), for Fanon, 'the very place of identification, caught in the tension of demand and desire, is a space of splitting'. The colonised subject is forever caught between his demand for recognition (which requires the assertion of a coherent identity) and his desire for transformative negation (which requires the assertion of difference, of self as critical other). This ambivalent desire of the colonised self to be recognised as simultaneously identical and different, both 'certifies its existence and threatens its dismemberment' (Bhabha 1994: 45). Subsequent generations of postcolonial theorists have tended to take up one or other of Fanon's positions, without always addressing the ambiguity his work produces. Thus, Fanon's rejection of a pan-national universal has mostly influenced poststructuralist postcolonial theory, while his insistence that the nation acts as the arena for cultural unity, identification and a politics of recognition, has been highly influential for Marxist and communitarian postcolonial analysis.

However, for Fanon, the crucial problem of subject-formation and recognition faced by an oppressed class is vexed, not only because of the constitutive tension between recognition and negation which ambiguously both affirms and deconstructs notions of unity and identity, but also because this tension emerges from a dialectical structure of ontology, in which the negating or deconstructive position is defined according to its negative identity in relation to a given positivity. The constitutive tension that generates the subjectivity of the negating class thereby relies upon the unequal political distinction between identity and difference. To put this another way, the subjectivity of the negating class is generated by a causal negativity – the inequality of the political relation between identity and difference. Determined and defined by negativity, the resisting class has a perverse interest in preserving this negativity, which is the condition of its existence and recognition as such. Since culturalist nationalism (and negritude) arises in the context of colonial (and white) claims to superiority, the oppositional values it seeks to promote are themselves partly a construct of the colonial condition. The very need for a resisting nationalist or 'black' identity arises in response to colonial/racist oppression. Thus, from its inception, 'blackness' is marked as oppositional, as a difference circumscribed by the requirement that it define itself against, and in relation to, the colonising class it opposes. Even when self-identified, blackness arises from the condition of opposition, conceived in terms of a dialectical relation, which is

> by no means chaotic but is inscribed with order and direction . . . what negation generates is not random otherness but a determinate other marked with the specificity of what is negated. It is a negative shaped by its opposite. (McCarney 2000: 86)

Postcolonial Appropriations

Writing from her childhood experience of French colonisation in Algiers, Hélène Cixous explains how this dialectical generation of alterity maintains the political distinction between the colonising agent and the colonised object:

> [W]hat is called 'other' is an alterity that does settle down, that falls into the dialectical circle. It is the other in a hierarchically organized relationship in which the same is what rules, names, defines and assigns 'its' other. (Cixous 1986: 70–1)

This remains the case even when the identity of the resisting class is self-defined. In certain respects, it is inconsequential whether blackness is affirmed as 'sensual', or 'communitarian', or 'irrelevant from a humanist perspective', or 'open to being anything at all', since the salient feature of blackness is its oppositional situation within the system of colonial domination and subordination. It remains other, defined by its relation of opposition to the dominant political class. Whatever else it is, the fact of colonial history renders blackness always the negative term, the negating other, and it is the internalisation of this negative being-other, the spiral towards 'self-hating', that Fanon explains is most insidious and damaging for colonised individuals: 'for unconsciously I distrust what is black in me, that is, the whole of my being' (1967a: 191).

Cixous comments further upon how dialectical progress promises liberation, but always-already implies another, suppressed story of oppression:

> [T]he white (French), superior, plutocratic, civilized world founded its power on the repression of populations who had suddenly become 'invisible' . . . Invisible as humans . . . Thanks to some annihilating dialectical magic. I saw that the great, noble, 'advanced' countries established themselves by expelling what was 'strange'; excluding it but not dismissing it; enslaving it. A commonplace gesture of History: there have to be *two* races – the masters and the slaves. (Cixous 1986: 70)

This is most significant if dialectical struggle is *the only* ontological model perceived to account for the shape of history and processes of social transformation, for as Sartre points out:

> negritude appears as the minor term of a dialectical progression: The theoretical and practical assertion of the supremacy of the white man is its thesis; the position of negritude as an antithetical value is the moment of negativity. But this negative moment is insufficient by itself, and the Negroes who employ it know this very well; they know that it is intended to prepare the synthesis or realisation of a human society without races.

> Thus negritude is the root of its own destruction, it is a transition and not a conclusion, a means and not an ultimate end. (Sartre 1976a: 15)

The minor position exists not simply for its own sake, but in support of the development of the dominant position, which is transformed in the process of their confrontation, but never stops being the dominant position, since it will always be the focus and the agent of its own history. Dialectical history describes the *particular* story of the subject: it represents the histories of others only in so far as they intersect with and confront the subject on its path of being. The subject transforms as it incorporates or assimilates the other, but it always reaffirms its active and dominant historical role as it acts upon the other to restore the difference that determines it. The other, by contrast, facilitates the transformation of the subject, but it is always acted upon, assimilated, and in teleological versions of dialectical thought, is finally eliminated (fully assimilated) when its transformative function has been satisfied.

As a 'minor term', the negating class is always the other, the 'not-yet' of history: 'Historicism – and even the modern, European idea of history – one might say, came to non-European peoples in the nineteenth century as somebody's way of saying "not yet" to somebody else'(Chakrabarty 2000: 8). Dialectical history reduces the Negro to a supportive role that enables 'human' (non-Negro) subjectivity to unfold inexorably towards completion. Negritude exists only to contest the adequacy of the idea of this subject on its journey towards completion; the majoritarian (white/Western/masculine/. . .) subject becomes more adequate, or more universal, as it assimilates and incorporates the values of negritude and makes them its own. Conversely, history is the story of the developing adequacy of the non-Negro subject, who must incorporate negritude to accomplish 'universality'. As the 'minor term', negritude is a necessary impetus for the developing self-concept of universal humanity, but the fact of this necessity denies negritude any real freedom or creative agency in the process of history-making. The Negro is reduced to an object in the history of the subject: 'And so it is not I who make a meaning for myself, but it is the meaning that was already there, pre-existing, waiting for me' (Fanon 1967a: 134).

In the end, the colonising subject has little to lose in 'recognising' colonised peoples in terms of the identity they assert for themselves, since this recognition simply facilitates the incorporation of the 'minor position' within the grand history of the (expanding, developing, colonising) subject. Accordingly, Fanon writes: 'One day, the White Master, *without conflict*, recognised the Negro slave' (1967a: 217). As he sees it, when recognition takes place without conflict, the other is denied agency and a creative role in history. Fanon's solution is therefore to restore conflict to the dialectic, to return violence upon the coloniser, to *make* oneself considered, in a form that is not simply amenable to assimilation or integration to the dominant position.[2] And for Fanon, as for Kojève and Sartre, the question of desire is central to this becoming 'actional':

> As soon as I *desire* I am asking to be considered ... I demand that notice be taken of my negating activity insofar as I pursue something other than life; insofar as I do battle for the creation of a human world. (1967a: 218)

Accordingly, Fanon asks the rhetorical question: '*What* does the black man want?' (1967a: 8). And, somewhat predictably, he answers that the black man desires to take the place of the white man, to possess the objects of the white man's desire; in effect, the black man desires to *be*, to attain the self-defining subjectivity already claimed by the white man through the recognition of his mastery over difference. Fanon wants recognition as a desiring subject, as a subject who transforms and possesses the material world through the act of negation. Thus, he cleaves to the dialectical goal of reciprocal recognition between 'freedoms confronted as freedoms', with a Marxist inflection similar to Kojève's and Sartre's, which holds that subjects might acknowledge each other in terms of the negating agency each extends, upon each other and their world.

Again, at this point, Fanon returns us to the moment at which we left Sartre: the possibility of mutual recognition does not divert from the central problem of the imperial character of dialectical action, in that it does not contest the dialectical mode of subject-formation which takes place through the objectification of others, nor the project to realise self-certainty by the elimination of contesting alterity. Fanon's effort to think the conditions in which all humans might become 'actional' and recognise each other in terms of the negations they perform upon the world, is an attempt to make possible a universally equal capacity for social agency and a truly mutual recognition. However, like Sartre, Fanon does not challenge the character of this human agency or the nature of action associated with the dialectical verbs of recognition and negation (see Turner 1996).

Feminist postcolonial theorists have drawn attention to the

masculine-identification of social agency and the problem of subject-formation through the objectification of the feminine other in the decolonisation theory of Fanon (for example, Chow 1988: 55–73), also suggesting that the debates within postcolonial theory may be seen to elide the more basic question of the *kind* of agency enabled by Hegel's (or Kojève's) dialectic of desire and recognition. Although Fanon places desire at the centre of postcolonial critique and reconstruction by asking: 'What does a man want? What does the black man want?' (1967a: 8) his question bypasses the primary problem of the *form* such desire takes, and the political effects it produces. While Fanon arguably poses a *post-colonial* question, the question properly raised by *postcolonialism* is subtly different: it asks '*How* does the postcolonial individual want? Or, *how* can we make a *postcolonial* desire and power work to disrupt effectively systems of *colonial* agency, rather than simply to reproduce such systems?' The question most pertinent for postcolonial theory then becomes: what critical and constructive actions can be imagined, that will not become perversely bound up within the structures they are opposed to and seek to transform?

Post-colonial resistance and the deconstruction of colonial desire

However, postcolonial theory tends to think resistance and socially transformative action according to the established terms of discourse adopted (though problematised) by Fanon, emphasising either collective identity and a power of recognition, or difference and its power of negation, as grounds for transformative action. Anti-colonial resistance struggles are conventionally characterised as collective class actions, which are often violently oppositional, and aim to return due authority to colonised peoples by re-inscribing an authoritative presence in national life. Often coupled with an explicitly Marxist revolutionary agenda critical of imperial economic exploitation in the colonies, resistance struggles tend to be articulated in terms of Marxist notions of political agency and emancipatory practice, which are drawn from the dialectical tradition of progressive transformation and grounded in representations of authoritative and oppositional identity (see Parry 1994a). Avowed through discourse which asserts and demands recognition of the identity and goals that define a resisting class and a national culture, these representations have authority precisely to the extent that they can claim to be representative; that is, to the extent that they exhibit a unified coherence and integrity of form (Brennan 1990). As an integral part of the project of national liberation, anti-colonial resistance has therefore not only been directed towards the negation and overthrow of colonial authority, but also to the positive articulation of well-defined political and cultural identity, expressed, for example, in postcolonial nationalist literature. Indeed, Simon During (1995: 125) asserts that 'the post-colonial desire is the desire of decolonised communities for an identity'. More generally, the creation of a canon of seminal texts of 'Third World Literature' gives collective voice to the wider experiences of colonised peoples, broadly identified in terms of the common situation of colonisation.[3] In choosing their own terms of representation for themselves and their histories, colonially oppressed peoples of the world can at times claim a certain unity of experience, which can be used to undermine the logic of colonial authority, by discrediting, decentring and dismantling the repetitive discourses that justified colonialism in diverse locations.

This conceptualisation of resistance has been supplemented, and somewhat contested, by the relatively recent inclusion of poststructuralism and deconstruction as critical methods relevant to theorising the post-colonial condition. In particular, Edward Said (1978) found Foucault's early work on discourse and discipline helpful for thinking about the powerful cultural practices of colonialism, and Gayatri Spivak's translation of Derrida's *Of Grammatology* (1974) introduced the 'deconstructive' potential of Derrida's work as a critical technique relevant to postcolonial theory. Although he is also deeply influenced by Fanon and by Lacanian psychoanalytic theory, Homi Bhabha significantly develops this deconstructive technique of post-colonial analysis, by reading the colonial archive with the intent of discovering the hidden gaps and anxieties in colonial discourse, which can be seen to mark moments of instability in the exercise of colonial dominance. While Spivak and Bhabha have often been criticised by Marxist postcolonial theorists, including Benita Parry and Aijaz Ahmad, who accuse them of deconstructing and neglecting the importance of collective conditions of resistance, it is also possible to see that Bhabha's 'work stresses and extends the agency of colonized peoples, whose participation in resistance to colonialism has often been underplayed when it does not fit our usual expectations of violent anti-colonial opposition' (Huddart 2006: 3).

In fact, much of Bhabha's work is committed to disrupting the conceptual boundaries between the oppositional classes of self and other, not by dialectical sublation, but by attending to the 'liminal' spaces at the 'edges' of identity, or 'between' identities, where the hybrid creation of meaning takes place in the shifting spaces of their relationship. According to Huddart (2006: 6), Bhabha's disinclination to credit the critical politics of dialectical opposition is a deliberate and political choice:

> [I]f you know where your identity ends and the rest of the world begins, it can be easy to define that world as other, different, inferior, and threatening to your identity and interests. If cultures are taken to have stable, discrete identities, then the divisions between cultures can always become *antagonistic*.

For Bhabha, then, the deconstructive technique of exploiting the insecurities, weaknesses and fissures in discourses of identity is a preferable critical strategy, because it resists reinforcing a problematic relation of antagonism through the discrimination and Manichean separation of oppositional identities (see also JanMohamed 1985).

Whereas the early Said (1978) was most interested in tracing the ways in which colonialism established and maintained its identity and its dominance through the repetition of colonial utterances, forming a coherent and consistent discourse of racial difference and imperial superiority, for Bhabha (1994) the most significant feature of colonial discourse about the other is not that it constructs a false representation that mobilises a justification for a political end, but that it reveals aspects of colonial subjectivity that suggest its own internal lack of coherence. As Robert Young comments: if 'Said shows that misrelation is the secret of Orientalism, Bhabha demonstrates that oscillation is at the heart of the colonialist' (Young 1994: 13–14). Bhabha's own analysis therefore attends closely to the process of colonial subject-formation, which he – like the (post-)Hegelian philosophers discussed in the previous chapter – sees as a process structured and compelled by desire (Bhabha 1994: 66–84, 85–92). He draws attention to the ways in which colonial desire is marked by ambivalence, evidenced by the moments when colonial discourse is conflicted by simultaneous attraction towards the allure of the exotic and unknown delights of the other, and revulsion at the apparent baseness of the other. According to Bhabha, by manipulating the tension between this simultaneous desire to appropriate the attractive other and to repel the base other, colonial subjectivity can be contested or unravelled from within, collapsed by its own internal instability (1994: 102–22).

In his book on desire and miscegenation in the context of colonisation, Robert Young (1995) expands upon the characteristics of 'colonial desire' and subject-formation described by Bhabha, with respect to sex as the most explicit site of desire in action.[4] He details the anxiously fastidious colonial labelling of kinds of bodies produced by miscegenation (quadroons, octoroons, half-castes, full-bloods, mulattos) and their evaluation according to a hierarchy of acceptability, and draws attention to an overt colonial discourse of disgust provoked by such racial mixing, which nonetheless evidences a covert fascination with the other as an object of desire. His purpose is to argue that the construction of such a detailed and formal bank of 'scientific' knowledge about race and miscegenation demonstrates not only a covert fascination for such transgressive couplings,[5] but also an attempt to contain the threat to the identity of the dominant subject posed by such blurring of bodily boundaries: colonial revulsion indicates a fear that contact with the other might contaminate or blur the distinction between self and other, between colonising subject and the objects of colonisation. By naming the difference posed by miscegenation, it can be safely appropriated as knowledge, even while miscegenation is repulsed by common codes of decency. Once again, we are reminded how the dialectical tension between desire as the force of identity-formation and desire as the force of transgression and transformation constitutes a central ambivalence in the desiring subject, which explains both the effort to assimilate, contain and control difference, and the effort to banish all traces of contaminating difference from the boundaries describing one's own identity.

With this constitutive dissonance in mind, Bhabha elaborates 'mimicry' as a resistance strategy. Whereas 'ambivalence' refers to the role played by the desiring subject in the process of identification/disavowal that signifies the inevitable loss of colonial control, 'mimicry' refers to the potentially subversive role played by the desired other in this process. In assimilating to colonial culture, the other mimes the colonial subject – takes on the pretensions of the 'superior' culture, affects the speech, values, system of production and fashion of the coloniser – and so is at once recognised as 'similar', yet disturbingly 'dissimilar': not quite/not white (Bhabha 1994: 87). The mime starkly confronts the colonising subject with a 'menacing' and 'partial' reflection, rearticulating and alienating the (absent, unstable) identity of the coloniser through the act of mimicry, and returning the gaze of the colonised upon the coloniser so that the constituting ambivalence of the desire that structures colonial identity is plainly visible: the desire to assimilate and the desire to differentiate is at once marked upon the visage of the colonised mime. In this way, the crucial characteristic of colonial identity that is captured through mimicry is *absence* of fixed identity, and the mimed reflection of this absence thus collapses the self-certainty associated with colonial authority. Self-consciously practised, 'mimicry marks those moments of civil disobedience within the discipline of civility: signs of spectacular resistance' (Bhabha 1994: 119). However, since it is limited to the deconstruction of the dominant (colonising) power, mimicry surely falls somewhat short as a resistance strategy. It offers no alternative vision of society, no positive reconstruction of an alternative relationship.

While Bhabha arguably extends the reach of post-colonial resistance by drawing attention to the ways in which colonial identity can be disturbed by quotidian acts of uncanny relation, the resisting subjectivity of the subaltern (as it has conventionally been conceptualised) is also undone by the same deconstructive tool of critically reading social texts and representative discourses to uncover their points of incoherence and instability. In her important and acclaimed essay 'Can the Subaltern Speak?' (1985), Spivak challenges the rather facile assumption (in the context of Spivak's critique, made by Deleuze and Foucault in discussion (1977), but also evident in much Western political theory) that colonised peoples can adequately represent themselves within the established terms of Western political discourse, in order to recover a lost or silenced, definitively 'subaltern', speaking position. In fact, she insists that the colonised individual is never a stable site of resisting agency, being always already inscribed with multiple, at times contradictory, sites of identification, including gender and economic class. Where the subaltern might exercise agency within one system, this agency is simultaneously effaced by the other systems of representation. As a result, 'there is no space from where the subaltern (sexed) subject can speak' (1985: 129). She occupies no discrete position of enunciation, but is ever manipulated, displaced and rewritten, either as an object of imperialism, or of patriarchy. As Robert Young comments:

> It is not a question, therefore, of being able to retrieve the lost subaltern subject as a recovered authentic voice who can be made to speak once more out of the imposed silence of history, because that subject is only constituted through the positions that have been permitted. (1990: 165)

Spivak's intention is to deconstruct the power and centrality of the notion of representation that lies at the heart of Western political philosophy by destabilising its methodological and epistemological underpinnings, and her analysis incidentally attends to the ways in which postcolonial theory and resistance practice problematically derives its terms of reference from the discourse of the coloniser. However, in pointing to the multiple, contradictory and unstable sites of subaltern identification, Spivak denies the coherence of a representative resisting class capable of 'speaking' an alternative history, and so collapses subaltern identity as a stable ground for resistance.

For this reason, deconstructive postcolonial theory is criticised by Marxists; it is accused of being a 'repressive and bourgeois' (Ahmad 1992: 36) discourse produced by a privileged intellectual class, which is problematically uninterested in questions of collective action and the cultural and socio-economic conditions of determination of identity and relations of dominance, and of theory itself. Thus, Benita Parry writes:

> The significant differences in the critical practices of Spivak and Bhabha are submerged in a shared programme marked by the exorbitation of discourse and a related incuriosity about the enabling socio-economic and political institutions and other forms of social praxis. (1987: 43)

For Marxist postcolonialism, the capacity for critical speech is understood primarily as a concern of the community in which such speech is produced, rather than an issue of subjectivity. Postcolonial theory influenced by deconstructive poststructuralism is seen to privilege discourse and text as the products of the 'speaking subject' under analysis, thereby neglecting the primary cultural, social and economic determinations of enunciation (Parry 1994b). Accordingly, poststructuralist postcolonial theory is accused of being politically ineffectual, little more than an ideological tool lacking basis in political reality, which shifts political attention away from the material causes of oppression, and towards a privileged class preoccupation with identity and subjectivity.[6] In fact, by emphasising the fragmentation of identity and history, deconstructive poststructuralism is claimed to obscure analysis of the 'real politics' behind imperialism and exploitation: global capitalism (Ahmad 1992: 18–23). By claiming the impossibility of certain or stable forms of representation, such theory is also perceived to undermine the concrete efforts of resistance made by certain nations and narratives of nationalism, against their engulfment by the uniforming forces of globalisation

(Parry 2004). In destabilising, multiplying and fragmenting their meaning, poststructuralism 'debunks all efforts to speak of origins, collectivities, determinate historical projects' (Ahmad 1992: 38), and so fails to acknowledge the political salience of unifying concepts and categories, such as nationalism, actually used in concrete forms of practical resistance. Worse, this failure suggests the worrying possibility that poststructuralism is a theoretical perspective which is politically motivated by the desire to deflect and deny due recognition of resisting subjects, in a deliberate construction of a disabling politics coinciding with the emergence into subjectivity of previously subjec*ted* peoples: '[T]he concept of postmodernity has been constructed in terms that more or less intentionally wipe out the possibility of post-colonial identity' (During 1995: 125). On this view, poststructuralism is a conservative discourse, which works to preserve existing political dominance and to disempower locally resisting peoples. In response, Marxist postcolonialism seeks to restore the possibility of identity and recognition to the political process of dialectical struggle for social progress, and thus to reaffirm the critical role of negativity and negation in the play of the productive and transformative tension between well defined, oppositional categories.[7]

While Marxist and deconstructivist impulses within postcolonialism tend to divide and, to some extent, polarise the field of study, they are nevertheless united in their common emphasis on the critical power of the negative. In Marxist postcolonialism, this negativity is rendered in the dialectical play of opposition; in poststructuralist, deconstructive and psychoanalytic postcolonialism, critical negativity inheres in the crucial lack or absence at the ontological heart of the subject, destabilising its authoritative certainty from within. In both cases, negativity transforms the problematic presence or positivity of an authoritative structure, either by directly opposing its legitimacy with a contesting form, or by undermining the ground upon which its legitimacy stands.

Thus, in both formulations, postcolonial theory is a definitively critical theory, and postcolonial critique is grounded in negativity. In either case, difference (the negating class, the lack at the heart of the subject) is the negativity that prompts transformation. Critical negativity therefore arises from this fact of difference in its various forms, including not only opposition and contradiction (Marxism), but also the ambivalence signalled by the uncanny surfacing of repressed alterity (poststructuralism). However, in both strains of postcolonial thought, transformation occurs through the struggle to negate the uncomfortable tension provoked by difference, and this action generates novel forms of unity or presence: opposing forms are sublated and transformed into new unities; one's uncomfortable encounter with uncanny difference creates new self-understanding and prompts alternative ways of repressing the destabilising foreignness within oneself. The concluding section of this chapter will problematise the collusion of negativity, critique, difference and postcolonial agency, but firstly some practical effects of this collusion can be identified, by analysing the discourses of indigenous disadvantage, resistance and postcolonial reconciliation that currently characterise relations between indigenous and non-indigenous communities in postcolonial Australia.

Post-colonial Australia: constitutive disadvantage and resistance

Irrespective of whether the British colonisation of Australia was justified in international law by the assertion of Australia's status as a *terra nullius*,[8] it is clearly the case that popular colonial discourse constructed indigenous Australians as *civil nullius* – as primitives, lacking proper (i.e. European) structures of government, law, religion, agriculture, history, moral decency, self-awareness and rational foresight. In short, at the time of Australia's colonisation, indigenous populations were perceived to lack 'civilisation'. Thus, in 1824, *The Sydney Gazette* affirmed the consensus among settlers that:

> the very notion of property, as applicable to territorial possession, did not exist among them [indigenous peoples]. They had no civil policy, no regular organised frame of society, on the regulations of which the distinction of landed property depends . . . Each tribe wandered about wherever inclination prompted, without ever supposing that one place belonged to it more than any other. They were the *inhabitants*, but not the proprietors of the land. This country was then to be regarded as an unappropriated remnant of common property; and, in taking possession of it, we did not invade another's right, for one only claimed that which was before unclaimed by any (cited in Lattas 1987: 48).

The aboriginal inhabitants of Australia were accordingly entrenched in the colonial imaginary as being too primitive to be considered as sovereign peoples, thereby paving the way for the representation of the territory itself – in public discourse, at least – as a *terra nullius*, a land without a sovereign, available for appropriation and settlement.

These doctrines of *civil* and *terra nullius* did not only ignore the presence of indigenous Australians as a matter of colonial convenience. They also actively constituted a colonial culture which represented indigenous peoples and their culture in negative ways, with subsequent implications for the development of the social and political institutions that continue to structure problematic forms of relationship and representation in modern Australian society. This underlying principle of a general association of indigeneity, difference and negativity was seen to be an *a priori* justification for colonisation, since the introduction of 'civilising and Christianising' missions was argued to be duly and morally *required* to fill the void of civil humanity that apparently characterised aboriginal Australia. In our time, indigenous Australians continue to be defined in negative terms regarding their relative invisibility and absence from national life. Similarly, just as colonial media often represented indigenous people negatively, as morally dubious, degenerate and depraved, 'disordered, violent, amoral beings existing beyond the margins of normal human sociality' (Lattas 1987: 41), the association of indigeneity with overwhelmingly negative imagery continues today in popular (largely, but not exclusively, non-indigenous) public discourses of concern about indigenous communities in crisis, hopelessly beleaguered by drug and alcohol abuse, crime, unemployment, welfare dependence, social and domestic violence, and amoral 'cultural' practices including child sex abuse (see Langton 1993). Furthermore, these discourses continue to mobilise justifications for heavy-handed intervention in indigenous affairs and communities, as evidenced in June 2007, when after years spent ignoring the evidence and concern consistently voiced by indigenous people (Behrendt 2007; Atkinson 2007), the Commonwealth suddenly declared a 'state of emergency' in relation to child sexual abuse in the Northern Territory and, using a military presence, took direct control of communities, overriding the authority of State and local government structures and the self-governing measures existing in these indigenous communities (see Altman and Hinkson 2007).

The racist principle underlying the doctrine of *civil nullius* and its extended legal version of *terra nullius* was therefore not simply a non-recognition of existing difference. In fact, indigenous culture was clearly recognised, but as different *and as negative*, in relation to a Eurocentric point of view embedded in European, Christian, capitalist culture. Indigenous difference was constructed through negative imagery – in terms of all it was *not* – by a colonial culture, which simultaneously imagined and represented itself in contrasting positive terms, as culturally and morally superior, as the product of accomplished and progressive civilisation, as substantively and historically *present*. The recognition of indigenous difference as negative absence, deficiency, or depravity, as being without history, is recognition of a difference circumscribed by the requirements of the defining colonisers, which allowed the colonial assertion of justified political dominance. The negative aboriginal state is constructed as a problem, which a 'civilised' presence can, and must, rectify. Mick Dodson comments:

> Since their first intrusive gaze, colonising cultures have had a preoccupation with observing, analysing, studying, classifying and labelling 'Aborigines' and Aboriginality. Under that gaze Aboriginality changed from being a daily practice to being 'a problem to be solved'. (Dodson 1994: 3)

The problematisation of aboriginality occurred through the colonial association of indigenous nature with generalised lack or negativity. As Paul Patton suggests, the

> principle of *terra nullius* was implicated not just in doctrines of international and domestic law, but in the whole complex of measures which give effect to the legal invisibility of indigenous peoples, as well as in the beliefs and attitudes which made these measures possible. (1999: 64)

With the 1992 ruling on the *Mabo* case, the Australian High Court decisively rejected the racist principle of *terra nullius* with respect to native title (*Mabo v Queensland*; see Bartlett 1993). In recognising the prior existence and continuation of native title, the court implicitly recognised the prior existence and continuation of indigenous custom and law as a source of native title, which therefore impacted upon the foundations of Australian constitutionalism (see Webber 2000). *Mabo* therefore represents a significant shift in domestic legal practice, away from the association of aboriginality with negative absence in the doctrine of *terra nullius*, and towards acknowledging indigenous presence. However, the recognition of native title and indigenous presence is not enough to reject the full principle behind *civil nullius*, which does not only refer to indigenous absence, but also to other modes of negativity, such as inferiority, degeneracy and deficiency.

In fact, in *Mabo*, the common law 'recognises' indigenous law, but still asserts its inferiority in a colonial hierarchy, which affirms Western assumptions about the proprietary nature of the relationship to land (an assumpiton that is not traditionally shared by indigenous peoples), and leaves unchallenged the colonial State's authority to extinguish native title, as indeed the Howard Government chose to do following the *Wik* decision in 1998.[9] This hierarchy is also reflected in the courts' understanding of the sort of property rights that native title gives to indigenous peoples. Native title does not fully equate with standard property rights, which include a usufructuary right to exclude, transfer or dispose (Pearson 1997a; Bartlett 1996; see also McNeill 1997). An indigenous right to native title is an inferior or lesser type of property right, which is recognised only in so far as it does not compromise the possessive enjoyment of the title claimed by Europeans upon settlement.

In certain respects, *Mabo* left the relation of power largely intact and unchallenged: indigenous peoples remain positioned as disadvantaged supplicants for recognition of 'special' native rights, by a reluctant State and a mainstream community that has the power to be selectively responsive. Nevertheless, with the formal rejection of *terra nullius* as a principle of colonial justification, *Mabo* does represent a benchmark decision in Australian jurisprudence and political culture. One task of Australian political philosophy in the wake of the *Mabo* and *Wik* judgements is to give expression to this practical development (Patton 1999: 77–8). Australian postcolonialism might now best focus on *how* indigenous presence is recognised in discourse, honouring the courts' rejection of *terra nullius* by creating concepts that would enable its more complete overthrow in social discourse and institutional practice. (Indeed, one way to contribute to this task is attempted here, by imagining a philosophy of process predicated upon a positive conceptualisation of difference, with corresponding concepts of critical and constructive, transformative practice.)

Such conceptual intervention is necessary because the association of aboriginality, difference and negativity persists in contemporary discourses – indigenous and non-indigenous – about the 'problem' of indigenous disadvantage with respect to cultural enjoyment, national participation, and legal and social status. Reconciliation is proposed as a solution to this 'problem of aboriginality'. In its first report to Parliament, the Council for Aboriginal Reconciliation (CAR) presented reconciliation as 'the satisfactory resolution of the disadvantaged situation' faced by Aboriginal and Torres Strait Islander peoples in Australia (CAR 1994a: xiv). Chairperson Patrick Dodson claimed that this 'disadvantage can be traced directly to dispossession', which took place 'without rights, without consultation, without negotiation, without compensation, and little in the way of equal human interaction' (1994a: 4–5). The legacy of historical dispossession is now seen in the 'disadvantage and inequality of Aboriginal people in all areas of life where comparison is possible between Aboriginal and non-Aboriginal people' (1994a: 5), and is clearly reflected in Indigenous people's 'poor health, substandard housing, poor education outcomes and low levels of employment' (1994a: 8). Reconciliation is needed to address the 'community division, discord and injustice to Aboriginal people' (1994a: 9), and in particular, the Council is concerned to instruct government in the 'special measures' that 'will be necessary to overcome the disabilities being experienced by so many people of Aboriginal descent' (1994a: 11).

The Second Report, delivered to Parliament in 1997, also frames the problem in terms of a discourse of indigenous disadvantage. It perceives that the statutory responsibility of the Council is 'to promote, by leadership, education and discussion, a deeper understanding of the history, cultures, past dispossession and continuing disadvantage of Aborigines and Torres Strait Islanders and of the need to redress that disadvantage' (CAR 1997: 12). It reaffirms that this 'disadvantage is tragic: Indigenous people have lower life expectancy than non-Indigenous Australians, suffer a high burden of illness and higher rates of infant mortality, have higher unemployment and are over-represented in custody and arrest statistics' (1994a: 12). In its final report to Parliament in 2001, the Council similarly concludes: 'continuing acute disadvantage, discrimination and racism suffered by Aboriginal and Torres Strait Islander peoples remains the biggest challenge for reconciliation'(CAR 2001: 101).

In other contexts, reconciliation is similarly perceived as a necessary response to indigenous disadvantage. For example, in the international arena, the United Nations Committee for the Elimination of all forms of Racial Discrimination (CERD) has expressed concern about the continuing denial and lack of enjoyment of indigenous Australians' human rights, coupled with the lack of confidence expressed by indigenous peoples in the reconciliation process as a means of addressing this disadvantage (CERD 2000). Some commentators have also argued that reconciliation is needed as part of Australia's international responsibility for the preservation of the world's fragile and endangered indigenous cultures (Reynolds 2000).

Presenting reconciliation as the solution to the problem of indigenous disadvantage employs several problematic subtextual representations. The concepts and categories used in this discourse of indigenous disadvantage position indigenous peoples and non-indigenous peoples in certain ways in relation to reconciliation, which is then already inscribed, like colonisation itself, as a 'phenomenon which emerges from the power relations inscribed in the very structure of categories' (Lattas 1987: 40). Carol Bacchi argues this is important because 'concepts and categories are shaped by political goals and intentions. Contests over the meaning of concepts, it follows, are contests over desired political outcomes' (1996: 1). She elaborates:

> [T]he way in which a social 'problem' is conceived and/or represented limits the range of possible responses... this sequence is not coincidental but serves the purposes of those who wish to moderate change to protect their status and power. (Bacchi 1996: 12)

In the dominant, 'white' discourse on reconciliation, indigenous peoples are the focus of the problem. Their representation as 'disadvantaged' constructs them as deviant, deficient, delinquent and substandard in relation to a standard of 'normal' (non-indigenous) society, which is not directly problematised, and in which they are presumed to seek inclusion. The discourse of indigenous disadvantage diverts critical attention away from the standard, and from the colonial processes of exclusion and the relations of power that produced the standard in the first place.

By comparison, indigenous people commonly assert that their continuing disadvantage stems from the fact that their policy initiatives have consistently been unsupported and they have been prevented from pursuing their alternative approaches to government, law, religion and culture (CAR 1994b: 13–28). While this claim does imply criticism of the dominant standard and a desire to pursue alternatives, indigenous people frequently present themselves as supplicants to a heartless State and passive victims of colonial dispossession: 'when our land was taken we lost our economy, our lifestyle and our culture, all under the rule of law' (CAR 1994a: 4). By contrast, colonial or white Australia is perceived in active terms, as the cause of indigenous disadvantage, through 'dispossession; marginalisation; rejection of their cultural identity, land rights and legal and political rights; and the forced removal of children from the families' (CAR 1997: 12; see also Keating 2000).

The structuring discourse of indigenous disadvantage then perpetuates negative representations of aboriginality that are central to both indigenous and non-indigenous understandings of 'the problem'. It reinforces 'pain and loss as the defining characteristics of Aboriginality' (James 1997: 74). The presentation of the problem as indigenous disadvantage also constrains the development of strategies for the transformation of this problematic present. Even though injustice perpetrated and perpetuated by the State should be a civil concern of all Australians, as the focus of 'the problem', indigenous peoples (and their non-indigenous 'supporters') have generally endured the responsibility for action against the social injustices they continue to experience because of the colonial dispossession of their land and the colonial policies that dispersed their communities and eroded their cultures. In effect, reconciliation is perceived as an issue that primarily concerns indigenous Australians and the problems of disadvantage faced by indigenous communities: matters of social injustice relating to indigenous peoples continue to be portrayed as 'Indigenous Problems', rather than as issues of injustice affecting the entire Australian community. Indigenous peoples are then positioned as petitioners to the State and civil community, burdened by the responsibility of proving their disadvantage,[10] and disillusioned by the exhausting process of extracting funding and policy initiatives from a reluctant and recalcitrant government. While some of these 'indigenous concerns' have at times pricked the public conscience (for example, those around the issue of the 'Stolen Generations' of indigenous children removed from their families and communities), State and public responses to 'indigenous issues' have generally been reluctant and inadequate. This failure of response is exhausting for indigenous activists, and reinforces the sense of powerlessness and invisibility felt by many as real obstacles to the success of any action (Dodson 1994; see also Watson 1998; Langton 1994). As Mick Dodson quips: 'if the diseases don't kill us then trying to get some action most likely will' (1998: 22).

Accordingly, most indigenous activists perceive their empowerment to be the most basic solution to the problem of their structural disadvantage. Their fundamental interest is to inscribe an indigenous authority upon social practices and in discourses, or in other words, to author an indigenous subjectivity. Patrick Dodson (2007: 24) insists: 'the recognition, respect and resourcing of Indigenous authority by the dominant society is fundamental'. Mick Dodson affirms: 'Nearly suffocated with imposed labels and structures Aboriginal peoples have had no choice other than to insist on our right to speak back . . . To build and represent our own world of meaning and significance' (1994: 4). Public recognition of an authoritative, representative indigenous identity is understood to allow indigenous Australians to 'speak for themselves', thereby challenging the assumed unity, and so also the representative authority, of the existing 'Australian' national identity produced partly through the colonial construction of the negative aboriginal other.

Such a challenge incidentally prompts the transformation of national social institutions, such that they might better cater for the more adequately representative civil body incorporating indigenous being. This strategy of indigenous empowerment as a means of social transformation is fundamentally dialectical. Indigenous Australians are the negating element combating exclusive narratives of 'Australian' society. They generally seek recognition of their difference, that the specificity of indigenous being and native title might be included as part of a national existence. Such recognition of difference negates the claim to universality of the dominant (non-indigenous) national identity, and thereby compels its transformation. In striving to be authentically representative, the 'Australian' nation is forced to expand the structures defining its character, to accommodate better indigenous being, thereby developing a more adequate universality.[11] In this way, reconciliation represents the developing harmony of the Australian national body, as differences are acknowledged and then transcended, reconciled within a more adequate unity.

In thinking about and practising subject-formation and social transformation, indigenous activism has not only spontaneously developed from concrete experience in the Australian colonial situation, but has also often been influenced by international developments, such as the black civil rights movement in America.[12] More recently, the emergence of a global indigenous community that shares a common historical experience of 'internal colonisation' has created

> a world community of Indigenous peoples spanning the planet; experiencing the same problems and struggling against the same alienation, marginalisation and sense of powerlessness . . . united by our shared frustration with the dominant systems of our own countries and their consistent failure to deliver justice. (Dodson 1998: 19)

Indigenous Australians also have a history of engagement with, and contribution to, the international field of postcolonial theory. Like decolonisation movements in general, indigenous actions of resistance and social transformation have usually involved their assertion of a positive identity derived from the fact of aboriginality as a ground for action and their demands for recognition (see Gilbert 1995; Jordan 1984). However, like Fanon and other participants of decolonisation struggles internationally, Australian indigenous people have also often found this assertion of a cohesive identity limiting and difficult, as establishing a representative indigenous body has often meant unrealistically excluding the actual variation in ways of being indigenous (Oxenham et al. 1999, esp. pp. 51–91).

Indeed, the boundaries of indigenous unity are essentially and necessarily contested, since this identity must simultaneously invoke their right to 'equal treatment' as Australian citizens, and also a degree of 'special treatment' with the recognition of their particular rights to native title and the enjoyment of their special roles as the nation's 'First Peoples'. Accordingly, indigenous unity is variously imagined at different levels of organisation, and in terms of the apparently conflicting discourses of cosmopolitanism and community. Indigenous activism consequently appears polarised in two directions, at times claiming authority on universal grounds, through the liberal human right to equal justice; at other moments asserting a particular authority deriving from authenticity grounded in communities of practice. However, there are a variety of overlapping standpoints between these two extremes of the global and the local, each invoking a normative unity at some level. Furthermore, each standpoint is identified not only by the ways in which it establishes its internal unity and coherence, but also according to the ways in which it asserts its own particularity against the other available positions by expelling or assimilating contesting differences.

The first strategy employed by indigenous activists is structured by a discourse of moral cosmopolitanism. Advocates claim a human right to equal treatment, and point out the disparities between non-indigenous and indigenous Australians' enjoyment of their basic human rights to health, education and adequate housing, employment opportunities, and childhood development. This stance claims an authoritative identity grounded in world citizenship:

> As members of the world's peoples, we are the subjects of international law. We are entitled to be the full and equal beneficiaries of that law and make claims over our rights. That holds true whether we live in New York or Bolivia or Murray Bridge (Dodson 1998: 19).[13]

Principles of cosmopolitan right are drawn from a concept of impartial justice, emphasising the equality of individuals, claimed in virtue of a common humanity that transcends claims to cultural particularity. Universal principles of human rights are liberal principles, in that they are 'fundamentally individualistic', designed to 'determine and limit the form of any state (or of any unit of collective control)' (Charney 1999: 841). Indigenous individuals claim their human right to protection against unjust and harmful state policies that perpetuate racial inequality in Australia, as was pointed out in the Report of the Human Rights Commission to Government on the subject of the Stolen Generations:

> To know who you are, where you are from and to whom you belong is a basic human entitlement. It is essential to the realisation of the 'dignity and worth of the human person' which underpins the Universal Declaration of Human Rights. (HREOC 1997: 17)

The second approach employed by indigenous activists asserts a global indigenous identity, 'a world community of Indigenous peoples spanning the planet' (Dodson 1998: 19). The international indigenous perspective asserts itself in criticism of a global humanity that does not address itself to the particular set of rights and requirements demanded by indigenous peoples, such as collective rights to culture and native title. The *United Nations Declaration on the Rights of Indigenous Peoples* was adopted by the General Assembly of the United Nations in 2007. The *Declaration* was drafted with the aim of making the cosmopolitan vision of individual human rights more comprehensive, enabling collective rights to be better recognised as human rights. In company with Canada, New Zealand and the United States, Australia originally voted against the adoption of the resolution on the basis that the partiality implied by a special set of indigenous rights devalues the principle of cosmopolitan universalism embodied in a human rights perspective (see Davis 2007).

The second indigenous approach thereby signals the philosophical crisis in liberal theories of justice. Critics, such as the international collective of indigenous peoples, charge that the moral universe given in such theories of justice is not truly universal, but is rather drawn from the culturally specific context of Western liberal democratic society. Western society is claimed to privilege individualist civil and political liberties at the expense of other values, such as 'culture' itself, which may become more pressing in a non-Western context, or in a context where this value is threatened, as is the case with indigenous peoples. Some thinkers, including Duncan Ivison (2002) and Will Kymlicka (1995), argue that the right to culture can be realised from within a (transformed) liberal framework, and indeed the transnational indigenous approach seeks to expand the liberal human rights vision to include the collective right to culture. However, globally, indigenous peoples also claim a specific set of native title rights over and above universal human rights, which expressly challenges the cosmopolitan equality of universal humanity, which also suggests limits to justice conceptualised wholly in terms of impartiality (Pearson 1997b; Poole 2000; Chesterman and Galligan 1997: Chap. 7). Problems associated with the liberal framework as a basis for postcolonial public reason and consensual deliberation will be discussed in Chapter 6.

A similar challenge to claims about the universality of Australia's *national* models of liberal justice and jurisprudence is suggested by the third kind of indigenous perspective, which asserts indigenous authority at the national level, constructing an indigenous Australia represented in bodies like the (now defunct) Aboriginal and Torres Strait Islander Commission (ATSIC), the Aboriginal Provisional Government (APG) or the Council for Aboriginal Reconciliation (CAR). This expresses a tenuous unity born out of an actual multiplicity of diverse indigenous communities, by claiming a common experience of colonisation together with a shared opposition to the exclusion or erasure of indigenous identity from nationalist discourse and to the erosion of indigenous particularity that occurs with its assimilation within the dominant nationalist frameworks and mechanisms of government (Chesterman and Galligan 1997). Indigenous discourses of nation also resist dominant (non-indigenous) nationalist narratives, which exclude aspects of Australia's inglorious colonial past by glorifying colonial race relations, glossing over the violent history of colonial massacre and the disturbing history of indigenous resistance, or incorporating a 'safe' indigenous presence through 'noble savage' imagery. Indigenous nationalists and their supporters engage in rewriting Australian history so that pre-colonial, post-colonial and current indigenous roles are accurately represented (Huggins 1990: 168–9; e.g. Reynolds 1988). Part of this project is the shifting of national structures, to represent better indigenous interests, including the recognition of co-existing structures of indigenous law, culture, knowledge and governance. Indigenous nationalism nonetheless contrasts with communitarian and liberal nationalisms. While indigenous nationalism is asserted against the *false* unity of an existing national identity, communitarian and liberal nationalisms are asserted as a necessary context for meaningful identification, against *abstract* global universality (see Walzer 1990; Miller 1995; Tamir 1993). Even so, in either case, 'the conveniently ambiguous term of "national culture", leaves open the question of whose nation and what kind of nation is to be developed' (Bhabha 2000: 3). As with Fanon's writing on national culture, this ambivalent tactic of asserting a universal in order to contest another universal remains a vexed theoretical strategy.

Indeed, this ambivalence is compounded by the fourth strategy informing indigenous politics, which claims authentic indigenous voice exists only at the level of particular communities, thereby asserting authority in terms of a cultural and territorial unity based in a discourse of authenticity related to traditional cultural practices. This strategic claim to authentic forms of representation has been important for indigenous people working in community-based interventions, particularly in response to issues of health policy and environmental management. This identification has at times accompanied assertions of local indigenous 'nationhood', as with the Pintupi Nation (Central Australia), the Ngarrindjeri Nation (South Australia), and the Jawoyn Nation (Northern Australia). Claims to traditional authenticity are, however, also fraught with difficulties, particularly when they assume some version of cultural homogeneity and stasis. For example, the Native Title Tribunal demands some demonstration of 'authenticity' in recognising Indigenous claims to land. This has been disempowering for indigenous claimants, who mostly cannot claim to participate in an unchanged, traditional culture.

The four constructions of aboriginality represent four 'solutions' to the 'problem' of indigenous disadvantage, seeking to rectify the situation Michael Mansell (2007) refers to as 'the political vulnerability of the unrepresented'. Each of these particular levels circumscribing indigenous subjectivity asserts an internal coherence, not only with respect to its own identification, but also *against* the other positions of indigenous unity. For example, the 'global indigenous' stance celebrates the ways in which global technologies and interconnectivity can enhance communication among indigenous communities, identifying similarities that can support solidarity in action. It also supports the opportunities global technology provides for publication and expression of indigenous voice (Smith and Ward 2000: 9). However, traditionalists are more concerned that world globalisation can 'undermine traditional systems of power and authority that are the core of Indigenous societies' (Smith and Ward 2000: 4). How, for instance, might the predominance of young indigenous voices on the internet affect the structure of societies where power is traditionally held by older persons? . . . Reformulations of access to knowledge in digital contexts engender new areas of risk to traditional Indigenous ways of knowing; there are serious implications for social processes and structures. (Smith and Ward 2000: 8)

At the level of domestic politics, traditionalists also insist that indigenous individuals and communities experienced the colonisation of Australia in vastly different ways, according to their local relation to colonial policies such as those that destroyed family bonds, the presence or absence of 'civilising and Christianising' missions, the requirements of the local labour market and so forth. This fundamentally challenges other indigenous claims about national unity born out of a common experience of colonial oppression (e.g. Gilbert 1977: 203–4).

The underlying difficulty common to each kind of identification is that not all indigenous people are able to experience their aboriginality in the same way. Thus, speaking of her engagement with Navaho people in America, Pat Dudgeon comments upon how she felt inferior because she does not speak her own aboriginal language, whereas the Navaho generally do: 'I was actually feeling less Indigenous and authentic to them because I didn't speak my language' (Oxenham et al. 1999: 84). Differing criteria of 'authentic' experience force indigenous people perpetually to 'measure our Aboriginality' (Oxenham et al. 1999: 85) in order to decide who can legitimately claim the authority of indigenous voice. Consequently, and perversely, claims about a 'unifying' aboriginality have often been the basis of an exclusive politics.

At each level of representation, authority is claimed in terms of a unified and representative aboriginal presence, which is asserted against difference (contesting inscriptions of aboriginality) on the one hand, and against identity (the false inscription of colonial identifications) on the other. In this way, indigenous strategy remains caught in the tension of desire, which pulls the subject towards recognition and identity on the one hand, and negation or difference on the other. As with the postcolonial theory discussed in the first half of this chapter, indigenous strategy is torn between the need to affirm and the need to deconstruct identity, and faces the complication that the tools of deconstruction simultaneously undermine indigenous attempts at self-representation. However, indigenous strategy is not disabled simply by the apparent crisis of representation. The broader problem faced by resisting peoples everywhere concerns the conceptualisation of transformation as a dialectical process driven by a constitutive contradiction, and the position occupied by the agents of difference or negation within the structure of dialectical struggle. That is, the association of aboriginality (and difference in general) with negative imagery is reinforced by the dominant, dialectical view of social change as oppositional negation, here driven by indigenous action. Noel Pearson points out that these characteristics of transformative agency

> are largely white constructs. The colonists have defined the way in which our struggle is to be understood . . . The emergence of radical activism changed the way in which Australians were forced to take account of the victims, but it did not always change the stance and the position from which the victims spoke – as the powerless and oppressed minority . . . The language of victim politics positioned the rest of Australia as guilty perpetrators. It is an uncomfortable position and not one which will sustain a political cause (Pearson 1997b: 218).

On this view, reconciliation is driven by conflict and the Fanonian struggle to 'do battle for the creation of a human world' by transforming existing social and political structures (see Molnar 1995). Action for reconciliation is consequently perceived to be divisive, read as a 'threat' to national unity. 'Aboriginality, or race relations, is always the agent of disruption within the non-Aboriginal community' (James 1997: 70). Indigenous desire for authority is seen to conflict with existing structures of authority, which positions the rest of the community in fear of 'the theft of their enjoyment' of the status quo.[14] Significantly for 'settler' activists like myself who have been involved in practical efforts at reconciliation, this conceptual scaffolding also neglects to address and support the transformative interests and activities of the dominant settler class. While there is evidence of strong, broad-based public support for reconciliation, this tends to be devalued and subsumed under the assumption that there is a more serious 'cancer of settler hostility to Indigenous people that bubbles beneath the surface of Australian civil society' (Dodson 2007: 25). In fact, because progress is understood to be *driven* by subterranean hostility, such an assumption is, perhaps, necessary for dialectical forms of transformation. The sort of agency that is generally assumed to be appropriate in these struggles finally reproduces the structural relationships and suspicions that the notion of reconciliation contests. These are relationships of antagonism, which are characterised as a struggle for authority and recognition, and they continue to associate difference with negation, which positions indigenous people as the bearers of difference, negatively: 'Active aboriginal presence in public discourse is negative. It is anti-social' (James 1997: 71).

While reconciliation develops an ever-increasing, encompassing universality, it does so *because* its antagonistic, conflictive structure of difference is constitutive, and so is always sublated but preserved: difference resiliently resurfaces, reintroducing conflict to the process after every moment of unification, thereby propelling the movement on its continual, unifying trajectory. The difference that is preserved and reinstated each time is the relationship of antagonism between opposing terms. Difference here represents the *degrees* of separation or inequality of a class, in negative relation to a second standard class. Dialectical progression requires the continuing existence of a minor or negative term that is the bearer of this difference. If, on the other hand, a teleological resolution is permitted, the ideal end – the realisation of a postcolonial unity – suggests a possible elimination of conflicting differences and the establishment of harmony and equality. This end would eliminate the problematic differences in the *degrees* of power exercised by indigenous and settler Australians. The ultimate aim of reconciliation, as it is currently conceived, is thus to *eliminate the degrees of difference* of enjoyment or authority, either by equalising in sameness (equal justice for all) or through difference (empowerment of indigenous particularity). A postcolonial sensibility suggests the second of these impulses is more appropriate, for, as Cathryn McConaghy (2000) warns, an increase in indigenous voice is not enough to transform colonialist social structures. The goal of equal participation in national structures is important, but reconciliation also requires the recognition of difference as positive, not simply its elimination altogether.

However, it is precisely the *negativity* of difference that is associated with a capacity for the critical transformation of the present. Like transformative practices in general, reconciliation currently remains caught in a double bind thrown up by the concept of the negative. The underlying problem is that difference is positioned ambiguously in dialectical visions of society and social transformation. Difference is that which lacks being; it is incomplete, it is the 'not yet' of history. Further, dialectical difference is determinate, constituted as the negative term in relation to a primary and positive binary opposite. However, difference constitutes the immanent cause of history, its moving principle, and so is also figured as a necessary support for the progression of history towards a universal harmony of humanity. The problem is that the 'negation of the negative' has been the driving mechanism of critique, while simultaneously the basis of an imperial philosophy of difference. The challenge for the postcolonial critic is to think change alternatively.

In part, this challenge responds to the frustrating situation often described by the thinkers and activists I have spoken through in this chapter. That is, the nature of resistance is too often defined by the system of oppression it faces, with the result that 'the semiotic pawn signifying the indigenous person can only be moved in very circumscribed ways' (Ashcroft et al. 1995: 214). Marcia Langton points out that while indigenous resistance is presented through an indigenous discourse on Aboriginality,

> this fixation on [self-] classification reflects the extraordinary intensification of colonial administration . . . elaborate systems of control aimed, until recently, at exterminating one kind of 'Aboriginality' and replacing it with a sanitized version acceptable to the Anglo invaders and immigrants. (1994: 96–7)

Similarly, Mudrooroo (1995: 144) argues that indigenous self-representations that are aimed at attracting the recognition of non-indigenous Australia must conform to modes of presentation acceptable or tolerated by the mainstream media: they must 'establish an indigenous presence in a non-indigenous world which has been structured in certain ways, and one in which people are educated to present ideas and images in certain ways' (1995: 144).

The Hindmarsh Island Bridge Affair offers a striking example of this, demonstrating that where indigenous knowledge and practices do not conform to non-indigenous worldviews and understandings they simply cannot, or will not, be heard. In this case, Australian law did not accept the existence of privileged and sacred knowledge, accessible only to certain women. The revelation that 'women's knowledge' and specifically female Dreaming stories might have existed and survived off the public record, unknown to expert anthropologists and ethnographers, was simply not credible to the popular imagination. Because the sacred nature of the story meant that it was held by only a few women, and because each of these women held different parts of the story, the Ngarrindjeri community as a whole could not claim a unified awareness of this 'Women's Business', and nor could they speak about such Business, because of the access taboos and privileges associated with the information. This lack of community coherence further compounded non-indigenous scepticism about whether the claims were true or fabricated by 'anti-developmentalists'. According to Western cultural beliefs,

> knowledge is best shared, theories are there to be questioned, unpicked and interrogated . . . Publication is a measure of importance . . . Not all cultures are like this. In many Aboriginal cultures, secrecy is a measure of whether or not knowledge is important. Myths and Dreaming stories are layered. An outer layer is told to children. As the children grow older they learn more. . . . Sometimes the story changes in important ways . . . a child might be told a story about a man coming over the hill trailing a spear or a stick. Then later, they might be told that the stick was not a stick after all, but a penis. Later on, or in some other stories, the person might not be a man at all, but a woman. Or a goanna. Stories shift and change depending on the speaker and the listener. There is no written version. Nothing is fixed. And if something is widely known, then it is a sure sign that it is not central, and not important. (Simons 2003: 218)

As Spivak (1985) also suggests, it often seems that the efficacy of indigenous actions and of postcolonial transformations in general have been limited by the need to speak resistance in the language of the coloniser if these resistances are to be heard at all. That is, transformation is generally understood and interpreted through the dominant Western discourse of resistance grounded in dialectical philosophy, with its clearly defined criteria of validity and authority based in the representational categories of presence and opposition, identity and difference. This discourse describes both imperial practice and social progress as Western society has envisaged it, at least since the time of Hegel.

Desire, negativity and postcolonial agency

In the preceding chapter, I suggested that the problem of imperial agency is best perceived as an effect emerging from the ontological emphasis upon negativity and negation, such that action takes form as the attempt to satisfy a desire to fill an ontological void, by the appropriation and possession of that difference which is lacking. Agency is connected to the 'mastery', 'appropriation' and 'possession' of difference when subjectivity is grounded in a model of desire connected to a constitutive negativity. This is because desire is satisfied when action eliminates the negativity of lack or absence, by appropriating and possessing the object of desire. The desiring subject is compelled to become more adequate by incorporating difference, but in order to maintain a stable and coherent identity, contesting differences must simultaneously be expelled from within the boundaries of the subject. Subjective agency, when subjectivation is grounded in ontological negativity and a responding desire, thereby involves the ambivalent and imperial gestures of repulsion and appropriation of difference.

Representations of desire, power, subjectivity, causation and difference in postcolonial theory remain consistent with this ontology structured by negativity. Accordingly, across both Marxist and poststructuralist versions of postcolonial theory, desire motivates a power of action, in the form of mastery over difference: in Marxism, politics involves the struggle for power to demand recognition from the other, or to withhold it; in poststructuralism, the colonising self struggles to repress the difference within, while resistance to colonial authority involves rendering this difference visible and uncomfortable. As Fanon makes clear, political inequality between economic classes biases this ontological struggle: in 'doing battle for the creation of a human world', subjects must therefore also fight for control of the means and the process of material and cultural production. Accordingly, the ontological struggle for recognition is also a battle over representation and perceptions of truth and falsity in contesting versions of reality – the discourse of the coloniser versus the counter-discourse of the colonised.

In each case, the desired outcome, for both dominating and dominated, is victory over the other. The goal of reciprocal recognition does not alter this constitutive desire for the control of difference, since recognition is occasioned by negation, by subjective action upon the objective world. In mutual recognition, each recognises the other in terms of their desire and their negating activity in response to this desire; each recognises that the other has the power to negate (appropriate or annihilate) difference in the act of transforming it. Even where poststructuralist versions of postcolonial theory affirm the permanence and resilience of difference in the dialectical process, action remains structured as objectification, corresponding with the expanding adequacy of the subject as it develops better self-understanding about the difference it internally carries, accommodates and represses. The force motivating action remains the desire for mastery over difference.

Thus, postcolonial theory is confronted by difficulties, not only in the nature of representation – its impossibility and its necessity in resistance practice – but also because history itself, the process dominantly described in the West by the movement of the dialectic and its inscriptions of negativity, is complicit with an imperial epistemic. Robert Young comments:

> Hegel articulates a philosophical structure of the appropriation of the other as a form of knowledge which uncannily simulates the project of nineteenth century imperialism; the construction of knowledges which all operate through forms of expropriation and incorporation of the other mimics at a conceptual level the geographical and economic absorption of the non-European world by the West. Marxism's standing Hegel on his head may have reversed his idealism, but *it did not change the mode of operation* of a conceptual system which remains collusively Eurocentric. (1990: 3, emphasis added)

The imperial structure of dialectical subjectivation is therefore not just a problem for the resisting subaltern seeking identity as a ground for agency. It also calls into question the very possibility of *postcolonial* subjectivity, in so far as this is conceivable only in terms of a historical discontinuity, a rupture with that mode of subjectivity and sociality that is constituted by negativity and defined in terms of appropriative satisfaction. Again, postcolonialism is caught between a need to destabilise and a need to affirm identity. We have seen how the dominant debate within postcolonial theory focuses upon the need to destabilise the authority of the colonising subject position, while affirming the authority of the resisting position. There is also a need for postcolonial theory to critique the process of colonial (and post-colonial) subject-formation, while simultaneously affirming the process of becoming appropriate for postcolonial subjectivity. While postcolonial theory might affirm a *resisting* or *post-colonial* identity using dialectical categories of subject-formation and ontological opposition, a properly conceived *postcolonial* identity can only be affirmed when it does not replicate the structure of colonial subjectivity, or its process of formation by excluding or assimilating difference. While the ongoing process of *decolonisation* through the assertion of the counter-discourses and histories of the other might therefore remain (uneasily) complicit with the ontological struggle for recognition that compels dialectical progress, *postcolonisation* requires an alternative mode of subject-formation and social transformation. This alternative kind of postcolonial self must break with the notion of agency satisfying a primary and defining emptiness, through a desire to master, appropriate, repress (and finally annihilate), difference.

However, because the dialectic persuasively compels us to think being in terms of its becoming, modern critical and transformative philosophy remains seduced and captured by Hegel's work and by the critical notion of the negative. Gayatri Spivak therefore believes:

> our sense of critique is too thoroughly determined by Kant, Hegel and Marx for us to be able to reject them as 'motivated imperialists' . . . A deconstructive politics of reading would acknowledge the determination as well as the imperialism and see if the magisterial texts *can now be our servants*, as the new magisterium constructs itself in the name of the Other. (1999: 7; emphasis added)

As Spivak here suggests, remaining within a framework of critical negativity forces the critic to preserve the mastery *somewhere*. If difference is not mastered, the critic is left to show the ways in which difference actually masters, either by demonstrating the hitherto unacknowledged ways in which the self is deconstructively destabilised by reliance upon the other, or by insisting upon the permanence and resilience of negation in the dialectical process, which therefore undoes any claim to final unification. But a new oppression is instated when the master, the magisterial text, is made into the servant of the other. Surely, postcolonial philosophy and practice should strive to resist repeating structures of domination and servitude, indeed must disrupt such structures and encourage a different kind of critical and constructive practice altogether, in which difference is neither mastered, nor masters. While postcolonial theory might fruitfully acknowledge the role played by dialectical philosophy and by the privileged force of negativity in the determination of Western and critical theory, together with its role in Western imperialism, it must also strive to imagine, and work with, a wholly alternative philosophy of determination and transformation that is not predicated upon a connection between critique, difference and negativity. This kind of approach would move beyond that of Derrida, Spivak and others who similarly seek to conceptualise difference outside of the sphere of mastery, but try nonetheless to remain within the critical scope of the negative.

The task of 'thinking outside of the Hegelian dialectic' is, of course, fraught with difficulty. Simply to contradict dialectical thought is not enough, since contradiction is bound up with the modulations of dialectical critique. The critic remains caught up within a dialectical movement, in which the object of criticism is transcended, but preserved. However, the dialectic gives us a *particular* movement of becoming and a particular model of critique, a particular choreography that proceeds by the 'unrest of incompatibles', giving rise to a developmental process driven by ever-renewed contradiction and opposition. In its particularity, dialectics is not the *only* method of grasping the transformative principle of the becoming of being. While most cultures have concepts explaining creation and transformation, many of which could provide a good basis for thinking about postcolonial change, I will now turn to an alternative thread within the cultural tradition of Western philosophy. Deleuze's concept of different/ciation describes a method of critique which is not *directly* opposed to Hegelianism, but certainly offers the possibility of side-stepping the dialectical tradition by taking up a completely alternative philosophy of production and transformation, based upon a positive concept of difference.

Notes

1. The reference is to Benita Parry (1987: 31) on Homi Bhabha's 'annexation' of Fanon.
2. For an alternative reading of Fanon on violence, which argues that 'Fanon makes it impossible to choose, for violence or against', see Kawash (1999).
3. This strategy is fraught with the complexities involved when using a colonialist cultural medium ('literature') to decentre colonialist cultural dominance, as well as inherent difficulties associated with the very notion of 'Third World'. See Ahmad (1987).
4. For evidence of a contrasting anticolonial discourse linked to transgressive sex practices, see the discussion by Leela Gandhi (2006: 34–67).
5. For a related discussion about the relations between techniques of power and desire, see Ann Laura Stoler (1995).
6. Leela Gandhi (1998: 56–8) points out that when critics devalue the 'private' concerns of the subject and valorise the 'real politics' of the 'public' collective, they are susceptible to feminist criticism.
7. One way this is attempted is by opposing the accuracy or logic of poststructuralist analysis, thereby recouping a dialectical structure of critique: poststructuralism is accused of making falsely universal claims, which Marxism then negates in order to transform. For example, Aijaz Ahmad (1992) argues that when poststructuralism debunks universalising categories or narratives such as 'nation' or 'nationalism' *tout court*, it is itself falsely homogenising such narratives and failing to distinguish between different kinds of nationalism, including 'repressive cultural bourgeois', and 'liberating visionary'. Arif Dirlik (1990) makes a similar point.

8. On the debate about the legal status of Australia as a *terra nullius*, and the existence of this term at the time of colonisation see: Reynolds (1988, 2006); Connor (2005).
9. For discussions of native title issues relating to the *Wik* decision, see Mansell (1992); Patton (1995, 1999); Bartlett (1996). On the *Wik* decision, co-existing title and the backlash provoked in the national imaginary, see Nicoll (1998).
10. For example, the Council for Aboriginal Reconciliation finds: 'Despite overwhelming evidence that Aboriginal and Torres Strait Islander peoples are the most disadvantaged Australians, almost half the Australian people believe that they are not disadvantaged' (CAR 2001: 100).
11. Andrew Lattas (1991) points out that appropriations of Aboriginality in nationalist discourses do not so much force as *allow* the becoming of the ontologically empty, non-Aboriginal subject.
12. An excellent history of aboriginal resistances to the ongoing dispossession of their land, which includes discussion of international influences on indigenous action such as the 1964 Freedom Ride is given in Goodall (1996).
13. Historically, international law has evolved in order to protect the sovereignty of States in the arena of international relations. However, principles of human rights expand this focus, so that individuals can now also be observed as subjects of international law. In addition, some articles exhibit a collective dimension, which may give weight to claims for justice that are based on cultural considerations. These are articles 1 and 27 of the International Covenant on Civil and Political Rights (CCPR), article 5 of the Covenant on the Elimination of Racial Discrimination (CERD), and article 30 of the Covenant on the Rights of the Child (CROC). International Human Rights law can be used by indigenous peoples in the following ways: firstly, by enabling individual indigenous complaints about human rights violations to be heard in the international arena, via the complaints mechanisms established for this purpose; secondly, by the requirement that ratifying States report to the Human Rights Commission (HRC) on the progress of the implementation of human rights within domestic law, in accordance with article 40 of the ICCPR. Because the HRC accepts evidence from non-governmental organisations and uses this evidence to interrogate States on their human rights records, the report situation can be used to embarrass the State, particularly when it regularly submits its own reports that gloss over its violations of indigenous human rights and which pay lip service to international obligations in the most despicable fashion. See, for example, Australia's reports to the UN, available from the UN website: www.UN.org. Finally, international law sets standards that put pressure on the domestic implementation of

principles of justice in policy fitting the requirements of indigenous peoples. The Racial Discrimination Act 1975 (sadly eroded by the Howard government's 10 Point Plan in response to the 1996 *Wik* decision, and more recently by the implementation of the 2007 emergency legislation allowing the State to intervene in indigenous communities in the remote Northern Territory, is an example of this, being explicitly drawn from the International Covenant on the Elimination of all forms of Racial Discrimination (CERD). See Pritchard (1998).

14. This fear was strikingly evident in popular discourse following the 1998 *Wik* decision. See Nicoll (1998). Slavoj Žižek 's (1993) work on the 'theft of enjoyment' will be discussed in more detail in Chapter 5.

3

The Problem of the Actual

Every human problem must be considered from the standpoint of time. (Fanon 1967a: 12)

The dialectic models the ontological basis of a philosophy of becoming – of the formation and transformation of being – which privileges the roles played by difference in the practices of critique and negation. The dialectic also gives a model of human interdependence in the form of one's reliance upon others with respect to subject formation and social harmonisation. Oriented and structured by the (temporary or teleological) goal of ontological synthesis and the resolution of conflict, the dialectic is driven both by a final cause (ideal unity) and by an immanent cause (real difference), which together define a motivating force of causal desire. These concepts of causation ground a clearly defined concept of agency – both subjective (towards others), and collective (towards the process of history-making and social transformation).

However, the model of dialectical process is problematic from a postcolonial perspective, since the trajectory is driven simultaneously by difference, conceptualised negatively as lack or opposition, and by the desire to negate this difference in the movement towards unity and recognised presence. This structuring dynamic results in a mode of agency shaped by an imperial motivation: the desire to negate external difference by its appropriation or elimination. As we saw in Chapter 2, this motivating desire seriously complicates postcolonial theory and constrains post-imperial transformative practices, such as reconciliation. Postcolonial theory needs an alternative, *positive* notion of difference as a basis for thinking about critical and creative agency. In this context, the significance of Deleuze's philosophy lies in his insistence that there are two notions of difference, which dialectical philosophy falsely reduces to a single concept (1994; 1991b: 35–44; see Hardt 1993: 1–26). His theory of different/ciation describes an alternative, non-dialectical becoming, which is a complex process of development and transformation based upon

The Problem of the Actual

an absolutely positive notion of virtual difference. The focus of this chapter is Deleuze's critique of dialectical becoming, his alternative model of process, and the type of critical practice this enables and sustains.[1] Then, in following chapters, I will turn to the issue of constructive agency in order to elaborate the postcolonial potential implicit within Deleuze's model of ontological trans/formation.

Deleuzian ontology

Deleuze's critique of dialectical philosophy has two main points of focus: difference is conceptualised badly or inadequately; and the dialectic describes a 'false movement' of being (1994: 10, 52; 1991b: 44). However, Deleuze's method of critique is not directly confrontational. He does not set up his argument as an antithesis, which might then be recuperated back into a transformed, more adequate theory of dialectical ontology. In fact, Deleuze's critique of dialectical *ontology* is total: nothing is preserved in a moment of negation; no recovery or expansion of the original (dialectical) position is possible. Deleuze's argument with Hegel is not directly oppositional, but oblique, emerging as a consequence of his own ontology and philosophy of process. His critique does not so much establish the condition for his reconstruction or reconceptualisation of being/becoming, as his alternative philosophy at the same time establishes a critique of the dialectic as a model of ontological genesis (Hardt 1993: xvii, 1–2, 116).

Deleuze critiques the dialectic *as a model of ontological generation*, however he maintains a place for dialectical *transformation* as a process occurring between bodies that have already come into being through a different ontology, which he describes as actualisation. Thus, his description of this primary and alternative mode and movement of becoming reveals to us that the dialectical process describes a movement within a limited subset of Deleuze's own greater ontology. The dialectical representation of real causation is false, yet nonetheless has a certain efficacy in that it works as a persuasive illusion about being by claiming to represent a true and complete ontology (1991b: 21ff., 35). With this claim, dialectical ontology has in fact significantly shaped our thinking and social practice for the past few centuries. Deleuze's argument is not that the philosophy of the dialectic is inconsistent or incoherent, and can be made better, but that its coherence and its persuasive currency in practice belies the paucity of the reality it describes. In short, the dialectic is believable because it truly describes *a* process of ontological *transformation*, but it nonetheless presents an incomplete picture of the becoming of being. Deleuze's vision reveals being in its unlimited fullness, and simultaneously shows that dialectical ontology is only a partial representation of reality, and one kind of transformation among possible others, rather than the one true representation (see 1994: 45–50, 53–5; Boundas 1996). Indeed, Deleuze shows that dialectical 'ontology' is a mere surface description of *actual* reality, which emerges from a more profound ontology of *virtual* reality. In this way, Deleuze's critique is incidental, but complete.

In order to understand and appreciate the nature of Deleuze's quarrel with dialectical ontology, it is helpful firstly to consider his alternative ontology and philosophy of process, and the conceptualisation of difference he works with. For Deleuze, 'difference is not and cannot be thought in itself, so long as it is subject to the requirements of representation' (1994: 262). In dialectical philosophy, difference is attributed to a thing *externally* by virtue of its relationship to a representative or standard body (and the aim of dialectical unification is to internalise this external difference). By comparison, Deleuze's work initially attends to the difference *internal* to a body as it transforms over time, and then subsequently to external differences arising between bodies in the course of their individual and relational becomings. His early essay on Bergson (1956) and the texts *Bergsonism* (1966), *Difference and Repetition* (1969) and the *Logic of Sense* (1969) each explore this idea; while it does not form a philosophical system in a conventional sense, all of his subsequent work (both solo and with Guattari) refers in some way to the conceptual framework outlined in these early texts (1994: xv).

The dialectical becoming of being proceeds by incrementally reducing external difference and establishing an always-expanding, increasingly universal and representative unity. In some versions of dialectical thinking unification finally eliminates difference, while in other versions unity encompasses difference within an overriding structure of identity. In its various forms, the dialectic is thus characterised as a movement from conflict to harmony, division to unity, or difference to identity. Following an alternative philosophical tradition including Duns Scotus, Spinoza and Bergson, Deleuze argues that the becoming of being instead proceeds from unity to difference. All things emerge from a universal elementary ground, which divides and 'differenciates' to produce diverse types of actual bodies: 'A single voice raises the clamour of being' (1994: 35). The universal ground is characterised by Deleuze and Guattari as a chaotic milieu consisting of elementary bodies in networks of contact with other bodies (1987: 39–75; 1994: 50–1). This ground is chaotic in the sense that it displays no discernible pattern of regular, coherent order. The relationships binding bodies are flimsy and transient, constantly in flux. However, with time, complex orders or 'strata' emerge as these elementary parts settle into regular and enduring habits of relation to one another. The regular association of particles produces a complex body, which in turn relates to other complex bodies to form even greater degrees of complex organisation (1987: 254). Accordingly, a 'body' in Deleuze's sense need not be a material body. Concepts and discourses can likewise be thought of as 'assemblages' of elements combined into an enduring and coherent order. This physics of relational bodies and their emergent complexity through association is the basis of Deleuze's ontology. Everything that exists can be thought of as a body, which is in contact with other bodies, and which is composed of elementary parts arranged in a regular order to produce an enduring assemblage (see Deleuze and Guattari 1987: 327–34; 1994: 15–23, 122; Bonta and Protevi 2004).

Following Bergson, Deleuze considers this emergence of organisation to be the process by which *virtual* reality becomes *actualised*. This distinction Deleuze makes between virtual becoming and actual being is crucial (for our purposes), as it enables a method of critique based upon a purely positive concept of difference. Deleuze and Guattari describe the universal, formless ground from which all things emerge as a *virtual* unity, a 'plane of immanence', which is always-already present within actual things as the condition of their determination (1987: 265–72; 1994: 42, 50–1, 118–22). Being eventuates by a creative process of constructive emanation which proceeds from the 'groundless ground' of virtual chaos, upon which everything co-exists in various states of actualisation. Virtual chaos is

> a pure plane of immanence, univocality, composition, upon which everything is given, upon which unformed elements and materials dance that are distinguished from one another only by their speed and that enter into this or that individuated assemblage depending on their connection, their relations of movement. A fixed plane of life upon which everything stirs, slows down or accelerates (1987: 255).

More precisely, the becoming of being is a process of actualisation in which an original, uniformly chaotic ground both 'differentiates' to select and determine the content defining a virtual and problematic Idea, and then creatively 'differen*t*iates' to express individuated actual bodies as forms of solution that exist as responses to the particular problem given by that virtual Idea:

> We call the determination of the virtual content of an Idea differen*t*iation; we call the actualisation of that virtuality into species and distinguished parts differen*c*iation. It is always in relation to a differen*t*iated problem or to the differen*t*iated conditions of a problem that a differen*c*iation of species and parts is carried out, as though it corresponded to the cases of solution of the problem. It is always a problematic field which conditions a differen*c*iation within the milieu in which it is incarnated (Deleuze 1994: 207).

The formulation of an Idea differen*t*iates chaos; it 'carves out' and defines a 'plane of composition', comprising elemental forms of content relative to the problem given in the Idea, as well as rules for the assembly and complex expression of these elements in emergent forms of ordered being; so 'begins' the determination of actual order from virtual chaos. Actual being expresses a particular point or 'event' in the process of 'differen*c*iation' or actualisation that develops from this differentiated plane of composition. Being becomes actual at the moment in which a durable relation, or 'consistency', has been established between the elementary parts that constitute a body (Deleuze and Guattari 1987: 327–37). Virtual becoming and actual being can be distinguished by the particular quality of the relations governing their internal parts: 'They are distinguished solely by movement and rest, slowness and speed' (Deleuze and Guattari 1987: 254). Actual being is a point of fixture or arrest, when mobile and flexible relations of force between parts acting upon each other become consolidated into definite and rigid relations that define the form of the emergent body. Actual being is thus an imposition of *form* over relations of *force*,[2] an event of 'stratification', an emergence of organisational consistency or the consolidation of an ordered relationship between constituting parts (1987: 40ff.) These elementary parts initially assemble in a transient and tentative fashion, then certain constituting relations binding elementary parts become stable and consolidate, while others dissolve. In this way, the becoming of a body is a 'bloc' that occurs between 'parts', in the interstitial space of the relationship that binds elementary bodies into a more complex organisation (1987: 291–3).

According to Deleuze and Guattari, this process of the actualisation

The Problem of the Actual

of being has an immanent causation: as the universal, chaotic ground from which all actual order emerges, the virtual plane of immanence 'at every instant causes the given to be given, in this or that state, at this or that moment' (1987: 265). The virtual plane of immanence determines both the structure and the genesis of actual being, since it both provides the elements that comprise being (content), and specifies the mode of their association (expression) (1987: 43ff.) While to a certain extent the emergence of a complex body depends upon the initial chance encounter of elements that then combine together, the differentiation of the chaotic virtual into problematic Ideas that selectively determine content for relative processes of actualisation creates a causal principle of organisation or consistency. This principle is the facilitation and designation of 'an encounter, a conjunction' that draws together the elemental components of a body in compatible associations and consequently expresses their arrangement in particular configurations (Deleuze and Guattari 1994: 93). In this way (as will be discussed further in Chapter 4), the 'plane of immanence' described by the virtual is also a field of 'desiring-production', which is differentiated or 'coded' to define a 'plane of composition' that regulates the associations between elements, causing certain elements to draw together, specifying the intensity and nature of their conjunction, and bonding elements in particular relations of attraction and force. The 'plane of composition' can therefore also be thought of as a type of virtual 'grammar', which specifies 'concrete rules' of connectivity for the elementary parts that combine, thereby determining the process of differen*c*iation and the identity of emergent forms of actual being (Deleuze and Guattari 1987: 502–14; see Rajchman 2000: 8; Colebrook 1999).[3]

However, this 'developmental or organisational principle does not appear in itself', since it is a virtual phenomenon that 'is by nature hidden. It can only be inferred, induced, concluded from that to which it gives rise' (1987: 265). According to Deleuzian ontology, that the actual exists coincidentally attests to the existence of the virtual as origin and cause. The existence of the virtual is discerned through analysis of the actual forms that develop from it. The virtual is carried within the actual, as a 'hidden' principle of its development, an internal, efficient cause that determines the existence and the nature of emergent, actual forms. Furthermore, because complex organisation *naturally* emanates from the virtual plane of immanence that causes it, the virtual acts as a form of 'non-intentional' or spontaneous causation: '[D]ifferenciation . . . comes first and above all from the internal explosive force that life carries in itself' (Deleuze 1999: 51). In Chapter 5 I will return to this concept of immanent causation in order to consider Deleuze's suggestion, developed in later works but already evident in his early [1953] text on Hume (1991a), that empirical experimentation furnishes people with knowledge of how various bodies may (or may not) be happily combined. In this future chapter, we will discover how a constructive agency might deliberately experiment with the virtual and attempt to facilitate purposefully the emergence of a particular configuration of the actual.

Before coming to a Deleuzian understanding of subjectivity, it is necessary to appreciate more fully the diverse nature of the movement of virtual being in the process of its actualisation. In the complex process of different/ciation – the determination of the content of a virtual Idea prompting the actualisation of being as an individuated 'solution' to the 'problem' described by that Idea – difference is not limited or eliminated but created, affirmed and multiplied; in becoming actual, being has an unlimited potential to trace divergent paths of development, individuating multiple, novel and diverse forms. This is so, because of the primarily chaotic nature of the virtual 'plane of immanence' from which all forms of actual order develop. The virtual chaos is firstly restrained by the constitution of a problematic Idea, which collects a body of relative elements from the chaotic ground, and so defines the elemental content of the future-actual and carves out a 'plane of composition' for the assembly of this content. However, problems or Ideas are not already given, but arise or are constituted. There are infinite ways in which a problematic Idea might form or be formulated, each potentially restraining chaos in a novel way, involving a potentially different selection of elemental content from the flux of chaos, and constituting an alternative set of rules for the assembly and actual expression of the virtual content. It follows that, just as there are infinite possible ways of differentiating the virtual by selecting elements as content for composition, there are infinite possible paths of complex actualisation or differenciation. While the assembly rules specified by a problematic Idea might determine a range of possible and impossible connections between selected elements, to some extent the process of elemental connection depends upon the chance proximity elements share with one another; the connection and composition of elements into more complex forms of order might always be differently arranged, shaping different paths of actualisation and resulting in novel forms of actual being. In this way, for Deleuze, nothing in the world is given, but is developed, through an ontological process that always involves an aspect of chance, and which could always have taken an alternative path of development. Accordingly, 'the finality of the living being exists only insofar as it is essentially open onto a totality that is itself open' (1991b: 105).

Deleuze's description of ontological generation radically departs from the choreography of dialectical transformation. In fact, these two concepts of process signify 'two types of division that must not be confused' (1991b: 95). Whereas Deleuze's concept of becoming involves a process of *actualisation*, the dialectic traces a trajectory of *realisation*. Moving through a dialectical process, being is realised, made real, as it develops from a possible existence to real existence or facticity, through a movement governed by the two principles of resemblance and limitation (1991b: 97; 1994). The real resembles the possible, since reality is simply possibility plus existence in fact. As Elisabeth Grosz (1999: 26) comments: '[M]aking the possible real is simply giving it existence without adding to or modifying its conception.' The real is preformed in the possible; the process of development does not create novel forms of being, but rather draws a pre-given or predetermined reality from a range of possible alternatives, by limiting and 'culling' these alternatives (Grosz 1999: 26). There is nothing creative about realisation: everything that comes to be is already given in the realm of the possible, which history simply makes real by the elimination of difference (1991b: 98). Realisation therefore involves exclusion and limitation, in that real being emerges through the gradual elimination of other possibilities. In this way, dialectical realisation moves from possibility to reality, multiplicity to unity, or difference to identity.

By contrast, actualisation moves from virtuality to actuality in a way that allows a process of genuine creation and innovation, because unlike the relation of resemblance between the possible and the real, the actual in no way resembles the virtuality from which it emanates (1991b: 97). The difference between virtual reality and actual reality is a difference in nature between force and form, chaos and order, movement and fixture. The actual develops from the virtual, but does not resemble it: the actual and the virtual are different kinds of being. However, unlike the dialectical relation between possibility and reality, the difference between virtual being and actual being is not described by an absence of reality, nor is the virtual thought of as an impoverished or incomplete form of the real. The chaotic unity of undifferentiated virtual being *really* exists, as a kind of 'superabundant real that induces actualisation' (Grosz 1999: 26). In fact, both the virtual and the actual are real, co-existing and mutually constitutive, and the reality of the virtual makes possible the process of its actualisation. In contrast to dialectical philosophy, then, Deleuze does not conceptualise the difference between the levels of the virtual and the actual negatively, in relation to a lack of reality.

Furthermore, unlike dialectical realisation, which is a movement conceptualised in negative terms of opposition and negation, the process of actualisation is positively conceived. Being is described in absolutely positive terms as a creative process of constructive emanation: 'For, in order to be actualised, the virtual cannot proceed by elimination or limitation, but must *create* its own lines of actualisation in positive acts' (1991b: 97, 101–2). Whereas things are 'realised' through a dialectical movement from the possible to the real by rules of limitation and resemblance, actualisation describes a movement from universal virtual chaos to diverse actual forms, by a process of creative divergence: 'the creation of the world from chaos, a continual renewed creation' (1987: 502). Actualisation is therefore an open-ended process governed by principles of difference and novelty; whereas 'realisation' involves the unfolding of a predesignated possibility, actualisation involves the genuine creation of heterogeneous forms of existence. Where realisation proceeds by negation, actualisation proceeds by production and the connective synthesis of elements into semi-enduring forms of complex ordered being. Therefore, unlike the dialectical process, which is grounded in a negative concept of difference as lack or opposition and which proceeds by negation, Deleuze's ontology is not at all grounded in negativity. In fact Deleuzian becoming proceeds as a purely positive, creative movement, in which difference is not eliminated, but proliferates.

However, the characteristic open-ended positivity of Deleuze's 'cosmic vitalism' raises important questions for transformative political practice. Firstly, how is critique possible in this 'philosophy of unlimited affirmation', since criticism surely involves a capacity to negate, to refuse, to oppose, to say 'no'? (Hallward 2006: 161, 162; see e.g. Hegel 1969: 112; Marcuse 1960: viiff.; Coole 2000; May 1991). And secondly, if reality evolves creatively in a novel and open-ended fashion that is unpredictable and unforeseen, how can change be directed towards betterment? How is constructive agency possible, when actual reality spontaneously 'emanates' through a haphazard process of complex emergence? Can this auto-poetic emergence be shaped? Or is there nothing to prevent such social complexes from taking a terrible turn away from cherished ideals like equality, democracy and justice, towards fascism or imperialism? Before we turn to consider these issues relating to constructive agency, the remainder of this chapter will address the first question about critical practice.

Deleuzian critique

Central to Deleuze's critical method is the Bergsonian notion that the actual and the virtual support two distinct concepts of difference. For Deleuze 'difference' properly (or firstly) refers to a *quality* of relationship, composition or consistency, rather than to a *quantity* of deviance from a standard, or a measure of deficiency or 'disadvantage'. The virtual and the actual differ, not in terms of their reality, but in the nature of the 'multiplicity' they describe, in terms of the relationships that connect their elementary parts:

> One is represented by space . . . It is a multiplicity of exteriority, of simultaneity, of juxtaposition, of order, of quantitative differentiation, of *difference in degree*; it is a numerical multiplicity, *discontinuous and actual*. The other type of multiplicity appears in pure duration: it is an internal multiplicity of succession, of fusion, of organization, of heterogeneity, of qualitative discrimination or of *difference in kind*; it is a *virtual and continuous* multiplicity that cannot be reduced to numbers. (1991b: 38)

A 'multiplicity' is a collection or an assemblage of relationships. The multiplicities that make up the virtual and the actual constitute two distinct types of difference (1991b: 42–3). The actual is thought of as an *ordering* in space, in which things differ by quantitative degrees in relation to each other (for example, by degrees of perfection, or of deviance from a standard, or of freedom). The second, *virtual* type of multiplicity is conceptualised as an *organisation* in time, which differs qualitatively as it changes over time. In actual space or extension, a thing differs primarily in terms of comparison, via its external relation to others. In its virtual existence or duration, the thing differs primarily from itself, in an internal movement of difference or 'differenciation' that occurs as the relationships between its composing elements transform and shift with time.

In the realm of actually existing things, then, difference is understood as a comparative relation between identities already relatively fixed into concrete types of actual being. For example, in postcolonial societies, the categories 'indigenous' and 'non-indigenous' denote two fairly rigid 'bodies' or identities, which differ from each other by degrees of advantage/disadvantage, degrees of citizenship privilege and state protection, or in an older discourse, degrees of 'culture', 'civilisation', or 'history'. Actual difference, or the difference between actual things, is therefore best described as a *difference in degree*, which is a source of inequality and conflict, and is the impetus for the dialectical process of equalisation or unification (1991b: 34–8, 101). Accordingly, dialectical politics takes place in the realm of the actual. The difference between opposing categories of actually existing bodies measures degrees of deviance from a projected ideal unity, and this numerical difference is the basis of an opposition that compels the dialectical process of realisation or unification, which is achieved through the eventual elimination of these degrees of actual difference.

However, the realm of the actual is itself not given, but comes into being through a creative process of actualisation – the development of a virtual, universal chaos into diverse and discrete, actual forms of complex being. This process rests upon an alternative conceptualisation of *virtual* difference as different/ciation; as the creative division of a virtual and chaotic unity into multiple individuated forms of actual difference (1991b: 97–101, 1994: 207–22). The process of differenciation traces the morphing of bodies as they form, transform and develop over time. Whereas actual bodies differ from *each other*, virtual bodies constantly differ from *themselves* in the process of their becoming. Virtual difference thereby describes the difference internal to a body in the process of its becoming; this is a difference-in-itself, which represents a true *difference in kind* as a body changes qualitatively from one kind of assemblage to another when its constitutive elements shift and combine in alternative ways.

Thinking in terms of the virtual, or of the changes in things brought about by the internal processes of their assemblage and transformation, enables a distinction (but not an opposition) to be made between the actual and the virtual, and between differences of degree and the more profound differences in kind. Whereas the virtual is conceptualised in relation to duration or process, the actual is a stoppage of this process (1991b: 101–4). The actual develops from the virtual, but the existence of the actual constrains the creative flow of virtual differenciation. Therefore, while the virtual and the actual are two different kinds of difference, they nevertheless

The Problem of the Actual

share a complex relationship of mutual implication. The virtual and the actual must be thought together in terms of the process of actualisation (1991b: 94–106; 1994: 208ff.). Being moves through virtual differenciation in the process of becoming actual, and in achieving actual existence, is then defined in terms of its identity and its actual difference in relation to other actual bodies. However, the concept of virtual differenciation is most profound, since the actual is produced from the primary realm of the virtual. The concept of virtual differenciation is primary, productive, creative and purely positive, since it is the process of development of all things that come actually to exist.

While actual being is properly conceptualised only in relation to the process of its actualisation, differenciation or becoming, Deleuze explains that we generally perceive things to be real only when they *already* actually exist, that is, as they have already been identified or represented as such, or already come to be (1991b: 25–7, 104–5). Actual bodies are perceived as given things that exist in space or extension, while virtual entities have existence in duration or time, as things developing, or as bodies or identities in the process of their becoming. Thus, actual reality is an illusion about being which avows the apparent 'givenness' of existing bodies and obscures our better understanding that things have come to be as they are only through the productive process of actualisation, which formalises a contingent relationship between constituting parts. Furthermore, when the actual realm is falsely taken to be the whole of reality, difference can only be understood as a relation 'of gradation or opposition' between actual bodies, thereby obscuring the better understanding of virtual differenciation (1991b: 101).

For Deleuze, this tendency to conflate the two concepts of difference, and to reduce all difference to actual difference, is the source of 'badly defined' problems, which simply perpetuate the conditions of their existence as such.

> All our problems derive from the fact that we do not know how to go beyond experience [the actual] toward the conditions of experience [the virtual], toward the articulations of the real and rediscover what differs in kind in the composites that are given to us and on which we live (1991b: 26).

In fact, this is the crux of Deleuze's critique of dialectical transformation, which describes a process occurring between already given, actual bodies, opposed to one another in the realm of actual being.

The problem with dialectical transformation, according to Deleuze, is that it mistakes actual difference, or differences in degree, as the *only* kind of difference, and thereby fails to comprehend that critical transformation best refers to the more profound virtual differences in kind that produce actual being in the first place, and which guarantee that actual being could always be produced otherwise, according to alternative lines of development.

Deleuze accepts that the illusion of the actual is 'inevitable', since it is an illusion 'in which we are immersed' (1991b: 20). That is, we tend to think of things as we actually experience them, and to discern mere differences of degree between actual bodies, within this actual universe. However, a broader scope for critical practice opens when we become mindful that this actual 'universe' is not given, but rather created, drawn together from a virtuality that encompasses and surpasses the actual. Deleuze's critical practice hinges upon struggling against this illusion of 'givenness' and attending to the contingency inherent in the process of actualisation itself. The aim is therefore to 'struggle against illusion, rediscover the true differences in kind or articulations of the real' (1991b: 21). This 'struggle' is perhaps best understood as a contemplative labour of thought, in which the critic strives to develop an awareness of the presence of the virtual in actual bodies. The virtual reveals how the actual is 'a connection of components that could have been different' (Deleuze and Guattari 1994: 93). This provokes us to ask of the actual: 'What components are included in this configuration of being, and what components are excluded?' Also, 'What forces connect the components that comprise this form of actual being, and how could they be alternatively combined?' Furthermore, because cultivating awareness of the virtual existence of things enables our understanding that the actual is never given, but is in fact produced in a movement of becoming, the problematisation of the actual on the basis of the process of virtual differenciation involves questioning the stability of actual being: 'Why has this actual being stopped becoming? What constrains the open-ended creative process of becoming such that the transformation of being is blocked in this configuration?'

For Deleuze, then, virtual different/ciation is the ground of critique, enabling a specific problematisation of the actual in terms of its composition, and in terms of its fixture. This encourages us to think of bodies as involved in becomings, and also to imagine alternative ways in which the elements that constitute bodies could better relate to produce more cohesive complex organisations.[4] Virtual difference is thereby the absolute ground of critique, and also of reconstruction.

The Problem of the Actual

Because the actualisation of the virtual is essentially creative, producing diverse and heterogeneous series, the effect of the relationship between the virtual and the actual is to leave open the permanent possibility of the reconstruction of the actual according to alternative lines of development. The virtuality internal to actual being suggests questions that might guide transformation: 'What different components could be included? What different virtual connections could be made to produce the organisation and formal order of the actual?' Like dialectical processes, this critical and trans/formative practice is compelled by a notion of difference. However in this case, causation and change is thought in terms of the creative power of the virtual, rather than in terms of contradiction. Difference as creative immanent potentiality, rather than 'the negative in general' is the compelling principle of actualisation and transformation:

> For one has only to replace the actual terms in the movement that produces them to bring them back to the virtuality actualized in them, in order to see that differentiation is never a negation but a creation, and that difference is never negative but essentially positive and creative (1991b: 103; also 1994: 207).

This critical 'counter-actualisation' involves imagining the decomposition of actual bodies back into the virtual and elementary conditions of their formation. This allows a critical, retrospective tracing of the process of emergence of actual bodies, which form as complex entities through the regular and habitual association of their constituting elements. Since the initial meeting of these constituting elements is contingent upon chance and circumstance (when elements meet in an originally chaotic context), an alternative emergence is always possible if the constituting elements are related in other ways, or if the assemblage becomes composed by other elements. Different/ciation counters the apparent 'givenness' of actual reality, in so far as the transformation of the existing configuration of the actual according to alternative lines of development remains a permanent possibility. Counter-actualisation is then Deleuze's primary concept of critical practice, which facilitates a capacity for 'thinking otherwise'. Critical agents are chiefly responsible for 'counter-actualising' reality; imaginatively returning a constructed reality to a virtual, decomposed state, in which it becomes possible to reconfigure that which has previously come to pass. This endless weaving between the virtual and the actual is Deleuze's description of the formation and radical transformation of being.

Unlike dialectical philosophy which problematises the negativity of difference conceived as an opposition between unequal classes within the realm of the actual, and which ultimately aims to resolve the problem by negating this negative, Deleuze's concept of different/ciation translates into critical practice as the problematisation of the positive: the actual or the given 'solution' that has been historically constructed in response to the 'original' differentiation of a virtual and problematic Idea. The constructive aim of different/ciation is then to make possible an alternative process of actualisation by reconstructing an alternative foundation, a new virtual Idea or 'plane of composition', in response to which systemic inequity or select privilege would no longer be produced. This in turn suggests a way of reconceptualising postcolonial reconciliation and transformative politics, which allows a new kind of performance of critical practice, no longer grounded in a concept of the negative. In particular, it is helpful to think of postcolonisation as a new solution to the problematic Idea of social organisation *and* to the problematic actuality that is described by the continuing colonisation of indigenous peoples on their own territories. By placing the problematic actual in direct relation to the virtuality from which it has developed and thinking the actual in terms of its process of actualisation, we can articulate the conditions that have determined actual problems as such, and then resist these conditions by imagining other (virtual) conditions, which could conceivably determine the actualisation of new realities, 'new earths, new peoples', in which the problem does not appear.[5] Globally engaged in postcolonial reconciliation, participants might access, through a careful historiography, the virtual foundations of existing (local, concrete) forms of sociability, in order to actualise new alternatives to the problematic situation that is described by the continuing legacy of colonisation, inhering in the relations and institutions of the present (see Clendinnen 2003; Bignall and Galliford 2003). A central task for postcolonialism to employ is the disruption and 'counter-actualisation' of the problematic *post-colonial* present that remains tied to the virtual conditions of the emergence of colonisation, and the subsequent reconstruction of an alternative *postcolonial* present by drawing upon the resource of an alternative virtual sociability, in order to create new conditions of bodily or community interrelationship and complex social composition.

Of course, this task includes the problematisation of actual difference – established relations of inequality and opposition between actual bodies, such as exists between indigenous and non-indigenous peoples. However, the crux of the problem is not the difference, inequality or disadvantage represented by the indigenous other, but the way systemic inequality has come to be established and maintained through historical processes of social formation. In fact, neither aboriginality nor non-indigenous identity is problematic in itself, and the opposition of these unequal classes of identity is, on a Deleuzian view, neither ontologically given, nor structurally causal in their projected equalisation; the negative relation that exists in the present has been planned and manufactured over time, arising through a particularly colonial path of virtual different/ciation, which has been a historically and globally common causal force of actual social becoming. The underlying political problem is that the present, in diverse locations, has been actualised through an imperial mode of sociability or elemental connection; in many places, social relations and institutions were shaped in the context of colonial invasion, which inflected the initial attitude of orientation between indigenous and non-indigenous elements of society. The crucial problem to be addressed by postcolonisation accordingly concerns the way processes of colonial settlement and conquest have produced the continuing inequality of relational identities, by defining a relationship that was originally virtual and flexible and could have taken alternative happier forms, but has now become habitually unfriendly and unjust, and entrenched as such in the realm of the actual. It follows that:

> [i]f postcolonial theory is effective in bringing about a change in the relationship between colonizing Subject and colonized Other, it is not by appeal to rights and freedoms in a juridical sense, nor through retrieval of a lost identity, but rather through a genealogically informed critique of the mechanisms through which identities have been created. (Clifford 2001: 169)

In this way, Deleuze's philosophy enables a form of critique by problematising actual identity (and actual differences occurring between actual identities) on the basis of the primary productive force of virtual differenciation. However, Peter Hallward (2006) has criticised the apparently abstract nature of Deleuzian critical practice, which he believes 'looks for ways to evacuate the creatural so as to renew the creating that sustains it', and consequently worries 'inhibits any consequential engagement with the constraints of our actual world'. Because it privileges virtual creativity, Deleuzian politics is seen to be abstract and immaterial: it provides 'little more than Utopian distraction'. On Hallward's view, Deleuze gives no satisfactory account of actual relations between bodies; his is 'a philosophy of (virtual) difference without (actual) others', and 'there is no place in Deleuze's philosophy for any notion of time or history that is mediated by actuality'. Finally, this 'disqualification of actuality' leads to a paralysis of the subject or social actor: in privileging the critical imagination of alternative virtual foundations for actual existence, Deleuze 'disables action in favour of contemplation'(Hallward 2006: 160–3). If well-founded, these criticisms are damning indeed, suggesting a derailment of the project attempted here: the orientation of Deleuze's critical and constructive practice in a concretely grounded, postcolonial theory of agency. Fortunately, I think a suitable response can be made, and the following initial reply will be fleshed out in subsequent chapters.

Firstly, Hallward mistakes the interaction of virtuality and actuality as a 'unilateral relation' (2006: 162), when in fact they are always-already co-implied. The virtual exists in so far as it is carried within actual forms; the actual exists, not as given, but because it has been determined by a process of virtual different/ciation. Accordingly, engagement with the virtual conditions of creativity can only be done with respect to one's actual situation, which materialises the virtual in actual states of affairs. A constructive and transformative access to virtual creativity is only possible through concrete engagement with a 'here and now' actuality, via a critical understanding of the way actual structures have come to embody the abstract virtual in particular and contingent configurations of reality. This is why Deleuze and Guattari in fact caution against the complete 'evacuation of the creatural', warning that

> outside [actual] strata or in the absence of strata we . . . are disarticulated . . . How could unformed matter, anorganic life, nonhuman becoming, be anything but chaos, pure and simple? Every undertaking of destratification . . . must therefore observe concrete rules of extreme caution: a too-sudden destratification may be suicidal, or turn cancerous. In other words it will sometimes end in chaos, the void and destruction . . . (1987: 503)

Because access to virtual creativity is always necessarily mediated by actuality, Deleuze's critical philosophy is constantly addressed towards the concrete problematisation of the constraints presented by the actual. It is only through this problematic activity conducted with respect to actual relations and actual situations, that one can begin to critique and thus to rethink the virtual foundations of actual existence, in order to envision new virtual Ideas, corresponding with

The Problem of the Actual

new forms of becoming and new forms of actual existence, in which those constraints would not appear.

Secondly, Hallward reduces Deleuze's critical practice to a simple form of 'subtraction' or 'evacuation' from actuality, which obscures the fact, for Deleuze and Guattari, that counter-actualisation 'is never simple, but always multiple and composite' (1987: 509). While the complex nature of counter-actualisation will be discussed in following chapters, it is useful to note at this point that Deleuze and Guattari take care to distinguish between 'absolute' and 'relative' kinds of transformation, which they refer to as the 'deterritorialisation' of the 'territory' that the actual has consolidated from the virtual chaos that determines it. The first of these, absolute deterritorialisation, involves the kind of critical practice already outlined above, in which an actual state or situation is counter-actualised by destabilising its virtual foundations and setting out an alternative virtual 'plane of composition' for the construction of an alternative actuality. By contrast, relative deterritorialisation 'concerns only movements within the actual – as opposed to the virtual – order of things' (Patton 2000: 106–7). Critical practices of relative deterritorialisation include many kinds of struggle characteristic of contemporary politics of resistance and social transformation. These commonly aim to bring about change in actual states of affairs, not by destabilising and reconstructing the virtual foundations of actual structures and institutions, but by using mechanisms existing within the actual system (for example, human rights to equal treatment and opportunity) to apply pressure and prompt change, or by inventing new mechanisms (for example, new laws, pedagogies or institutions) that can be accommodated within the existing system and operate to bring about changes in actual relations. Dialectical, class-based conflict and oppositional politics likewise exemplify a movement of relative deterritorialisation in so far as this struggle takes place at the level of actually existing bodies, which problematically encounter each other in unequal ways and which transform each other in the process of finding improved harmony. However, class conflict will involve absolute deterritorialisation if, as in revolutionary Marxism, a virtual mode of production (immanent to actual capitalism) is forcefully redefined and reconstituted in terms of a new 'grammar' connecting productive elements in new and different ways, such that a wholly alternative form of economy and sociability develops as a result.

In a post-colonial context, absolute and relative forms of

deterritorialisation are exemplified by the distinct forms of resistance that James Tully (2000) refers to as 'indigenous struggles *for* and *of* freedom'. Relative deterritorialisation occurs from within established forms of society as a struggle *of* freedom: '[T]he struggles of indigenous peoples on the ground have primarily involved attempts to modify the techniques of government to gain degrees of self-government and control over some of their territories, rather than direct confrontation with the background structures of domination' (Tully 2000: 38). This relative deterritorialisation modifies the system from within, through the attempt to exercise a freedom to move critically within the dominating structures. This exercise of freedom includes not only practices of dissent and insubordination within the acceptable limits set by the regime, but also the 'mostly quotidian acts of protecting, recovering, gathering together, keeping, revitalizing, teaching and adapting entire forms of indigenous life that were nearly destroyed' (Tully 2000: 59). On the other hand, absolute deterritorialisation corresponds to that which Tully refers to as indigenous struggles *for* freedom, in resistances 'against the structure of domination as a whole and for their freedom as peoples' (2000: 50).

Accordingly there is no reason to assume, as Hallward does, that 'Deleuze's work is essentially indifferent to the politics of this world' and that his 'philosophy precludes a distinctively relational conception of politics as a matter of course' (2006: 162). Deleuzian philosophy maintains a place for the dialectical struggle of unequal, relational classes, but insists that this is a politics that generally takes place in the actual 'order of things', and so remains fettered to established categories of identity and action that finally reinforce the structures of actual existence that the resistance aims to upset, as indeed was observed in Chapter 2. In privileging absolute deterritorialisation or 'struggles *for* freedom' and describing a politics of virtual composition, Deleuze expands prevailing concepts of resistance by drawing attention to a (less often thought, less obviously evident) relation between virtuality and actuality as the basis of an alternative kind of critical practice and constructive process.

In fact, Deleuze's criticism of the actual resonates with the emphasis of much critical theory, which contests the ossified positivity of established forms of presence (e.g. Derrida 1974; Bhabha 1994; Marcuse 1960; Adorno 1973; see Coole 2000; Olkowski 1999). However, critical theory most commonly challenges authority and given identity by calling attention to an excluded negativity – an oppositional alterity, or an undecidability, ambiguity, or uncertainty – thus grounding transformative politics in a negative concept of difference, which as we have seen, occasions difficulties for postcolonial theory. In Deleuze's view, identity is problematic not because it is essentially lacking or ambivalent, but because it interrupts the flow of creative differenciation of things in the positive process of their becoming. The ascription of identity to a thing involves the illusion of a stoppage to this process of differenciation, since the recognition or representation of the identified thing requires that it be 'fixed' into some degree of stability and certainty of being. Identification thus sets artificial or imaginary constraints upon a body, which might in fact have already 'moved on' and become something else. In this sense Deleuze understands that the materiality of actual bodies is the 'inversion of movement', and that matter is the 'obstacle that the creative process of life must get around' (1991b: 101). Whereas the virtual, creative flow of differenciation is primary and positive, the fixed form of actual identity introduces a blockage of this process; this stoppage is problematised by Deleuze, not on the basis of a causal ontological negativity, but on the basis of the primary and positive force of differenciation in the virtual. Deleuze's critique of actual identity is therefore conducted neither in terms of its essential incompletion, nor through its telltale ambivalence towards the (colonised) other, but through the positive concept of virtual difference or differenciation.

Furthermore, Deleuze's critique of actual presence is not only relevant for theorising new forms of virtual politics and absolute deterritorialisation, but also suggests an alternative 'positive' focus for strategies of relative deterritorialisation, which appears similarly promising for postcolonial programmes of anti-colonial resistance. Whereas dialectical strategies of equalisation or unification have often sought to remove indigenous *disadvantage*, either by empowering particular indigenous aspects of culture, or by striving to ensure indigenous people have an equal opportunity to enjoy the benefits and rights of mainstream society, or by a combination of both of these strategies, the Deleuzian critique of actuality shares more common ground with a critique of *advantage*, such as is suggested by critical studies of 'whiteness', as well as by some feminist strategists working against masculine dominance. For example, Joan Eveline argues that 'in the discourses and strategies of equality politics, both the reality and the representation of advantage are repressed' (Eveline 1993: 53). She argues that the failure to attend to the problem and the politics of advantage has meant that equality politics has been conducted solely through a discourse of disadvantage, in which 'claims against inequality are relegated to a defensive position that implicitly reinforces the practices the claims seek to challenge' (1993: 54). Ultimately Eveline argues for a strategic reversal that acknowledges advantage as a register of the problem of actual difference, or inequality. She points out that where unfair advantage is perceived to be unremarkable, it is 'simultaneously normalised and obfuscated', thereby stabilising the relation of power between classes defined in terms of their respective statuses as 'standard' and 'deviant'. She also suggests that, while it has been useful in raising awareness about actual political differences, the discourse of disadvantage has had a number of alienating effects on those whom it presumes to represent. Interestingly, the Australian Council for Aboriginal Reconciliation agrees that, in its current form, reconciliation in Australia is not relevant to many aboriginal people, who like many women, remain 'convinced that the discourse [of disadvantage] does not apply to them ... alienated by its being read as deficiency' (Eveline 1993: 57, 58; CAR 2000: 27).

This 'positive' strategy of critique associated with identifying actual advantage or beneficiary whiteness as problematic is potentially useful in the relative deterritorialisations attempted as part of postcolonisation. Drawing attention to the problematic status of inherited settler advantage suggestively alters the position of indigenous resistance in discourses of reconciliation and social justice. It redirects indigenous activism for social justice away from a mode of supplication. It simultaneously disrupts the tendency to construct aboriginality as a deviation from an unquestioned standard, or as otherwise 'problematic'. In so doing, it refuses the ground of justification of those commentators who seek to portray indigenous activism as a cause of social disorder or degeneracy, or as a force of division in the community. On the contrary, such activism does not seek to destroy and disrupt 'normal' society for the sake of (unfairly) advancing particular indigenous interests; it seeks to subject the production of 'normality' itself, and the selective, unfair advantages this process reinforces, to critical scrutiny. Furthermore, responsibility for redress is more actively directed towards the beneficiaries of unfair advantage, who might consequently be less inclined to resist postcolonisation, and more helpfully, might more clearly appreciate and ratify their obligation to participate in the postcolonial processes of just social transformation (see McKay 1999).

Conceived problematically, the production of the actual implies an associated problematisation of the historically selective domination

The Problem of the Actual

of constructive agency, and therefore also foregrounds a problem of exclusive or privileged access to constructive processes. Colonial processes of national development formalised inequitable relationships between bodies, and the identities of indigenous and non-indigenous people alike were produced and maintained by dominant forms of constructive agency that even now continue to manipulate the construction of the actual to certain settler advantage. Foregrounding the actual as a focus of the problem of colonisation enables criticism of the way the present has taken form, by an agency which consolidates certain relations of advantage and disadvantage between bodies. Placing 'advantage' in the virtual context of the process from which it developed raises the genealogical questions: by *what* process of actualisation and *what* mode of agency did the advantage come about?

Fairly obviously, the systemic advantage currently globally enjoyed by 'white' or 'Western' society came about through colonisation. Less obviously, the actualisation of advantage came about through a *particular* form of social agency, a particular kind of social orientation, practice and interrelation. This is not to say that indigenous agency is a negligible feature of colonial history, nor that the production of settler advantage did not meet with resistance. Of course, there have been many instances and traditions of successful indigenous and non-indigenous resistance to colonial domination. However as we saw in the previous chapter, in order to be understood or heard at all, this resistance is mostly compelled to work through the same mode of established agency – involving a claim to unity of identity and therefore authority, in opposition to other identities and other structures of authority. Perhaps as a result, on the whole, colonial society was able to contain and repress indigenous resistance, and even now preserves its social advantage through the same type of agency of social construction that works to perpetuate imperial modes of sociability.

While this mode of agency has been dominant in Western history, it is not the only mode of interaction available to constructive agents. Indeed, placing the concept of imperial agency in the context of the virtual from which it emanates denies the self-evidence of this particular concept of agency. It also makes it possible to imagine alternative forms of agency, which potentially actualise alternative forms of sociability. Taking a Deleuzian view, a significant task faced by postcolonial theory is to conceive of a mode or modes of agency and social composition that will disrupt the politics of advantage and disadvantage, and reconstruct a postcolonial sociability, which will not strive to eliminate actual difference (arguably a futile and imperial aim), but to reorient it. Here, the challenge postcolonialism faces is to make actual difference ethical, not discriminating. An alternative actualisation of a postcolonial future-present can begin to take form through the carefully attentive practice of an alternative, postcolonial attitude and agency of relation, defined by orchestrating a virtual 'plane of composition' which can orient an appropriate association between the elements comprising a society. The description and promotion of this alternative mode of agency arguably remains a most pressing task for postcolonial activists, and it is to this constructive task that I will turn in subsequent chapters.

However, there is another aspect of critical practice that needs to be addressed, before we proceed to these reconstructive and reorienting tasks. So far, I have been arguing that Deleuze's philosophy enables a form of critique by problematising actual forms (of identity, and relatively, of actual difference) on the basis of the primary productive force of virtual difference. However, transformative postcolonial practice is best conceptualised as *collective* action. Like some other postcolonial theorists, Peter Hallward worries social transformation depends upon 'more resilient forms of cohesion, on more principled forms of commitment, on more integrated forms of coordination' than (Deleuze's) poststructuralist philosophy can sustain (Hallward 2006: 162; Parry 1994a, 2004; Ahmad 1992, 1995). Is Deleuze's critical practice capable of an active solidarity that can forge postcoloniality?

Unity, cohesion and commitment

Pragmatic concepts of collective 'solidarity', 'people' and 'commitment' remain undeveloped in Deleuze's work. However, concepts of unity, co-ordination and consistency are not entirely absent from his philosophical lexicon. Indeed, the theme of association lies at the heart of Deleuzian philosophy: the relation and connection of elements to form consistent collective assemblages is the basis of Deleuzian ontology, and his and Guattari's 'philosophy of desire' is the basis of a social and political theory of groups. However, in this thought, two main problems arise for conventional forms of political resistance and transformative practice. The first concerns the nature and scope of the commitment it is possible to make to an actual assemblage (or the actualisation of an assemblage), without insisting upon its fixed or ultimate form; the second concerns a problem of application regarding the

The Problem of the Actual

general relevance of a particular collective form as a preferred basis for organising resistance and transformative action, when diverse forms of assemblage are possible. The following discussion begins to draw out a Deleuzian understanding of cohesion and commitment, which corresponds with his notions of association and unity and his style of philosophical thought, and which might be put to use in attempts to theorise collaborative postcolonial movements for social change.

Like Etienne Balibar (1995) and Judith Butler (1996), Deleuze suggests that the concept of 'universality' is undone by its internal multiplicity or the 'insurmountable *equivocity*' (Balibar 1995: 48) rendered by its ambiguous existence as ideal more so than real (for Deleuze, as virtual rather than actual), and its consequent contingency within the cultural context in which it is defined. In these essays, Balibar and Butler both distinguish between three moments or 'points' of universality: as 'real'; as 'fictive'; and as 'symbolic/ideal'. Their notions of 'real universality' loosely correspond with Deleuze's notion of 'actual' unities or assemblages 'which together build what we call the World: institutions, groups, individuals' (Balibar 1995: 49). The problem for universal theories and principles is that, despite globalisation, real 'standards of universality are historically [and culturally] articulated' (Butler 1996: 47) 'in the constitution of social hegemonies' (Balibar 1995: 71), with the consequence that instead of being unified and univocal, 'the universal is a contested term' (Butler 1996: 47), and each of its articulations is complicit with a form of hegemonic normalisation (Balibar 1995: 71). However, this essential ambiguity or contestability of universals also gives rise to a 'performative contradiction' that is productive because it 'constitutes one way to expose the limits of current notions of universality, and to constitute a challenge to those existing standards to revise themselves in more expansive and inclusive ways' (Butler 1996: 48). Thus, claims about 'real universality' are constantly revealed as 'fictitious universals' in fact, but Butler explains that this revelation 'that the universal has not yet been articulated is to insist that the "not yet" is proper to an understanding of the universal itself'; that is, a universal works best as a 'postulated and open-ended *ideal*' that has not (yet) been adequately realised. In this way, for both Butler and Balibar, ideal universality is the 'futural anticipation of a universality that has not yet arrived . . . [and] . . . for which we have no ready concept' (Butler 1996: 49). Thus, 'ideal' universality 'establishes the universal as that which is yet to be achieved and which, in order to resist domestication, may never be fully or finally achievable' (Butler 1996:

52). 'Fictive' universals (discursively presented as 'real') are our necessarily fallible but productive mechanisms of identifying or positing the conditions of the 'ideal' universality in progress.

Butler's and Balibar's descriptions of the 'different realms' situating 'real', 'fictive' and 'ideal' types of universality clearly resonate with Deleuze's insistence that actually represented universals are 'illusory'. On his view, there is no final perfect society, no uniform 'aboriginality', 'whiteness' or 'nation', and no global principles of 'human' rights or 'good' existence. In fact, these are simply convenient categories, which are necessary since they allow us to make sense of the world, but which impose an illusory stability on real diversity. The 'illusory universes' of the actual are therefore essentially contestable, problematised from the perspective of a greater, virtual unity: the understanding that everything is primarily diverse and differentiating, rather than essentially similar and converging. Deleuze and Guattari describe this virtual unity as 'an unlimited One-All', a universal ground which is 'a Powerful Whole that while remaining open is not fragmented' (1994: 35). It can only be thought of in terms of the virtual duration or becoming of things, which is 'universal, univocal and unique' (Boundas 1996: 97). Deleuze thus thinks of unity in terms of 'a single time, a single duration, in which everything would participate' (1991b: 78). In short, duration expresses the univocity of being, which is said everywhere in the same way as a becoming over time. Only the virtual process of different/ciation is truly universal; actual unity is a constrained or limited subset of this universal process. Consequently for Deleuze, universal (we could add, postcolonial) humanity is conceivable only as a virtual 'future-people', a 'coming people', in much the same way that Giorgio Agamben (1993) describes the 'coming community', and Hardt and Negri conceive of 'the multitude' as a virtual force for inventing that which is 'not yet' (Hardt and Negri 2004: esp. 220–2). Again resonating with Butler's and Balibar's descriptions of the 'fictive' role of universals, Deleuze at times also suggestively champions the usefulness of the Bergsonian notion of 'fabulation', or 'telling-tales', in the politically strategic constitution of a people to come (1995: 125–6, 174).

However, Phillipe Mengue (2008) is critical of Deleuze's notions of 'people and fabulation', arguing that Deleuze's 'people' are depoliticised because they are always virtual and never actual, and that fabulation, for Deleuze, is consequently a 'minoritarian' tool of art, of artistic resistance and virtual creation, rather than a tool of politics proper, of co-ordination and cohesion at the macropolitical level:

> [B]y investing the concept of the people with a reality that is merely virtual, he misses the central and proper object of politics . . . the Deleuzian people, being always to come, is indeterminate (it has neither territory nor borders nor traditions), it is deterritorialised . . . [but] . . . politics has to deal with a people that is other than virtual, potential or yet to come. A people that fears for its safety, that has borders to defend, that hopes to improve its well-being, a people that is territorialized, such a people is the proper object of politics. (Mengue 2008: 230–1)

As a way of rendering Deleuzian thought more properly political (in his view), Mengue proposes the need for a 'doxic plane of immanence' as a political supplement to the immanent planes of art, science and thought that Deleuze and Guattari describe in *What is Philosophy?* This 'doxic plane' would consist of elementary 'opinions'; their co-existence and connection is what 'makes possible the existence of a people as *demos*' (Mengue 2008: 235). The doxic plane itself thus has a

> potential existence as fabulation – in other words it is what makes it possible to receive the thousands of little stories irrepressibly produced by the multitude, to compare them with one another, to analyse their phantasmal or delirious character, and to work towards an agreed decision on what is to be done. (2008: 235)

In this way, the 'common space rests upon a plane of doxic immanence that traverses the little stories and commands confrontation and the elaboration of a narrative that tends towards the common', which Deleuze 'would like to ignore' or 'tries to banish' (2008: 234).

While Deleuze and Guattari's failure to provide for an autonomous political field is certainly problematic and Mengue is right to address this, he is arguably too hasty in his condemnation and dismissal of the political potential suggested by the role of the virtual. In fact, virtuality is a notion of genuine universality (or commonality) that, for Deleuze, is the germinal basis of actual forms of common life, and also the common ground for the 'confrontation and elaboration' of improved forms of common existence. For Deleuze, a 'people' is already actual but could always become otherwise, and so is *simultaneously* virtual; this 'always otherwise' is a *universal* virtual condition of actual existence, but therefore only exists with respect to concrete forms of actual existence. Deleuzian 'people' are always 'to come', but this becoming is performed on the problematic basis of that which they already are. Furthermore, virtual unity is already *real*, but without being *actual*. This is exactly where Deleuze departs from Balibar, Butler, Lacan,

Laclau, Mouffe and others, who insist that unity is *ideal* and never to be *realised*, and that this gap is critical and productive. In keeping with a political commitment to *ideal* unity as a political solution to common life, these thinkers maintain a conventional understanding of the political problem of conflict: commonly in Western political theory, unity is conceptually organised at the level of the solution as an ideal, final harmony, a democratic consensus. Universal representation is, then, conventionally understood to be the ideal solution to real conflict, and the fissure between the real conflict and ideal harmony drives the common effort to materialise the ideal. By contrast, if the Deleuzian concept of virtual universality is able to inform the potential unity of common practices, it requires that we think of unity at the level of the problem, rather than at the level of the solution: '[O]nly the Idea or problem is universal. It is not the solution which lends its generality to the problem, but the problem which lends its universality to the solution' (Deleuze 1994: 162). In fact, this is just what Mengue proposes when he lays out a 'democratic plane of immanence', with the result that, for him as is already the case for Deleuze,

> the (democratic) people is indeed absent, for it is not actual and never will be in history. Yet at the same time the people is not absent, for it is the virtual reality of the democratic plane on which opinions are received and confronted – the only possible meaning to be given to the word 'WE' – and perhaps, if necessary, the thing on behalf of which and thanks to which the 'resistance' will rise up. (Mengue 2008: 236)

In the context of postcolonial reconciliation in Australia and elsewhere, 'we' might think of 'ourselves' united as nations in relation to our problematic actuality – the continuing colonisation of indigenous peoples upon their own territories. On this basis, we could also be united in our various struggles to think this problematic actuality as it might otherwise be, and to imagine and enact, through fabulation, the ethical and political foundations that would make possible various performances of postcoloniality in our relations with each other. While we might act together to confront the problem of the legacy of colonisation, if we are to respect each other's differences by acknowledging that there are multiple approaches to this problem, many tales to tell, the solutions we develop will probably be diverse and will not necessarily be commensurate with each other. The outcome should not be the formation of a seamless social unity, but a society that continues to be characterised by actual differences in the relations we form with each other. The challenge is deliberately to organise this difference in ways that are ethical – postcolonial and communicative, rather than colonial and segregating.

Whether this will be successful depends upon how we conceptualise a purposely postcolonial agency, one which is capable of actualising forms of common life in which constituting bodies can peacefully co-exist in a post-imperial fashion. In rejecting unity at the level of the solution, Deleuze's theory of practice rejects visions of utopian finality as organising principles of social transformation. But does it commit us to 'the more disconcerting idea of *un*predictable transformation' including, perhaps, our dystopian acceptance that society might well devolve into forms of systemic evil, if 'the movement of actualisation is the opening up of the virtual to what befalls it' (Grosz 1999: 17, 27)? Is it possible, on a Deleuzian view, to direct social transformation towards a preferred, postcolonial future? If universals are virtual rather than actual, what kind of commitment, affinity, fidelity or faith to a preferred form of actual society is possible? These questions return us to the problem of intentional agency and the notion of directed, immanent causation.

Notes

1. Aspects of this discussion appear as Bignall (2007a).
2. Chapter 4 will clarify how the explanation of structure in terms of force relations shows the influence of Nietzsche on Deleuze's thought. See his *Nietzsche and Philosophy* (1983), especially pp. 39–71. Deleuze also explains Foucault's thought, with its similar Nietzschean influences, in like terms. See Deleuze (1986: 70–93).
3. This notion of 'grammar' obviously borrows from Wittgenstein. The notion of a 'grammar' specifying rules for connectivity is also employed in other, recent work on complex systems and self-organisation. For example, see Kauffman (1993: 387–402). On Deleuze's relationship to complexity theory, see Bonta and Protevi (2004).
4. Discussion of the nature of the ethical evaluation implied by 'better' assemblages is beyond the scope of this chapter, although this theme will be taken up in Chapters 4 and 6. However it is useful to note here that this is the point where Deleuze turns to Spinoza, potentially allowing for an ethics of assemblage based upon Spinoza's notions of 'desire', 'joy' and 'conatus'. See Deleuze (1988b) and the commentary by Michael Hardt (1993: 56–112).
5. Mark Galliford and I have considered how re-enactments of history can provide examples of this idea operating in practice in our (2003) article on 'Reconciling Replicas: The Second Coming of the *Duyfken*'.

II
Constructivism

4
Power/Desire

[T]he analysis of desire is immediately practical and political . . . for politics precedes being. (Deleuze and Guattari 1987: 203)

Central to the creation of a postcolonial concept of agency is the need to reconsider the nature of power and desire, which together constitute the conditions and the impetus for social action.[1] The first aim of this chapter is to present an alternative perspective on power, not conceptualised in relation to mastery. This is found in Deleuze's interpretation of Nietzsche, and in Foucault's elaboration of this in *Discipline and Punish* and the *History of Sexuality*. However, Foucault's analysis is largely limited to the constitutive effects of power upon the subject, and the scope for constructive agency is often not understood or is obscured in readings of Foucault's work. I will suggest that this problem arises because Foucault does not adequately emphasise desire as a causal component of agency. While there are constant references to desire made in the context of his history of sexuality and his later work on the ethical practices of the self, ultimately Foucault shows how a *concept* and *practice* of 'desire' is produced in modernity as an effect of power, captured by discourses of sexuality and morality, and reduced to an aspect of pleasure. This obscures the way the *force* of desire itself acts as a cause in the production of social forms.

The second aim of this chapter is therefore to place Foucault's causal concept of productive power in relation to a complementary concept of desire, which is not conceptualised in relation to ontological lack and appropriative satisfaction. Deleuze has developed this concept of 'desiring-production' in detail, especially in his work on Spinoza, as well as in his collaborative work with Guattari. By positioning Foucault's theory of power in an explicit relation to this theory of desire, I hope to clarify how poststructuralist political philosophy can think of a productive, transformative and ethical agency, which is also potentially *postcolonial* because it is grounded in a non-imperial ontology of selfhood, and not defined by the desire to master, appropriate or exclude the other.

Causal forces

Deleuze (1983) offers an interpretation of Nietzsche's philosophy that posits the concept of the 'will to power' as the immanent causal principle of constructive action. Underlying this interpretation is the particular view of ontology that was the subject of Chapter 3: Deleuze thinks of existence as order emerging from an immanent field of virtual difference that becomes organised through various events of actualisation. With Deleuze's reading of Nietzsche, this ontology comes to be thought in terms of a field of differential relations of force between bodies, themselves conceived of as forces. By framing his analysis of existence in terms of the types of forces and force relations that constitute and define bodies, Deleuze reads into Nietzsche's philosophy an implicit ethics and a method of evaluation of bodies and their actions. The concept of the will to power assumes a central importance in this reading, since it is identified as the active principle of the actualisation of the virtual, now conceptualised as the active principle of the organisation of relations between forces.

Deleuze begins his discussion of Nietzsche by explaining how bodies can be thought of as complex forces, themselves constituted by relations of force. Any given body is the product of a relation between dominant or 'active' forces, and dominated or 'reactive' forces.

> What defines a body is this relation between dominant and dominated forces. Every relationship of force constitutes a body – whether it is chemical, biological, social or political. Any two forces, being unequal, constitute a body as soon as they enter into a relationship. (1983: 40)

A given force will dominate in a relation with other forces according to the degree or quantity in which it is expressed. The quantity of force exerted by a body in its various relations with other bodies then defines a quality of that body. A body composed mainly of dominant forces will be 'active', whereas a body composed mainly of dominated forces will be 'reactive'. These distinctions between dominating and dominated forces, and active and reactive bodies, provide the basis of a genealogy of the sense and value of things, since 'the sense of something is its relation to the force which takes possession of it, [and] the value of something is the hierarchy of forces which are expressed in it as a complex phenomenon' (1983: 8). Attending to the way bodies have been constituted by particular kinds of relations of force therefore prompts the genealogical questions: what force has taken hold of this body? And what value has been attributed to this body because of the order of forces that have taken hold of it? However, in Deleuze's opinion, these genealogical questions will be poorly understood unless it is first made clear what is meant by Nietzsche's claim that there is a 'will to power' at work in every relation of force.

Deleuze explains that the will to power is not equivalent to the desire for power (1983: xi, 82–3). Rather, the will to power is best interpreted as an internal, efficient cause of being, where being is understood as a complex force which itself emerges from a relation between forces. The will to power is 'added to force as the internal principle of the determination' of force and force relations (1983: 51). As the 'internal element' of the production of bodies through relations of force, the will to power is 'the element from which derive both the quantitative difference of relative forces and the quality that devolves into each force in the relation . . . the will to power here reveals its nature as the principle of the synthesis of forces' (1983: 50). However, this activity of the will to power is only partially the cause of existing things, since existence is always constrained by chance – Nietzsche's throw of the dice – which is the ultimate cause of encounters between forces. While 'chance is the bringing of forces into relation, the will to power is the determining principle of this relation' (1983: 53). The will to power is the determining element in a force relation in so far as it influences the *way* forces come to be hierarchically positioned in that relationship.

Deleuze clarifies this claim by distinguishing between two qualities of the will to power. These two 'primordial qualities of the will to power' can impose upon a force relation in two distinct fashions; one affirmative, the other negative: a will to power can shape a relation of forces, either in a spirit of affirmation, or in a spirit of negation. A body that is oriented to another in terms of an affirmative will to power is an active body, which affirms itself by affirming the differential relation of force it is immersed in. Conversely, a body that is oriented in its relation to others by a negative will to power is a reactive body, which asserts itself only by denying or depreciating the differential in the relationship (1983: 54). The will to power therefore evaluates the forces in the relationship, qualifying them as active or reactive in their orientation towards each other.

It is apparent that the two different qualities of the will to power suggest criteria for the evaluation of forces. The affirmative tendency of the will to power, and the active body this affirmation qualifies, are primary in relation to the negating quality of reactive forces. This is because reactive forces are constituted as such only 'in relation to and on the basis of the active' (1983: 42; see Patton 2000: 65). In the context of his writing on Nietzsche, Deleuze's argument against Hegel is framed by his description of the dialectic as a relation of forces dominated by reactive bodies and a negative will to power (1983: 196; see Schrift 1995: 253–4). In a dialectical structure of relationship, each body has its character conferred upon it from without, through the active recognition of the other. Each body is thus reactive, defined against and by the other, and each seeks to eliminate the differential described by their relationship in order to achieve an ontological harmony and agreement between self and other, subject and object of recognition. The bodies arranged in a dialectical conflict are reactive forces oriented towards each other by a negative will to power, each seeking the negation of the difference between them.

The evaluative criteria that privileges active bodies and affirmative relations supports a practice of ethical relationship, which I will begin to elaborate here. In particular I will start to outline a postcolonial ethics by building from this notion that bodies, which initially encounter other forces by chance, ought to strive to become oriented in these relations – and indeed actively to forge and facilitate meetings – according to an active and affirmative will to power. However, even at this early stage, it is possible to discern the beginnings of an ethics and an evaluative perspective in Deleuze's interpretation of Nietzsche. In particular, it is apparent that Nietzsche's method of genealogical critique is properly addressed to the will to power that is the immanent principle of the organisation, qualification and evaluation of forces. Analysing the sense and the value that is attached to a body requires an analysis of the will to power that is the determining element of this sense and value. The genealogical question is properly conceived as: which will to power has taken hold of the forces in this thing to make it what it is? The ethical question is then properly conceived as: which will to power is required, in order to allow a preferred complex form to emerge from a relationship between constituting forces? However, before turning to address the character of the ethics, agency and subjectivity that might be combined with the analytical and speculative tasks of genealogy in order to produce a poststructuralist philosophy of transformation, it will be helpful first to consider how Foucault develops Deleuze's reading of Nietzsche's will to power into a theory of social power, with particular reference to modern disciplinary societies.

Power

Foucault thinks of society as a network of power or force relations. On his view, power

> traverses and produces things, it induces pleasure, forms knowledge, produces discourse. It needs to be considered as a productive network which runs through the whole social body, much more than as a negative instance whose function is repression. (Foucault 1980a: 119)

As a relation between bodies, power refers to a subject's capacity to act upon another's actions (Foucault 1983b: 221). In this sense, power operates at a local, 'micropolitical' level, but through its circulation it becomes concentrated in general 'macropolitical' institutions such as prisons, schools and State apparatus, and structuring discourses such as delinquency, health and morality. This distinction between the micropolitical and macropolitical levels of the operation of power is generally perceived as a spatial distinction, leading us to conceive of micropolitical relations as small scale relations of force carried out between individuals or small groups, and macropolitics as large scale political relations involving the structures of class, discourse and institutions.[2]

As Said explains in *Orientalism* (1978), the establishment of a body of persuasive colonial discourse that could function as a disciplinary 'regime of truth' was central to the success of imperialism. However, as Bhabha (1994) points out, Said's Foucaultian analysis of colonial discourse tends to portray colonialism as wielding a complete and hegemonic control over the colonised people, and so assumes a seamless and unconflicted colonial subjectivity and the utter debilitation of the colonised people. The political operation of colonial discourse extends over the entire social field, and thus any space outside of this discursive operation from which resistance might be formulated is rendered negligible. In fact, this is symptomatic of many critiques of Foucault's theory of power, including the criticism later presented by Said himself (Said 1986). Critics of Foucault's theory of power as discipline or normalisation tend to perceive that 'the disciplinary society is a *society*, a social whole' (Walzer 1986: 57; Said 1986: 154), with the result that there is no critical distance available in a society of diffuse and pervasive 'microforms of discipline' (Walzer 1986: 59). In addition, they worry that activism has no focal point when power is undifferentiated, locally effected and broadly dispersed. On this view, Foucault totalises the social space in terms of discipline, despite his explicit refusal of totalisation as a theoretical strategy. These critics therefore interpret Foucault's reading of the social wholly in terms of disciplinary social space, into which both micropolitics and macropolitics are compressed, as different *degrees* of disciplinary relations of power. Micropolitics is identified as small scale, local, or minor relations of power directly bearing upon the individual, and macropolitics is defined as the large scale, structural relations of power embodied in institutionalised discourses and practices.

This common reading of Foucault leads to the understanding that his differentiation of the macro and micro categories of power has been made solely in terms of space or extension and differences of degree or scale. However, at a few explicit moments in Foucault's work on power there is a more profound distinction in kind being made. This is a distinction made in terms of time, duration or movement, in terms of differential speeds and slowness, flux and stoppage. For example, in *The History of Sexuality*, Foucault (1990: 93) distinguishes 'power' and 'Power' according to the different dynamics of the force relations that compose them. The first is conceived in terms of 'the moving substrate of force relations which, by virtue of their inequality, constantly engender states of power; but the latter are always local and unstable'. The second, Power, which 'insofar as it is permanent, repetitious, inert and self-reproducing, is simply the overall effect that emerges from all these mobilities, the concatenation that rests on each of them and seeks in turn to arrest their movement'. Both Foucault and Deleuze and Guattari elsewhere identify this as a distinction between molecular and molar forms of power relations, or between micropolitical and macropolitical practices.[3] The crucial point is that micropolitical or molecular forces of power are unstable and flexible in nature, while macropolitical or molar forms of power are stable and characteristically fixed. It is in the context of this distinction between the forces and the forms of power that Foucault's claims about power are best understood. Power must be understood *in the first instance* as the multiplicity of force relations 'immanent in the sphere in which they operate and which constitute their own organization', as processes, and as strategies, which crystallise into strata (Foucault 1990: 92–3). *Subsequently*, macropolitical structures or Power in 'the sovereignty of the State, the form of the Law, or the overall unity of a domination . . . are only the terminal forms power takes' (Foucault 1990: 92).

This temporal distinction between the two kinds of power relation offers an initial response to the criticism that Foucault's theory of power disables effective resistance to structures of domination in society. In fact, such criticism misconceives the complex nature of power in Foucault's social theory. This is not surprising, however, since Foucault is not consistent in distinguishing the two types of power, and in fact it is only in his later works that this distinction is articulated with clarity. In addition, his analyses of power usually focus upon disciplinary spaces and the way in which the subject is produced by Power, rather than the ways in which the micropolitical capacities of the subject can be used to disrupt this established Power.[4]

Nonetheless, this distinction, properly emphasised, is a basis for the conceptualisation of resistance. Macropolitics is a practice that establishes and manipulates structures and strata, a politics of form. Micropolitics does not describe a different degree of the same kind of practice – 'small forms' or 'miniature structures' – but a qualitatively different practice, implying a movement that differs in kind from macropolitical struggles (Deleuze and Guattari 1987: 208–32). Deleuze names this movement 'deterritorialisation', and explains that its objective is the transformation of established arrangements and values. Micropolitics is in this sense opposed to macropolitics and bears upon macropolitical structures. Where macropolitics is a politics of form, micropolitics is a politics of transformation. Micropolitics is a politics of movement, of contestation, of difference, of the creation of novel identities through shifting political relations between selves. Macropolitics is a politics of consolidation, of stability, of the reproduction of identity by the fixture of power relations into regular hierarchies of dominance and subordination.

Micropolitics or deterritorialisation describes the goal and action of resistances directed at the 'permanent, repetitious, inert and self-reproducing' structures of domination that constitute the 'state-form', the 'terminal forms' of Power, which function by delimiting a conceptual 'territory' defined by its rigidity and its capacity to preserve its form (Patton 1984). This delimitation is a strategic closure, an assertion of authority through a claim to self-evidence. In the spatialised discourse of power, closure inscribes a conceptual interiority, which nonetheless remains relative to an open exteriority that threatens to disrupt it. In fact, the space of interiority retains its structure only by excluding that which remains excessive to it, that which disturbs it: an outside space that 'claws and gnaws' at it (Foucault 1986c: 23). This is why, for Foucault as for Deleuze and others, the thought of the 'Outside' is a thought of resistance.

Foucault's theory of power offers an explanation of how transitory relations of power are the ground for the emergence of structures of social domination. In this way, Foucault contributes to critical theories that seek to explain how individuals can be complicit with the forces that repress them. Foucault's work also challenges the grounding authority of sovereignty, showing this to be an effect of power, rather than its foundation. In contrast to the 'repressive hypothesis' of power, in which power is contained by a sovereign subject, and takes the form of mastery or imposition over others, the notion that power is primarily positive and productive permits its alternative conceptualisation outside of the sphere of mastery. This is clearly of use in attempts to think of a genuinely postcolonial political practice. The critique of sovereignty is important in other relevant respects, too, supporting the resistance strategies of some indigenous activists such as Taiaiake Alfred (1999), who worry that sovereignty is a dominant Western political concept, which has been instrumental in the practices and justifications of colonialism, and may therefore be quite inappropriate as a mode of expression of indigenous politics, and indeed Alfred is far more sympathetic to a Foucaultian understanding of power.

However, in challenging grounding political concepts such as sovereignty, Foucault's theory of power simultaneously challenges conventional understandings about human rights, thus threatening the basis of much argument for progressive social transformation. On his view, rights do not flow from a given universal human nature endowed with inalienable sovereign entitlements, but on the contrary represent an established moral discourse about values and social obligations, emerging in concrete social and historical circumstances and constructed by individuals with specific interests that these claims of right are designed to protect. While a detailed consideration about the nature and place of rights in Foucault's political theory will remain beyond the scope of my discussion here, it is important to note that Foucault's philosophy does not deny the existence of rights, and indeed he continued to use the language of right to urge broad political engagement in many of the actions he was personally involved in, such as prison reform, refugee accommodation and gay activism. In fact, Foucault's work is conducive to a new understanding of rights: they are never foundational, but arise in the context of actual relations of force between bodies. Rights are thus embedded in power relations, and represent the 'recognised and guaranteed degrees of power' a body may legitimately be disposed to practise upon another (Patton 2004: 47ff.; see Golder and Fitzpatrick 2009:

122–4). Rights are a necessary delimitation of the spheres of influence of relational bodies, since each body exists only as a force in relation to other forces. Each body in a relationship has a necessary duty to preserve the capacity of the other to exist and maintain some degree of power, in order to preserve the relationship that produces and sustains them both. Because they originate in the context of the power relations in which they are embedded, concepts of right constantly shift according to changes in these relations of power. However, while a micropolitical practice of right necessarily accompanies every transitory and unstable relationship of force between bodies in order to guarantee the survival of the constituting forces, regular repetition of these rights across many instances of relationship also consolidates a general conduct of bodies, producing an emergent macrostructure of right, a metastable discourse of rights and responsibilities, tacitly associated with relations of power in general. Chapter 6 will consider a similar notion of rights implicit in Deleuze's work on affective embodiment.

Foucault's theory of power (and associated rights) provides us with a conception of micropolitical practice that is qualitatively different from the colonising practices of the state-form and macropolitics. It thereby points the way to a platform for the evaluation of resistances, when it leads us to question: which practices are macropolitical and which are micropolitical? In the context of postcolonisation, we might then ask: how can we act in order to shift the strata of established values and norms and so destabilise the colonial basis of a given society, without simply becoming included in the strata? However, this politics remains underdeveloped and problematic, since, as Nancy Fraser (1981) and others point out, if history is simply a succession of power structures that orchestrate and manipulate different regimes of truth and right, there appears to be no normative criterion for the evaluation of the sorts of power relations or the truths that progressive transformative action such as reconciliation would seek to establish. This in turn raises an important problem of agency: why resist? Why should agents resist established power, if the only outcome of resistance is the re-establishment of a power relation? And further, while its natural opposition to macropolitical structures enables us to identify a focal point for micropolitical practice, how can micropolitical agency itself be conceptualised? What kind of active freedom is a micropolitical subject capable of? What ethical responsibilities accompany micropolitical subjectivity?

In his final works, Foucault began to develop the ethics suggested by his theory of social power and micropolitical resistance. In the third volume of *The History of Sexuality* (1986b), he develops an ethic of 'the care of the self', which can be read as a return to Nietzsche in a manner that explores the ethical implications of the notion that the will to power is a determining cause of the form taken by a relation of power. Because micropolitical relations of power constitute the ground for the emergence of structures of domination, a collective and critical awareness of the nature of the will to power that is implicated with existing emergent macropolitical structures potentially influences the transformation of both micropolitical relations and the macropolitical institutions that have emerged from these relations over time. The challenge is then to cultivate an ethical sensibility 'that informs the quality of future interpretations, actions and relationships' (Connolly 1998: 111).

If 'the political' is a register that concerns the entire realm of one's collective relations with others, and particularly how these relations bear upon subject-formation, 'the ethical' concerns one's interior relation with oneself, particularly one's awareness of self-conduct in relations with others (Patton 1998: 69; Connolly 1998: 114–15ff.). While they show different orientations of the subject in her or his relationships, these registers are clearly not able to be detached from each other, since one's capacities and constraints in relations with others are simultaneously constitutive of one's subjectivity and sense of self. In every relation of power, individuals are both subjects of power and subjects of ethics. Both of these registers of the ethical and the political also concern one's relation to broad social discourses of truth, which inflect how one interprets these relationships with self and with others (Patton 1998).

However, I want to emphasise a distinction here between the political register and the ethical register of action, in terms of the kinds of orientations or dispositions that the will to power is capable of producing. I suggest that the political register essentially concerns the *quantity* of force the subject is capable of exerting in a relation, while the ethical register essentially concerns the *quality* of the force relation or the way forces are organised in a relationship. The main focus of politics is the body and the expression or repression of its active capacities, while ethics really concerns the nature of self-conduct shaping the relation between bodies. In so far as a subject's will to power organises the *degrees* of force in a relation, the *political* subject must seek to orient herself according to an active or dominant will to power, which will maximise the 'feeling of power' or

Power/Desire

capacity to act, within that relation. In addition, the *ethical* subject must attend to the *nature* or quality of the will to power with which she conducts herself in relationships with others. I will argue that this distinction enables us to see that while Foucault's social theory does have scope for a normative political practice, he cannot provide satisfactory criteria for a normative ethical practice because he does not allow a causal role for desire, which is the qualitative force of association.

In outlining the kind of politics and ethical sensibility suggested by Foucault's social theory, it is useful to draw from the use he makes of the notion of 'governmentality' (1991; see Hindess 1998). For Foucault, government is a question of 'disposing things ... to arrange things in such a way that, through a certain number of means, such and such ends may be achieved' (1991: 95). Foucault's analyses of how 'things can be arranged' are usually conducted in the context of his work on discipline. He shows the ways in which established Powers govern by manipulating behaviours through hegemonic rules of self-conduct, so that social relations follow fairly regular channels. However, while Foucault does not often directly address this, his formulation of 'governmentality' leaves open the possibility of an alternative subjective agency, capable of manipulating relations of power in a way that transforms existing Power structures by changing the conditions of their emergence. The suggestion here is that subjects of power relations are agents of government in so far as they are capable of 'disposing' their relations with others to be as non-dominating as possible (Foucault 1988: 19; see Hindess 1998: 55).

The ethic of the care of the self develops the notion of governmentality from the perspective of micropolitical practice, such that the political subject must 'develop the art of manipulating relations of force' in ways that will maximise her or his liberty (Foucault 1991: 90). Because the self is always embedded in a network of power relations, this freedom will never be absolute, and will always be situated, relative and contextual. The freedom to act is found within the realm of human powers and capacities in relation to others. For Foucault, freedom is essentially found in the capacity to affect another's actions. This means that 'liberty is a *practice*', which consists of striving to organise one's relations of power in ways that maximise the capacity to affect others (Foucault 1984c: 245).

Because established regimes of truth limit one's freedom to think otherwise, the practice of liberty requires subjects to maintain a permanent critical reflexivity to all aspects of society, and to challenge these truths, where necessary, in their own relations. This, then, is another aspect of a subject's practice of liberty, exercised by a 'genealogical politics' (Brown 1998) of the sort also discussed by Deleuze in terms of deterritorialisation or counter-actualisation. This genealogical practice of liberty detaches 'the power of truth from the forms of hegemony, social, economic and cultural, within which it operates at the present time' (Foucault 1980a: 133). It is in this sense that Foucault argues: '[T]he problem is not changing people's consciousness – or what's in their heads – but the political, economic, institutional regime of the production of truth' (1980a: 133).

In Foucault's social theory there is, then, scope for a normative, prescriptive political practice. Agents should resist established Power, even though the result will be the institution of another set of power relations, because resistance can transform both micropolitical and macropolitical relations of power such that they operate with a minimum effect of domination upon the subject, or a maximum degree of subjective freedom. Agents should cultivate critical reflexivity in their approaches to their political relations, and should strive to institutionalise mechanisms that encourage and foster this reflexivity. All this is part of an ethic of care for the self, which aims to maximise one's capacities for action, within the natural constraints of political society.

However, Foucault has no satisfactory normative solution for ethical relations. An active and critical will to power affirms and increases the capacities of the self in its relations with others. The political subject should relate to others in ways that increase this capacity. But why should we monitor our conduct towards others in ways that increase *their* capacity for freedom? While he suggests an ethic of care for the self should develop 'friendly' relations of power based on mutual respect, this seems to be largely justified by the idea that behaving ethically primarily benefits the self, since character is constituted through these behaviours and modes of relating to others. Foucault's ethic of care does not *normatively* extend towards care for the other, for the sake of the other, and therefore Foucault's ethic of the care of the self seems to miss something important about ethical conduct.

Missing in Foucault's work is an adequate analysis of the way desire can inflect the way power takes form in social relationships. When Foucault privileges 'power' as the causal force of social existence, he fails to attach an equal or significant causal role to the notion of 'desire' as a force in the construction of social forms and relations. According to Scott Lash,

> The problem is that Foucault, unlike Deleuze, operates without a developed notion of [causal] desire or its equivalent; thus Foucault's body is only the prey of reactive forces – normalising or individuating forces, and Foucault's genealogy remains incomplete. (Lash 1984: 7)

Others have drawn attention to this lacuna in Foucault's work. For example, Ann Laura Stoler (1995) agrees with Foucault's primary thesis that power is productive, and that 'desire follows from, and is generated out of, the law, out of the power-laden discourses of sexuality where it is animated and addressed'. She adds that colonisation and colonial relations of power produced a particular discourse of colonial desire, restraint and moral propriety, that in turn pervasively informed colonial culture and created new forms of political justification in the form of civilising the unrestrained and therefore dangerous desires of the 'savage' other.

However, she also argues that desire *itself*, the *act of desiring* the exotic other, is a significant causal force in the formation of colonial relations of power, bodies of knowledge about the other, and the formation of discourses regulating 'the colonial order of things' (Stoler 1995; see also Young 1995). Accordingly, she affirms that while in some respects power produces discourses of desiring, thereby disclaiming the repressive hypothesis that power is the force that bears upon desire and restrains it, she also insists upon the productive nature of colonial *desire* for the exotic and unknown other, and so contests the simpler argument that power is the force that produces desire. Indeed, on her view, the desire for the other, the desire to *know* the other, instigates the association of bodies or forces in the first place, and thus produces the relation of power that enables the formation of such knowledge.

Deleuze offers a similar analysis of Foucault's contention about the causal relationship between power and desire, indicating that he and Guattari take a different view, attaching a primary causal role to desire, rather than to power (1997b; see also Guattari 1996). For Deleuze, desire is the force of association that operates in the primary realm of micropolitical relations between bodies, whereas power is the force of consolidation or capture that binds bodies in macropolitical relationships (1997b: 185). On his view, 'it is not the *dispositifs* of power that assemble [*agenceraient*], nor would they be constitutive; it is rather the *agencements* of desire that would spread throughout the formations of power . . . [accordingly] power is an affection of desire', rather than its cause (Deleuze 1997b: 186).

This emphasis on the causal role of desire in the production of political forms and relations of power allows a renewed understanding about agency and resistance. While 'power' primarily concerns the relative *quantity* of force exerted by subjects in relation to others, 'desire' essentially concerns the *quality* of the power relation. By privileging 'power' and reducing 'desire' to a power effect, Foucault obscures how 'desire' itself is a causal force, as the *qualitative and ethical* aspect of a will to power. The following section of this chapter therefore turns to Deleuze's treatment of 'desire', in order to expand upon the ethical practice suggested by Foucault's social theory based on the causal force of the will to power.

Desire

Chapter 2 described the development of postcolonial theory as influenced by both a Marxist commitment to progressive and collective transformation and a poststructuralist destabilisation of 'the subject', and argued that each influence has in turn been significantly shaped by a philosophical emphasis upon generative negativity. Because desire/lack operates as the motive force in the activities of critique and construction, it is central to both the Marxist and the poststructuralist variants of postcolonial theory. Both history and the subject are produced through desire, negatively conceptualised in relation to lack, and each remains 'impossible' or incomplete, so long as desire remains (permanently) unsatisfied. I also argued that this negative feature of desire, which is grounded in a primary absence, loss or lack, supports an imperial philosophy of difference that makes it unsuited to the promotion or generation of postcolonial society. There is, however, an alternative tradition of 'desire' in philosophy, which I would like to suggest is germane to the formation of postcolonial subjectivity. The nature of this postcolonial subjectivity will be the focus of following chapters. For now, the second half of this chapter aims to contribute to existing postcolonial and feminist scholarship by exploring the positive conceptualisation of desire as 'desiring-production' developed by Deleuze and Guattari.

In fact, the conceptual linkage between desire and lack has a long history in Western philosophy (Silverman 2000; Fuery 1995). It extends from Plato, through Descartes, Hobbes and Locke, to Kant, Hegel, Marx, Freud, Lacan, Sartre and beyond, to much postcolonial theory. However, alongside this dominant tradition, there exists an alternative discourse on desire, which 'focuses on the motivational force of the *desiderare*, the act of desire, as productive' (Schrift 2000: 176). This alternative discourse on desire can be traced from the recent work of Deleuze and Guattari, back through Nietzsche and Spinoza. This theory of desire has two definitive moments: one critical, in which the traditional association of desire and negativity is denied; the second constructive, in which an alternative, positive concept of desire as productive and affirmative is promoted (Butler 1987: 205).

Early in their *Anti-Oedipus*, Deleuze and Guattari claim:

> [T]o a certain degree, the traditional logic of desire is all wrong from the very outset: from the very first step that the Platonic logic of desire forces us to take, making us choose between *production* and *acquisition*. (1983: 25)

They argue that when desire is conceptualised in terms of the acquisition of that which is missing or lacking, it immediately becomes separated from reality: the desired object is missing in the subject's lived experience. In response to this primary lack in the real world, desire produces a fantasy or an ideal in which the lack would no longer exist. On this view, desire produces, but only in the realm of the ideal, or of fantasy, which can then have only an indirect and ameliorative effect upon the real. In Australia and North America, for example, it is clear that the desire for reconciliation is usually conceptualised in this way. The discourse of reconciliation is structured by a fantasy of national unity, which is presented as a response to a lived disunity or disadvantage in the real, material conditions of post-colonial society. The hope is that the desired ideal will indirectly regulate this reality, encouraging citizens to 'realise' the ideal in our social fabric, presumably through the mediating activity of the State.

Deleuze and Guattari counter this kind of idealism by asserting, 'the objective being of desire is the Real in and of itself' (1983: 26–7). As they see it, desire *produces* reality rather than being *caused* by a perceived lack in the real: 'If desire produces, its product is real. If desire is productive, it can be productive only in the real world and can produce only reality' (1983: 26). Desire immediately invests the realm of social production, so that every instance of material production is simultaneously an instance of desiring-production: 'The truth of the matter is that *social production is purely and simply desiring-production itself under determinate conditions.*' Consequently, 'there is only desire and the social, and nothing else' (1983: 29). For our purposes, there are two implications that flow from this: firstly, the material disunity or disadvantage in post-colonial society is itself the creation of desire; and secondly, postcolonial reconciliation must therefore involve a transformation of material reality, at the level of desiring-production. The primary task of the remaining discussion is to explain what this transformation through desire involves.

Like Foucault's theory of power, desire is here understood to be co-extensive with the entire social field. Unlike psychoanalytic interpretations of desire and selfhood, this desire is not located in a subject who invests it in appropriate channels of development. While it is directed towards the production of being, it is not directed towards an object that is lacking in the subject. Nor is it directed towards achieving or regaining unity or establishing a 'complete' or fixed identity. In fact, desire is directed primarily at the proliferation of desire. Desire aims to produce: this production is itself the process of desire. The process of desiring-production satisfies desire by creating it, in a perpetual feedback motion, which is not driven by negativity in the form of lack or absence, but by creativity and the positivity of production, and by the feeling of intensity that results from the creative transformation of being. In this process, the subject is produced by desire, but not as an intended aim or end point of the process. The subject forms alongside processes of desire as a 'residue' (1983: 17). However, as we shall see in Chapter 5, this subject created by desire can exercise social agency by cultivating a critical awareness of the particular and concrete *type* of desires that have been invested in his formation as such, together with a critical awareness of the *types* of desires he practises in the associations and relations that come to compose the social body at large.

Desire brings about a process of the association of bodies, which creates new forms of existence. As the cause of the emergence of all forms of material existence, including social organisation, desire is immanent to the productive process. However, like Deleuze's notion of the virtual, desire is itself actualised in concrete relations along with the assemblages it brings about. While desire is an abstract cause of all order, it can only be analysed in terms of the particular instances and the concrete assemblages in which it is actualised: '[D]esire is encountered not in theoretical abstraction as a timeless essence, but only in the real relations that exist between people. The knowledge of desire only arises from an immanent engagement with the social field' (Goodchild 1996: 41). For every desire, one must analyse how it is actually embodied, and for every assemblage, it is necessary to ask: *which* desire has brought about this particular arrangement?

Deleuze and Guattari suggest that there are two basic forms of desire in assemblage. The first is found in 'molecular' assemblages, 'in which new connections and new forms of relation to the outside are always possible, even at the risk of transforming the assemblage into some other kind of body' (1983: 77). The second form of desire is found in 'molar' assemblages, which limit their relations to other bodies in an effort to retain their structural identity. In this kind of assemblage, desire is complicit with its own repression: the assembled body resists the creative transformations that new desires and associations could bring about. For Deleuze and Guattari, this auto-repression of desire constitutes the primary problem of politics. Accordingly, they propose that any adequate political theory must analyse concrete instances of repression in order to promote a 'liberation of desire' (see Goodchild 1996: 163ff.).

The reception of *Anti-Oedipus* was marked by a general tendency to interpret this 'liberation of desire' as an irresponsible and naive politics, or an anti-politics in celebration of the irrational, the chaotic and the anarchic, that revels in undoing all forms of established order, particularly 'civilisation' and 'the subject'. However, this reading does not fully appreciate the implications of the idea that desire is an immanent cause of all forms of order, rather than a goal or an endpoint, which would arrive once order is dissolved. Desire is not simply opposed to existing structures of power, since it is always already co-implicated with them. In fact, when Deleuze and Guattari prioritise desire, they do so in order to provide an ethical complement to Foucault's theory of power and resistance. Both liberation and ethics come with an *awareness* of how desire and power operate together as components or moments within the causal principle of the will to power, and an *effort* to transform existing modes of desire and power, when they create repressive bodies or bodies that seek their own repression.

According to Deleuze and Guattari, desire is the immanent force that animates all the processes of material production. As we know, Deleuze thinks of this productive process as the ontological actualisation or self-organisation of being. All things that exist have developed through a process of actualisation: bodies form when transient relations of force stabilise into regular connections between elements. In *Anti-Oedipus*, the authors argue that all production is 'machinic' in that productive processes involve the connection and aggregation of elements into a complex product. 'Desiring-machines' shape the productive process by coupling elements together, or dividing them up so that they are free to couple with other elements. This makes desire 'the principle of . . . composition which determines the existence of any machinic assemblage' (Patton 2000: 72). In this respect, Deleuze and Guattari's theory of desire is an interpretation of the actualising ontology from the causal perspective of desire, rather than power, as is the case with Foucault or with Deleuze's earlier reading of Nietzsche.

Deleuze's interpretation of the Nietzschean will to power defined an efficient, immanent cause of the self-organisation of being. A given will to power disposes a body to act with a certain degree or quantity of force. This *quantity* of exerted force then qualifies or characterises the body as active or reactive in the context of its relations with other bodies and forces. In *Nietzsche and Philosophy*, Deleuze also suggests that there is a second, *qualitative* aspect to any given will to power. A will to power disposes a body to act not simply with a particular degree of force, but also with a particular quality of force, which qualifies or characterises the relationship between bodies as affirmative or negative. Although both desire and power are the forces operating in any relationship that forms between bodies, desire is best understood as a *qualitative* or ethical force of association that concerns the nature of the disposition or orientation of bodies towards each other and thereby expressing a 'grammar' of attraction and connection between bodies, while power is best conceptualised as a *quantitative* or political force exerted by relational bodies upon each other. Desire is primary in so far as it causes the association between bodies in the first place and disposes their practices of interaction in particular ways; power relations subsequently emerge from the practices of association bodies then engage in.

Deleuze's shift in focus from Nietzsche to Spinoza enables him to develop the idea of ontological actualisation in terms of desire. He then presents the Spinozan concept of desire or *conatus* as 'the first foundation, the *primum movens*, the efficient and not the final cause' (Deleuze 1988b: 102). With Spinoza, Deleuze's attention shifts from types of bodies and actions, to the types of sociability they engage in and produce. While the power or force exerted by a body qualifies the activity or passivity of that body, desire orients a body in its relation to another, such that this orientation or disposition 'typifies' the relationship, in the sense of giving it a particular character. Different modes of desire dispose bodies to particular types of relationship or sociability. Deleuze finds in Spinoza a method of social analysis that evaluates different types of social relation by considering the nature of productive desires at work and the types of sociability produced.

As Moira Gatens (1996: 108) explains, this encourages us to contrast 'the *sociability* of compatible bodies with other forms of association, for example, those built on *utility* or *capture*'. However, as we shall see in coming chapters, this turn to Spinoza, desire and sociability enriches Deleuze's earlier Nietzschean analysis of the causal force of the will to power, rather than replacing or superseding it. An ethical political practice involves the creation of *both* active bodies *and* forms of sociability in which individuals strive to meet with others in ways that mutually enhance their capabilities.

The Spinozan concept of *conatus* describes the fundamental desire of any existing body to persevere in its being. However, according to constructivist ontology, bodies are never 'given', but are always in a process of being constituted by their relations with other bodies. These relationships compose bodies and define their character, but can also decompose or destroy bodies, or diminish their capacities to act and to persevere in their being. Consequently, *conatus* properly refers to the fundamental desire of bodies to form compatible or 'joyful' associations that will maintain or enhance their power to exist, and to avoid incompatible or 'sad' associations that will detract from their existing powers. Here, joy is 'nothing but the process of the increase of our power, and thus it is the guiding thread of any ethical and political project' (Hardt 1995: 27). This makes *conatus* the basis of an 'ethic of joy', which is left underdeveloped in Deleuze's own philosophy, but which I will suggest is a useful guide for postcolonial practice, because this logically requires the creation of compatible associations in which participants in the relation refrain from destroying, detracting from, or diminishing each other.

Moira Gatens (1993; 1996: 108–25, 95–107; Gatens and Lloyd 1999: 100–7) develops the notion that Spinoza's ethics is best explained in terms of an ethological reading of bodies and the power relations they enter into. Ethology 'considers bodies in terms of their powers and capacities for affecting and being affected' (Gatens and Lloyd 1999: 100). An ethological assessment of bodily affects involves a distinction between two kinds of affects. The first are passive affections, or passions, which are caused by chance encounters that act upon the body, and which may therefore bring about either sadness or joy. Active affections or actions, on the other hand, are caused by the directed action of the body in its encounters; the *conatus* of a body entails that these actions should tend towards the creation of joyful encounters. An ethological evaluation acknowledges the constitutive effects of social context upon the individual, and will reveal what is beneficial in that social context, as well as what is harmful. As a consequence, ethological interpretations judge an action in the context of its occurrence, rather than in terms of a universal moral code. Ethology traces the processes through which individuals develop their powers and capacities, in their concrete relations with others. Thus, over time within a given context, ethology reveals a conceptual map of the types of associations that tend to enhance one's capacities, and those that are inclined to weaken one: 'An ethological appraisal will reveal what a given body seeks out and what it avoids' (Gatens and Lloyd 1999: 100). In particular, ethology indicates the 'compossibility' of individuals whose natures agree, and who can unite to form a compatible association that will mutually enhance their respective capacities. An ethological interpretation therefore assists individuals actively to select their associations, or strive to make their existing associations compatible, in order to develop a richer unity with greater power.

In this way, ethology involves an awareness of what one may become, if one makes the effort to desire in a way that initiates and sustains joyful encounters and modes of sociability (see Gatens and Lloyd: 1999: 107). Furthermore, ethology suggests a normative ethical practice: *every* body should be disposed to act in relation to others according to a type of desire that will bring about joy. As will be discussed in coming chapters, the experience of joy is necessarily mutual since joy is the creation of enhanced power of being, through the development of a more complex and richer community. Where the association detracts from one of the participating bodies, it will not bring about a richer unity, and therefore is not joyful. The creation and experience of joyful associations benefits every body; every body ought to organise their associations according to a desire that will produce a joyful satisfaction. Accordingly, Deleuze's theory of desire, read through the lens of Spinoza's ethics, provides a normative framework for ethical action that is missing in Foucault, even in his later work on the ethics of the care for the self.

By taking Deleuze's reading of Spinoza and desire or *conatus* into account in appraising their social and political philosophy of desiring-production, we are better able to understand what Deleuze and Guattari intend when they encourage a 'liberation of desire'. In the first instance, this sort of liberation involves a practice of critical genealogy, in order to evaluate the 'immanent modes of existence' determining actual practices (Deleuze 1990: 269). The genealogical moment of transformative practice involves understanding the present by imagining a return to the conditions of causation, and by analysing what kind of desire or force of sociability has influenced the emergence of contemporary society. Secondly, liberation involves developing the 'art of organising encounters', in order to create the causal conditions necessary for the emergence of preferred, because 'joyful', types of sociability. The way in which one desires or conducts one's relations with others will directly affect the kinds of collective existence that come to be formed. Associations between compatible bodies, whose meeting enhances the powers of each to persist and develop in their being, will result in preferred types of sociability.

Deleuze explains why, for Spinoza, the formation of 'common notions' is central to 'this art of organising encounters' (1990: 262). The experience of joy permits the recognition of something in common between two bodies. Initially, the experience of joy arises from the chance or passive encounter between two bodies whose natures agree. However, an ethological mapping of these passive joyful encounters reveals a diagrammatic image or a collective awareness of combinations that tend to be joyful, enabling the development of a common understanding about which combinations might be pursued to bring about joyful associations (Gatens and Lloyd 1999: 103–4). From this ethology of passive joyful affects, then, common notions are formed. And common notions then enable individuals and communities actively to seek out and organise those types of associations that will bring them joy. Common notions therefore represent the point at which social practice is directed towards the experience of joy that is no longer contingent or passive, but a joy born of reflexive understanding, that we bring about ourselves, in community with others (Gatens and Lloyd 1999: 105; Hardt 1995: 28–9). Whereas the genealogical moment of practice is critical and directed towards the effects of the past in the present, the ethological aspect of practice is constructive and speculatively directed towards the future. The coming chapters will expand upon this idea, in relation to the collective task of creating a 'common notion' of the postcolonial.

Through his combination of critique and constructivism, Deleuze provides a basis for a strategic political philosophy, though this remains latent in his own *oeuvre*. The notion that social organisation has an immanent causation involving the constructive forces of both power and desire makes a significant contribution to contemporary political thought, enabling a novel conception of agency that evaluates the relational qualities of a chosen action, as well as an individual's degrees of capacity. Because this conception of agency develops from notions of power and desire primarily defined as creative, productive and associative (rather than imposing, dominating and appropriative), it seems a fitting model of agency for practices of postcolonial selfhood. In this chapter, I have argued that Deleuze and Guattari's social philosophy of desiring-production should be interpreted in light of Deleuze's reading of Spinoza's ethics. This enables us to discern, within their philosophy, appropriate tools for a future-directed social practice guided by an ethic of joy or compossibility, which we may put to work in the incremental development of a 'common notion' of the postcolonial and in practical efforts at postcolonisation, as will be discussed in Chapter 6.

This chapter has expanded upon the notion that social organisation has an immanent productive cause, in order to describe a positive concept of causation that will now be put to work in theorising a version of postcolonial agency. Simply put, power and desire are positive, constructive forces that cause bodies to associate into complex organisations. Following Deleuze, I have suggested that power is best conceptualised as a quantitative force that determines the degree of activity or passivity of a body in relation to others. Desire, on the other hand, is best conceptualised as a qualitative force, which influences the kind of associations bodies are disposed to practise in relation to others. On this view, there are various types of political relation and different modes of desire. The kinds of social organisations that actually form will emerge as effects related to the particular causal types of power and modes of desire with which bodies approach each other. This includes the production of lack and the desire for possession it engenders. Lack is not original, not always already given:

> Lack is created, planned and organised in and through social production . . . It is never primary; production is never organised on the basis of a pre-existing need or lack . . . The deliberate creation of lack . . . is the art of a dominant class. This involves deliberately organising wants and needs amid an abundance of production; making all of desire teeter and fall victim to the great fear of not having one's needs satisfied. (Deleuze and Guattari 1983: 28)

The structures of desire-lack that characterise colonial types of social arrangement could then always be otherwise; lack is not ontologically given and need not be produced or chosen as such. If we want to produce encounters that can be thought of as postcolonial, it is incumbent upon us not to produce lack in our modes of sociability, and not to produce modes of sociability that assume a posturing of desire based in a fear of lack. Desire-lack compels my satisfaction through actions appropriating the other in my relationships, or makes me fear that once I reach repletion, the other will attempt to steal my enjoyment from me. A postcolonial desiring-subject should not choose lack as a disposition to structure associations with the other. To pose the question of desire in this way is to ask simultaneously a question of the subject: 'What kind of agent desires? Or, more precisely, what agency is produced, and by what kind of desire?' (Spivak 1986: 186). Deleuze and Guattari insist that desiring-production is a non-intentional force of creation, connection and transformation. Agency, however, is about giving direction to this non-intentional desire by investing it with a particular strategy. Theories and practices of directed social transformation towards preferred forms of actual society must address the issue of directed causation or agency, bearing upon the way power and desire operate together as forces of social construction. In coming chapters I will argue that a passage of transition to postcolonial society relies upon participating communities to imagine strategically joyful modes of power and desire, and create these through common notions and local relations of practice, which, with repetition, can subsequently cause the broad emergence and establishment of postcolonial social existence. But what is involved in the subjective act of choosing a suitable replacement strategy of satisfaction? What kind of subject causes desiring-production and intentionally chooses the direction to be taken by things in their actualisation? Indeed, is not the subject itself a *product* of desiring-production, rather than the *producer* as such?

Notes

1. An expanded version of this chapter is published in *Angelaki* as Bignall (2008).
2. Most readings of Foucault assume this spatial distinction between macro and micro scales of discipline. See for example Walzer (1986). The conceptual connection made between space and power is in fact an important motif across much poststructuralist philosophy. See, for example: Deleuze and Guattari (1987: 474–500); Bonta and Protevi (2004); Grosz (1995); Soja (1989); Dumm (1996); and the volume of essays edited by Diprose and Ferrell (1991).
3. Deleuze and Guattari 1987: Plateau 9. See also Michael Hardt's 'Foreword' to Negri's *The Savage Anomaly* (1991: xii–xvi), where he notes that Negri makes a similar distinction in his interpretation of

Spinoza. One reason why this distinction is downplayed or ignored by anglophone theorists is that English translations of the original French tend to collapse the different senses of *'pouvoir'* and *'puissance'* into the single term, 'power'.

4. See, for example, Foucault's response when asked about the nature of the relationships engendered between the 'molar body of the population and the microbodies of individuals', in which he conflates the two types of power (1980a: 124).

5

Subjectivity

We need a new political ideology for indigenous political strategy. (Pearson 1997b: 218)

There is no ideology and never has been. (Deleuze and Guattari 1987: 4)

Directed transformative political practices, such as postcolonisation, require the collective deployment of a strategy.[1] Strategy is self-consciously expressed from a position of subjectivity. The subject is thus the *cause* of transformative action, which is organised via the strategy it expresses. However, according to Deleuze and Guattari, a subject emerges only as an *effect* of its becoming. A subject – like all forms of being – is a virtual assemblage, made actual. But how can a subject then be a cause of its own becoming, when it is actually an effect of this process? What makes a body a 'self', an active agent of its own formation as subject? As a produced effect or *object* of social relations of power and desire, how can a *subject* come to have a position that is critical and capable of taking those social relations as the object of her intentional action? When she only exists as a position already given, already made actual, how can the subject strategically choose her position of action and cause the transformations she wills?

This chapter will consider what notion of the subject is possible for constructivist philosophy like Foucault's or Deleuze and Guattari's. The discussion begins by revisiting the nature of the body as conceived by Deleuze and Guattari, in light of their complementary concept of the body-without-organs (BwO). I will then draw from the analysis of composition begun in the previous chapter, in order to define subjectivity as a 'styling' of becoming, which posits the agent as a strategic performance of selfhood that necessarily refers to the social forces of power and desire which compose it and which it embodies (see also Colebrook 1999: 117–41). In this performance, the subject is simultaneously cause and effect, a 'folding' of an already effected, actual self upon an immanent, virtual and causal pre-subjective plane (Deleuze 1991a, 1988a, 1986: 94–124). This folding makes it possible for a subject to attempt the active styling of the process of actualisation through which self and society come to be. The second part of the chapter considers how this process of subjective styling is carried out through one's 'bit by bit' encounters and complex engagements with others. The final section of the chapter considers Deleuze and Guattari's analysis of the particularly imperial style of subjectivity expressed as Oedipus. This section also compares the kinds of political society corresponding to the different types of satisfaction expressed as 'enjoyment' and 'joy'. The following chapter will subsequently ask: what is postcolonial? Or, what style of subject expresses a postcolonial ethos?

The body without organs

We know already that Deleuze and Guattari think of a body as a complex assemblage of elements organised into an enduring pattern of relationship.[2] In this sense, 'body' does not simply refer to a particular material entity, such as a human body, but to any form of stable organisation or being. Their idea of a body is therefore abstract, encompassing all kinds of things that can be characterised in terms of the stability of their form, including both material bodies, and bodies of knowledge or ideas.[3] Thus, the relationship between wasps and orchids or between grammatical predicates constitutes types of bodies (a sex organ and language, respectively), just as cellular and morphological relations between organs constitute animal bodies, or relations between people constitute social bodies.

In the third chapter of *A Thousand Plateaus*, they describe the formation of a body in considerable detail, by referring to the 'geology' of its organisation (1987: 39–75). Here, 'geology' does not simply describe the formation of rocks and mineral forms, but properly refers to the general phenomenon of organisation and the process of ordering that is common to the formation of all bodies. They begin by asserting that, prior to any possible conception of bodily form, there exists a 'body without organs' (BwO), which we have encountered previously in Chapter 3 as the 'plane of immanence'. The BwO is 'permeated by unformed, unstable matters, by flows in all directions, by free intensities or nomadic singularities, by mad or transitory particles' (1987: 40). Thus, the BwO is the undifferentiated material mass of elements that are yet to be organised into discrete forms of order. The BwO is the disordered chaos that becomes disciplined and settles into ordered forms, as its free moving elements cohere into regular and stable relationships that bind them into complex associations (bodies). The virtual BwO can therefore be expressed in infinitely variable ways, as an infinite variety of actual bodies or forms. Whereas bodies exist as actual forms or formed matter, a BwO exists as force. Yet virtual force (BwO) is always immanent in actual form (body), since force is the binding that associates elements to produce a complex bodily entity.

In their 'geophilosophy', Deleuze and Guattari give the name 'stratification' to this emergence of order upon the chaotic surface of the BwO. 'Stratification is like the creation of the world from chaos, a continual, renewed creation' (1987: 502; see Bonta and Protevi 2004: 150). 'Strata' emerge when transient and unstable relations of force morph into rigid or locked relations of form. Strata then describe 'belts' of ordered matter, which operate by 'imprisoning intensities or locking singularities into systems of resonance' (1987: 40). That is, they are 'acts of capture' in which the disorganised and flexible relationships of force that occur as chance encounters between free elements become pinned down, 'sedimentary', inflexible and predictable. Strata are the systems of organisation or classification that attract and trap disorganised matter. They collect disordered bodies and slot them into their particular system of organisation, creating a consistency that emerges as coherence. Strata are, then, signifying systems that arrange bodies into meaningful orders. For Foucault, strata are the discourses and practices that establish a 'regime of truth' particular to a social context.[4] Deleuze and Guattari list three major strata as examples of these systems of resonance: physicochemical, organic and anthropomorphic (1987: 502). Furthermore, each major stratum comprises substrata, which differ in certain respects, even though they have common principles of consistency with each other and with the major strata they comprise. For example, the classification system of organic life is comprised of two major substrata: 'plant' and 'animal', which differ from each other in terms of the cellular elements they combine, even while they both exist as modes of a common organic organisation, or life.

The problem addressed by Deleuze and Guattari in 'The Geology of Morals' is the problem of organisation (1987: 41). How does something take its meaningful form as a consistency that emerges from chaos? They explain that this creation of consistency occurs because 'there is a single *abstract machine* that is enveloped by the stratum and constitutes its unity' (1987: 50). This 'abstract machine' is best thought of in terms of the production abstractly generated by social interactions. The 'abstract machine' of social interaction and utterance produces or 'articulates' a stratum by establishing a grammar or a code – a system of rules for the organisation of coherence. Strata are then 'articulated' in two moments or phases, which Deleuze explains occur 'together' as 'different/ciation', as we saw in Chapter 3. *'The first articulation concerns content, the second expression'* (1987: 44, 502). In the first productive moment (differentiation), the 'abstract machine' selects elements for composition. In the second moment (differenciation), it establishes a code or rule of connection between elements and consolidates these connections into quasi-permanent relations and stable structures. A stratum is therefore defined by the particular content of its parts and by the specific mode of combination they express in relation to each other. The stratum is accordingly characterised by the diversity of the elements that compose it, and also by the unity of its composition, since it exhibits a consistent and characteristic rule for the formal connections between its elements. Furthermore, strata differ from one another, either when their constituting elements differ, or when their rule of assembly differs.

All strata are then abstractly comprised of forms, substances and codes. However each stratum is characterised by the particularity of its forms and substances, and the specificity of its codes. Nonetheless, strata are not fixed or closed systems of meaning or coherence, but are vitally mobile and relative to other strata and substrata. A body might occupy many classifications simultaneously, and can transfer between strata. The surrounding strata and substrata thereby constitute a 'milieu' that furnishes material for the composition of a particular stratum and constitutes an exteriority that ensures a stratum is always open, since its composition shifts with respect to the relations it enters into with other elements and other strata. Deleuze and Guattari exemplify this in their discussion, which mixes strata of biology, geology, philosophy and geography, sharing their elements and complicating their rules of coherence in a way that changes the consistency of each stratum as they come into contact and undergo a mutual 'becoming' (1987: 40). The neighbourhood of surrounding strata, as well as the underlying chaos that is the body without organs, thereby constitute a 'milieu' in which any particular strata or organisation of meaning subsist. At its points of contact with this milieu, the stratum is fundamentally unstable, as its elements combine, shift, transfer and pass between nearby strata, or change form according to the particular modes of composition they enter into with respect to the codes of assembly defining other strata. There are, therefore, possible 'passages' between milieus, enabling movements of destratification or the partial decomposition of established regimes of signification. In one sense, then, a stratum is a body, in that it is a unity or a consistency of elements organised into a form of coherence by the fixture of their relations. However, in a more precise sense, strata are really 'systems' of bodies that share a consistency of composition. Accordingly, Deleuze and Guattari distinguish between strata as the formations of abstract machines, and bodies as concrete assemblages. This distinction is important here, as the concept of the assemblage provides scope for agency in the constructive process of the formation of ordered, actual being.

For Deleuze and Guattari, then, 'assemblages are already different from strata' (1987: 503). An assemblage is produced within a stratum, but properly operates in the zone of indiscernibility or instability where the stratum touches the milieu of its neighbourhood with other strata (1987: 503). An assemblage is fundamentally a 'territory' that is carved out from the milieu. It is extracted in pieces from the various strata that make up the milieu. These pieces are then combined into a complex body by establishing a 'rhythm' that keeps the different parts working together. Thus, an assemblage is formed in a piecemeal fashion from strata and from the perspective of the particular stratum that 'grounds' it, and has its own principle of consistency or development. For example, from the grounding perspective of a 'psychology' substratum, a wasp is a collection of animal cells (organic strata, animal strata) bonded together (physico-chemical strata) to express an insect form (organic strata and animal and insect substratum) that displays certain regular behaviours with respect to orchids and spiders (plant and animal strata, insect and arachnid substrata). The wasp is a body: it is an assemblage composed from a variety of strata, is considered from the perspective of a particular stratum that grounds its territory at any particular time (this perspective is essentially mutable), and expresses a rhythm or consistency of form that emerges with respect to its internal principle of development, the code of expression that specifies its form as wasp.

It is not yet apparent how these notions of the body, strata and assemblage enable an understanding of subjectivity or agency. What is the correlation of wasp to human subject? As we shall see, subjectivity emerges in the play of assemblage as both noun (n) and as verb (v).[5] A body, such as a wasp, is an assemblage(n) that is composed of particular defining elements and expresses a particular form. But some bodies can also be *acts* of assemblage(v), which work to '*make the world by organising forms and substances, codes and milieus, and rhythms*' (1987: 502; emphasis added). The subject then emerges as a type of 'residue' to the formative process, *as or with* this act of assemblage(v), alongside the assemblage(n) that is produced.[6]

We might best access the subject in Deleuze and Guattari's philosophy by first recalling that they have a strictly Spinozist view on the relationship between mind and body: the mind is the idea of the body. For them, the body is an assemblage(n): a 'territory' produced within a stratum, always with reference to the contextualising milieu of other strata and the body without organs. Thus, the mind is the idea of this body, the idea of this assemblage(n) that is simultaneously body and non-body, structure and non-structure. Mind is effected as soon as there is an assemblage(n), but subjectivity is not yet active until the mind begins the act of thinking the body in relation to the body without organs. And subjectivity is *enacted* only through the set of practices that involve making oneself a body without organs. The mind/body then becomes a subject, through practice. Through a certain effort, the assemblage(n) becomes an assemblage(v). In Chapter 6 of *A Thousand Plateaus*, Deleuze and Guattari instruct their readers how to undertake this task:

> This is how it should be done: Lodge yourself on a stratum, experiment with the opportunities it offers, find an advantageous place on it, find potential movements of deterritorialisation, possible lines of flight, experience them, produce flow conjunctions here and there, try out continuums of intensities segment by segment, have a small plot of new land at all times. It is through a meticulous relation with the strata that one succeeds in freeing lines of flight, causing conjugated flows to pass and escape and bringing forth continuous intensities for a BwO. Connect, conjugate, continue: a whole 'diagram', as opposed to still signifying and subjective programs. We are in a social formation; first see how it is stratified for us and in us and at the place where we are; then descend from the strata to the deeper assemblage within which we are held; gently tip the assemblage, making it pass over to the side of the plane of consistency. It is only there that the BwO reveals itself for what it is: connections of desires, conjunction of flows, continuum of intensities. You have constructed your own little machine, ready when needed to be plugged into other collective machines. (1987: 161)

Unravelling these somewhat obtuse instructions enables a better understanding of the kind of agency possible in this philosophy where the subject is not *causa sui*, nor the primary location of cause at all, but rather the developed effect of a productive process.

The first instruction – to 'lodge' oneself, 'experiment' and 'deterritorialise' – must be understood in terms of the conditions of possibility of thinking or existing at all. For Deleuze and Guattari, the aim of thought is to think actual being in terms of the process of its actualisation, for only this allows the proper understanding of the nature of things. Thought, therefore, requires an effort to think being as it 'first' exists as a body without organs: a chaotic virtual unity, which then differentiates into distinct forms of order. Understanding things properly involves understanding how and why they have come to be as they are, namely by being cognisant of the process of the 'development of forms and the formation of subjects' and the ways in which the virtual plane of immanence codes possible and actual relations between elements and thereby 'assigns the eminent term of a development' (1987: 265).

The body without organs is presubjective and preconscious, but can only be discerned retrospectively, from a position capable of conscious and active thought (see Deleuze 1997a). The developmental or organisational principle of the plane of immanence 'is always concluded from its own effects' (1987: 266), but in itself remains 'hidden':

> [A]t every moment [it] causes the given to be given, in this or that state, at this or that moment. But the plane itself is not given; it is by nature hidden. It can only be inferred, induced, concluded from that to which it gives rise. (1987: 265)

Thus, to think of oneself as a body without organs, one cannot *be* a body without organs: 'You don't reach the BwO, and its plane of consistency, by wildly destratifying' (1987: 160). To think, one must occupy a concrete position of conscious being: one can only think as a self, as an actually embodied being, as a body 'lodged upon a stratum'. The purpose of subjective thought, then, for Deleuze and Guattari, is not to strive towards the impossible goal of 'absolute destratification' in order to become a formless BwO or to experience the pure creative positivism of unrestrained desire. Indeed, they warn:

> Outside the strata or in the absence of strata we no longer have forms or substances, organization or development, content or expression. We are disarticulated; we no longer even seem to be sustained by rhythms. (1987: 503)

To think adequately, one must seek consciously to inhabit one's position, to be conscious of one's location and one's perspective, and from that position to observe and analyse the kind of assemblage one has become, to interrogate and transform this identity and the assemblages one creates in society with others. For Deleuze and Guattari, then, there must always be a subject who thinks, and strata that organise thought:

> you have to keep enough of the organism for it to reform each dawn; and you have to keep small supplies of significance and subjectification ... and you have to keep small rations of subjectivity in sufficient quantity to enable you to respond to the dominant reality. (1987: 160)

Their philosophy does not announce the death of the subject, and they do not insist upon the fragmentation and collapse of meaning.

However, they do insist that although a body is always enmeshed in the institutions, discourses and practices that assign meaning and identity and regulate social relations and positions, these strata are never closed in upon themselves, but always open to an external, contextualising milieu. The site of the body itself, the assemblage(n), is the point where strata overlap and form conjunctions. However, these conjunctions are rarely seamless, but most often partially disjunctive: the difference between strata forms a zone of undecidability where meaning potentially shifts and mutates. Thus, by cultivating an awareness of the assemblage(n) one embodies, and hence of the 'meticulous relation' one has with the strata one occupies at any given moment, it becomes possible to identify these zones of undecidability: the sites in one's own self where one's identity is multiple and perhaps contradictory – simultaneously mother and professional, daughter and friend, public and private, selfish and caring, independent and bonded, active and passive and so forth. These apparent points of disjunction in one's own identity, where one occupies multiple classifications and meanings simultaneously and where the occupation of one stratum alters the position assigned by another, signal points where the constituting discourses are unstable. It is in seeking out and finding such points of instability, Deleuze and Guattari suggest, that a person becomes most 'advantageously placed' to 'experiment' with the assemblage(n) he embodies and with the BwO he might access in order to become identified otherwise.

The instruction to 'experiment' is not at all to be understood as a poor substitute for political engagement, nor as an encouragement to engage with a vague or unspecified difference or with 'alternative

Subjectivity

'lifestyles' as such. In fact, Deleuze and Guattari mean something quite specific, rigorous and radically transformative by their suggested practice of experimentation. Beginning with the conduct of a close self-examination that attends to one's relationship to the discourses and conventions that give meaning to identity, experimentation firstly involves problematising the self by thinking identity in terms of its inconsistencies, internal disjunctions and contradictions. This might be done by experimentally positioning one's complex identity in relation to dominant social discourses, which tend to reduce complex identity to simple features assimilable to the terms of the discourse. Alternatively, positioning one's identity in relation to 'minor discourses' might reveal a site of movement in oneself, where one's assumptions are challenged and shifted. Locating these fissures of signification in oneself thereby simultaneously makes apparent points of instability in the social discourses that constitute identity.

The second moment of experimentation is then made possible by applying pressure to these points of discrepancy or instability of the strata. By focusing upon the fragile points in a system of social meaning, it becomes possible to experiment with the meaning assigned by certain strata. By locating the points at which significance shifts and by experimentally combining strata in unorthodox ways, it becomes possible to question and transform established meaning by changing the context of its production. This aspect of experimentation thereby focuses upon the strata, and not simply upon the self. Here, the aim of experimentation is to find systemic 'lines of flight' and flows: the conditions and moments where established significations collapse and transform, making possible passages, bridges and shifts in established structures of meaning.

Identifying the 'flows and continuums' particular to a system of strata thereby enables its description in terms of 'what comes to pass and what does not pass, what causes passage and prevents it' (1987: 152). Such a description works as a 'diagram' of a social apparatus: a dynamic mapping of the strata that form its established discourses and practices, the milieu given by their arrangement in relation to each other, and the slippages and morphing that indicate the lines of escape from these established strata (1987: 141–8; Deleuze 1986: 34–44). This diagram thereby images a social formation, making it possible for us to 'see how it is stratified for us and in us and at the place where we are'. From another perspective, the diagram shows the strata as 'striations' that have formed upon the surface of the BwO: strata are here diagrammed as rigid, ordered forms, but remain open to the chaotic movements of the plane of immanence or consistency, from which they have developed their particular formations.

Thus, the diagram with its images of order and flux – the fundamental chaos, the emergent strata and the flows that escape them – enables access to the idea of the BwO immanent to any formation of self or society. Furthermore, once we are conscious of this immanent formlessness of any actual regime of signification, it becomes possible to analyse the process of emergence that has taken place upon the BwO. At this point, it becomes possible to ask of a body: which elements have combined to produce this body? And: how do they combine in order to produce this body? What principle of organisation directs their conjunction? In other words, *what is the content and expression of this stratum? What is the content and expression of this assemblage? How has this body been articulated?*

We exist as actual assemblages, composed from strata that have themselves emerged as distinct and particular structures of meaning, through a process that regulates chaotic force relations into ordered forms. However, this process of ordering is not inevitable and does not follow a predestined path of development. There is indeed something of a dice throw in emergence: the chance meeting of elements, the fortuity of their agreement and combination into a complex body, the unhindered endurance of their relationship safe from destruction by other bodies encountered by coincidence along the way. Becoming conscious of the immanent BwO accordingly allows us to perceive the actual as a contingent 'connection of components that could have been different' (Deleuze and Guattari 1994: 93), which then opens up a further activity of experimentation.

Before we come to this activity, however, it is useful to recall that 'the BwO is desire; it is that which one desires and by which one desires' (1987: 165). In reaching the BwO, then, we reach *desire*, the productive plane of composition, which causes forms to emerge and which consists solely of attractions, connections and intensities of associative force between bodies. In reaching the BwO, the focus of experimentation therefore shifts once more: initially from self to strata, and now to desire. At this point, then, Deleuze and Guattari urge a strategic experimentation with desire itself, which involves actively selecting elements for association and arranging their composition. Desire is the force of association that combines elements to produce an assemblage: experimenting with desire involves intervening with the productive process in order to create and cause a new emergence of being. In the act of experimenting with desire, the body

Subjectivity

thereby also makes itself an 'assemblage capable of plugging into desire, of effectively *taking charge* of desires' (1987: 166; emphasis added). This, therefore, is the point at which strategy and causation properly emerge in the experimenting subject.

In the act of 'taking charge' of the desires that constitute one's self, this self as assemblage(n) becomes an agent of assemblage(v). Deleuze and Guattari distinguish types of bodies in terms of the particularity of their content and expression. In this way, they outline a distinction, not only between strata and assemblages, but also between the two different types of assemblage. Like strata, assemblages are articulated doubly (1987: 40, 41). The first articulation concerns content: the quantity or range of element types that comprise the body. And the second articulation involves expression: the 'principle of connection' between these elements that defines the quality or style of the form that emerges from their interrelations. For assemblages, expression also concerns the action and passion of the elements. The body becomes the subject of its own formation when it actively selects certain elements that comprise it, and actively arranges these in deliberate styles of relation. For every assemblage, it therefore becomes necessary to ask what kind of body it is, or *what can the body do*: does it actively select its elements and deliberately arrange its emergence as such? Is the assemblage simply an object (the passive result of an emergence of form that occurs spontaneously or through the agency of another body), or is it also a subject (capable of the active styling of an emergence of form)? For Deleuze and Guattari, then, the subject is conceptualised precisely as the kind of being that actively intervenes in the process of 'desiring-production', to select content and shape the expression of the reality that is being produced. The subject therefore experiments with desire to shape its own particular emergence as such, as well as styling the emergence of other social assemblages that embody the strata. The subject is formed in the act of productive assembly, alongside and contemporaneous with the event of actualisation she works to bring about.

There are, of course, limits to this constructive and styling activity of the subject, which is never free to construct the world at will. For Deleuze and Guattari, the subject-assemblage always acts within the constraints of her existence as a 'collective enunciation' (1987: 79–80). By this, they mean that a subject is 'articulated' as a territory or assemblage drawn from a *collection* of strata, and hence is 'spoken' and 'acted' through multiple and various discourses and practices. As we have seen, it is this constitutive multiplicity of discourses that enables the subject to locate within her identity the points at which their meaning overlaps and shifts. The 'collective enunciation' of the self as assemblage thereby enables the critical practice of experimentation and transformation. However, as we have also seen, this practice does not involve the total collapse of meaning or social structures. A subject must remain 'lodged upon a stratum' in order to think or exist at all. In fact, a successful practice of chosen actualisation involves the conduction of a series of *partial destratifications or deterritorialisations*, in which only certain, selected aspects of actual being are identified as unstable, then critically decomposed and actively reconstructed, while other aspects remain consistent and momentarily uncontested, allowing the subject to exist in continuity even through the process of its transformation.

Accordingly, the subject is always significantly (even dominantly) constituted by existing discourses and practices, in ways that may not be immediately transparent. There are always rigid social strata that the subject acts within, even while acting against other strata. The task of locating points of instability in established strata is constrained by this rigidity and this lack of transparency. However, these constraints are themselves not final. They might always be shifted through the practice of experimentation by combining apparently fixed strata in novel ways, which then create points of disjunction where they potentially unsettle each other's coherence, and become revealed as unstable. The subject-assemblage is therefore always simultaneously an assemblage(n) and an assemblage(v). A body is only ever a partial subject; even when causally active, it remains partly passive. As an object constituted through social discourse and practice, a self is always at least partly defined by others. Being constituted by strata that are the product of collective actions and expressions, the subject is therefore a 'collective enunciation' in another sense. That is, the subject is not simply constituted by a collective of discourses and practices, but also by the social collective that produces these discourses. One is always partly constituted by one's social others, whose 'articulations' collectively emerge as strata, in ways which might not be those actively chosen by oneself.

The practice of 'experimentation' involves the careful empirical analysis of one's constitution, and of the constitution of social strata. In each case there is a need to analyse these bodies in terms of the nature of their composition, and wherever possible strive to select actively the content and expressions that articulate the world. The

Subjectivity

practice of experimentation thus describes the selective movement of Nietzsche's 'eternal return' (Deleuze 1983: 68–71). A given assemblage 'returns' to its immanent 'origins' as BwO or desire, in order to select actively content for its composition. In the process of active formation, only that which is reselected and hence affirmed, will be chosen to 'return' once more to the recomposed form. Furthermore, only that style of expression that is actively chosen, hence affirmed, will return as the recomposed form: 'The lesson of the eternal return is that there is no return of the negative. The eternal return means that being is selection. Only that which affirms or is affirmed returns' (Deleuze 1983: 189). The affirming test of the eternal return is thereby the basis of Deleuze and Guattari's suggested practice of experimentation, and it is through experimentation that we are then able to critique, transform and affirm the forms of being we live as and with. We are now better able to perceive that agency always involves both power and desire, and that both power and desire can define a body as either active or reactive. In becoming a subject, a body needs to identify its composition and style, to define its internal powers and desires in terms of their active or reactive effects, and each subjective body aims to select actively and determine its composition and expression, with respect to creating the kind of emergence that responds to individually preferred social forms, such as postcoloniality, which can provide a sympathetic contextualising milieu for the activity of self-constitution. Of course, individual preferences may not be held in common; the social task of forging collectively preferred forms of society will be considered in Chapter 6.

On this view of selfhood, there is never a state of existence unimpeded by relations of power. Agency is not action that is free from impediments. Freedom cannot be conceptualised as a transcendent ideal state 'beyond' politics, or as the goal of a political struggle to end oppression. Nor is freedom well understood here as a possession or an inalienable right of individuals. Thus, neither Berlin's 'two concepts' or MacCallum's 'triadic' concept of positive and negative liberty fit neatly to Deleuze and Guattari's model of subjectivity.[7] Nor can freedom here be conceived as self-mastery or as mastery over others, for here the subject is always also a part-object for others. As in much modern political theory, freedom does concern self-determination, but here, one does not determine one's own actions outside of another's sphere of influence, since a body is a force always defined in relation to other forces, and one's character is constituted by the influence and interplay of these forces.

In fact on the view elaborated in this chapter, freedom involves an act of 'folding' upon the virtual conditions of determination, which shape the actual determining structures, which constitute the self. Self-determination is therefore asserted not simply against the immediate determining structures and relations of force in which the self is embedded, but against the primary forces of emergence that produce these structures in the first place. Freedom here concerns an availability of choices, but the choices themselves are not simply already available, but must be actively created. In fact, this is how freedom is here properly identified: as a *practice* of creation and transformation, as a *practice* of effective power and desire. Freedom exists as the practice of experimentation, at the various levels of focus: the self, the strata and the BwO. More precisely, freedom is the practice of experimentation with actual bodies, in order actively to transform them. However, these 'corporeal transformations' are facilitated by 'incorporeal transformations' at the level of the BwO (Deleuze and Guattari 1987: 80–8). Incorporeal transformation is the practice that involves selecting virtual content for the composition of a complex actual body, and arranging this content in chosen forms of power/desire-relations. These relations define the quality and degree of the effect constituting elements have upon each other, and thus 'style' the complex body they combine to compose.

Thus, for Deleuze and Guattari, freedom is exactly the *practice* of subjectivity. Freedom is found in the act of assemblage(v), which effects the subject at the same moment as it produces the assemblage(n). The subject is, then, a complex expression of freedom and of power, a complex situating of the self, in terms of a selective identification with constitutive social meanings, which are sometimes fluid and transforming, at other times rigid and resistant to change. The subject does not 'have' expression, but emerges as the act of expression. The subject does not 'have' a style, but emerges as a styling of the productive process of actualisation. The subject does not 'have' a strategy, but is itself a strategy of assemblage. The subject is not already given as the determining location of causation: the subject is an event, a virtual made actual, is acted as an effect of actualisation. However, the subject becomes a cause of itself and the world, when it actively folds back upon itself and upon the social and productive forces of desire and power that produce the actual, in order actively to select and qualify that productive process.

Perhaps most importantly, however, the subject is an experimental performance of sociability. Through this performance, the subject

Subjectivity

positions himself as an element in a social assemblage. Through the utterances that take place in these performances of sociability, the subject helps to effectuate the strata, the system of social coherence that emerges with the consistent repetition of such utterances across a social field. He is also capable of approaching others with an attitude of desire and a style of political engagement appropriate to the construction of a favoured complex social body, which emerges from these interactions. The empirical practice of experimentation is central to the 'folding' process of subject-formation, and experimentation is also at the heart of one's capacity to form joyful encounters with others: only by experimentally entering into actual compositions with other bodies are we able to develop adequate understanding about the complex forms of compatibility and incompatibility that define our relations with the elements comprising our social existence, which in turn enable us to become active, seek out alternative ways of associating, and so cause agreeable and joyful compositions with other bodies (see Armstrong 1997: 48ff.). The following chapter will consider how this practice of subjective freedom might attend to the collective construction and performance of a postcolonial ethos, but firstly we will take a closer look at how Deleuze's concepts of stylised embodiment and complex partial-selfhood transform the conceptions of social encounter and subjective satisfaction that were explored in Chapters 1 and 2.

The encounter with the other

We have seen that for Sartre and other thinkers working within the post-Hegelian tradition of the politics of recognition, my encounter with the other is something I simultaneously desire and fear, since the other both brings me into being by 'looking at me', and threatens to steal my being from me by objectifying me with her gaze. This encounter with the other is experienced as a situation of mutual bodily conflict; my body uncertainly faces a body that is both seductive and dangerous, as is mine for her, and our encounter is essentially a struggle in which we seek the mutual management of this threat. The bodies engaged in this struggle accordingly trace a circle of desire, swapping between objective 'being-for-the-other', and subjective action aimed at making the other 'be-for-me'. Because relations with the other are structured by the negativity of desire/lack, motivating a generative ontological longing for repletion but also a fear of loss, they are here chiefly concerned with self-possession and limiting the threat the other poses to one's fragile self integrity. This situation writ large, the colonial encounter is also conventionally conceptualised according to this logic, as the event of 'worlds colliding' and the struggle for just recognition and redress that ensues when one culture and political territory, one 'identity', has been 'stolen' by another. In this meeting, whole civilisations are seen to oppose (and yet also entice and enthral) one another; the class differences internal to each body on the divide are subsumed by the greater or more urgent, more significant, political difference embodied by the colonial other.

For Deleuze and Guattari, this description of the encounter with the other as a meeting of distinct bodies, each attempting to stand firm against the other and to manage their meeting in a way that accommodates the other without forcing the loss of one's personal ground, grossly simplifies the event, since they insist that a social encounter can only be adequately understood with reference to the highly complex natures of the bodies involved in the meeting. For them, a body is not a discrete entity defined by stable boundaries and a set of fixed characteristics; rather, it is an assemblage of components bound into a coherent form, but this bodily consistency is only ever temporary and is always shifting. This is so, because the component parts of a body constantly change as they enter into new relations with other parts encountered by the assemblage in its interactions with its existential milieu. A body is, then, a 'composition of relations between parts' (Deleuze 1990: 218–19), where some of these relations are internal to the body, and some are external relations with other bodies. More precisely, it is a particular mode of expression of the infinite possible expressions of being, and that which is expressed is a characteristic relation of consistency between parts (Deleuze and Guattari 1987: 254).

Accordingly, a body is best thought of as the collection of relations its constituent parts enter into. These relations are conceptualised by Deleuze and Guattari in terms of their duration: the speed or slowness with which they form and transform (1987: 258). Fleeting relations describe bodily characteristics that appear only occasionally: a flash of jealousy born from a combination of loss and longing; a twinge of spite spawned by a momentary mixture of anger and envy; a burst of kindness prompted by sympathy and care. These elemental combinations cause the body to be affected, for example with jealousy, spite or kindness. More enduring relations between components define more stable characteristics of a body, expressing its regular ways of being affected. A body is therefore defined not only

Subjectivity

by shifts in the consistency of its internal relations, but more particularly by the affections these relations produce (1987: 258). In fact, however, there are two sorts of bodily affections. Firstly, the body is an extensive entity that is comprised of elemental parts, combined in particular configurations according to the ways in which they affect one another. Secondly, the body itself exists as an elemental part in a multitude of more complex assemblages formed with other bodies in its social milieu. Accordingly, a body forms a characteristic consistency according to the extensive relations involving its internal parts, and also transforms intensively over time as it is affected by its engagements with neighbouring bodies and the complex array of relations into which they enter. This means that,

> depending on their degree of speed or the relation of movement and rest into which they enter, [affects] belong to a given Individual, which may itself be part of another Individual governed by another, more complex relation, and so on to infinity . . . Thus each Individual is an infinite multiplicity. (1987: 254)

But how might this complex and abstract notion of the body as an 'infinite multiplicity' defined by its internal and external affective relations be politically useful in the social context of postcolonialism? How does the nature of this body, which is defined by its many affections and determined by the vast variety of its relations with neighbouring bodies, also determine the ways it is affected and the quality of the encounters it experiences? And how might a body actively create postcolonial encounters with other bodies?

Moira Gatens (1996) and Aurelia Armstrong (1997) indicate that Spinoza's theory of the mind as an idea of the body is crucial for understanding how notions of sociable agency might arise from Deleuzian philosophy. Because the body is constituted and defined by its relations, the mind necessarily 'thinks the body' in the act of the encounters that define its ways of being affected, and accordingly, in terms of the relations that comprise its existence at a particular time and the transformations that trace shifts in the body over time (Deleuze 1990: 220–1). Deleuze explains that, according to Spinoza, the mind may have either an adequate or inadequate idea of the body. Inadequate ideas are caused by the passive affections a body undergoes when other bodies impact upon it; these ideas are inadequate because they are cognisant only of what the body suffers and remain ignorant of bodily powers of action and active capacity, which describe 'what the body can do'. Conversely, adequate ideas are the mind's awareness of the affections a body causes in itself and to others, when it actively engages with other bodies. Adequate ideas think the full power of a body in terms of the chosen affects it can produce by 'striving to organise its encounters' (Deleuze 1990: 261). In striving to understand bodily composition, the mind 'thinks the body' in terms of its affective relations, and so transforms the body into a self-aware being that is increasingly capable of discerning which relations are compatible and enhance active capacities, thus bringing about joy, and which relations are experienced passively by the body, imposing upon the body and thus occasioning a feeling of sadness.

Here, self-awareness initially involves understanding how one is formed through constitutive relationships, but this initially reflective self-concept develops into a reflexive practice of self-formation as the mind develops knowledge of how the body can increasingly engage the kinds of relationships that maximise active affections. In doing so, a body increases its power to experience joyful affections, since the active relations the body chooses are naturally those that increase its existential capacities (the *conatus* of a body entails that it chooses relations that preserve or increase its powers), and hence are experienced as joy. Conversely, passions suffered by the body are the cause of sadness, which the body experiences not only when it is weakened by the impact of another body that imposes upon it in a way that destroys some of its capacities, but also because the experience of a passive affection, even when it is not destructive, does not allow the body to exercise fully its active and joyful creative powers of self-assemblage. Spinoza's concepts of sad passions and active joys thus point the way towards an ethics of self-conduct. Adequate ideas correspond with actively produced, joyful bodily experiences arising from relations with compatible bodies; to discover adequate ideas, one ought to 'concretely try to become active' (Deleuze 1990: 226), and this involves developing understanding of oneself and others, so that one can organise encounters by seeking out bodies with which one can form compatible relations.

However, a problem concerning postcolonial application is signalled here. What might this ethics of self-conduct augur for the other in my encounters? I ought to seek out compatible others and engage with them in agreeable ways that increase my powers of existence and affectivity because this will increase my experience of joy, but what are my ethical obligations towards the other, for the sake of the other? If a relation is compatible with my powers and enhances

Subjectivity

them, is it also necessarily compatible with the powers of the other? Is the joy of the other a relevant concern to me, or should I simply attend to maximising my own satisfaction, pleasing myself? In particular, the problem signalled here concerns the nature of joy as the bodily experience of an increased power to be affected. This appears to celebrate the active formation of new relations *per se*, without due regard for their quality and their impact on others, since the combining of elemental bodies evidently produces a common body with increased complexity and a greater power of affection. Thus, 'In any encounter, whether I destroy or be destroyed, there takes place a combining of relations that is, as such, good' (Deleuze 1990: 249).

But how might colonised indigenous peoples interpret this claim? Generally in the colonial meeting of indigenous and non-indigenous bodies, while one body was diminished and largely destroyed by the meeting, the union nonetheless increased the powers of each to be mutually affected, creating a common body with a higher degree of complexity. Deleuze explains that evil 'corresponds to the fact that the relation combined when two bodies meet, are not always those of the bodies themselves' (Deleuze 1990: 251). As was mostly the case in colonial encounters, the meeting might destroy the internal relation between parts that defines one of the individuals. But for Spinoza, this evil 'amounts to nothing' so long as the meeting produces a new common body with a new set of internal relations that is more complex, more affective, and thus more capable of joy (Deleuze 1990: 251). There is but one case in which evil amounts to something: when the mode of expression of being 'passes from greater to lesser perfection', when the resulting common body is a diminished power, less capable of actively exacting joy (Deleuze 1990: 251). Accordingly, it appears we do no great wrong when we destroy an encountered body's existing relation, so long as the union creates the conditions of an increased capacity for affection. At face value, this seems like a justification for colonialism.

In fact, Deleuze's interpretation of Spinozan ethics, and the use we might make of this in a postcolonial context, is poorly understood unless Deleuze's quite particular reading of Spinozan embodiment is taken into consideration. This reading details the complex nature of bodily encounters: a body is affected in many different ways and is characterised by the multifarious relations it forms with the great number of neighbouring bodies comprising its contextualising social milieu. Encounters are not simply events describing the meeting of whole bodies as they come into contact, but more precisely involve a multitude of engagements taking place at the many particular sites of the affections that describe a body:

> Existing bodies do not encounter one another *in the order* in which their relations combine . . . Relations combine *according to laws*; but existing bodies, being themselves composed of extensive parts, meet *bit by bit*. So parts of one of the bodies may be determined to take on a new relation imposed by some law while losing that relation through which they belonged to the body. (Deleuze 1990: 237)

When bodies meet 'bit by bit', only some elements of their complex composition enter into affective relations, while other aspects remain unaffected by the encounter.[8] Balibar writes: 'Spinoza's idea is simple, but daring: what is exchanged are *parts* of the individuals under consideration . . . a given individual . . . continuously abandons some *part(s) of itself*, while at the same time continuously incorporating some *part(s) of others*' (1997: 18). Sometimes certain elemental parts will enter into new relations with the encountered body, which alters their capacity to remain in the previous relations defining existing bodily configuration, thus transforming the internal composition of the body and changing its expression of consistency as a mode of being. However, other aspects of bodily configuration will remain untouched and unchanged by the encounter with the other. While one's identity constantly shifts and transforms according to social context and particular constitutive relations, such becomings are only ever partial and incomplete, since one is never affected all at once in one's entirety. Some continuity of identity is retained: '"I" preserve my essence provided the dynamic proportion that defines me as an individual is preserved' (Balibar 1997: 19).

This is true also of cultural encounters occurring with the colonial collision of communities: each body is transformed by the meeting, and old traditions and concepts shift and change as new connections are formed which alter the internal consistency of each body. However, 'there does not exist anything like a global *face à face* between indivisible individuals [or discrete cultures] . . . Individuals are related to (or "mixed" with) one another because they exchange "parts" . . . i.e. because they are continuously "analyzed" and "synthesized", de-composed in their constituent parts and re-composed as relatively autonomous units' (Balibar 1997: 20). Because encounters proceed by the 'piecemeal insertion' of select elements into new relations with others, some aspects of each culture naturally remain unaffected, relatively stable and intact, allowing it to persevere in some recognisable form. Colonial violence intending the wholesale destruction of a community or a culture is thus a perverse encounter, which disavows the natural partiality of the meeting, where such partiality preserves aspects of bodily integrity despite the transformations compelled by new environmental connections and relations. This suggests a normative notion of formal protection is needed, to protect a body from the wilful and wholesale destruction of the given relations defining it, and this will be considered further in the final section of this chapter and in Chapter 6. However, at this point we are now better placed to observe that no great wrong is done when (some aspects of) an encountered body's existing relation are destroyed in the transformative process of interaction, so long as the union creates the conditions of an increased capacity for affection. In fact, the destruction of established ways of being is natural in the ontological processes of identity formation and cultural transformation, when this occurs through the assembly of shifting and piecemeal affective relations with others.

Furthermore, because encounters take place 'bit by bit' and with a vast number of bodies simultaneously, at any particular time a body is comprised of both passive affections (passions) and active affections (actions). Some of my encounters will be actively chosen by me because I perceive, in the other, a compatibility with aspects of my nature; other relations will eventuate through my chance encounters with others. Because these chance meetings are not deliberately sought out by me, they may impose upon me in ways that are sometimes compatible and beneficial, sometimes harmful and destructive. These chance relations will cause me to endure passive affections, which may be the source of a fortuitous joy, but may equally affect me with sadness. However, the relations I actively seek out on the basis of my understanding of their compatibility with me will always be joyful, since I will always choose those relations that increase my powers of affective existence. By attending to bodily complexity and the affective meeting of bodies 'bit by bit', we can now better understand that the ethical tasks of 'becoming active' and 'organising one's encounters' properly entail that one must not simply strive to unite with bodies that one perceives to be wholly sympathetic and similar, but more precisely with the sympathetic facets of the diverse bodies that comprise one's social milieu, in compatible ways that will agreeably affect relevant aspects of one's body, potentially 'forming a *totality* of compatible relations' and thus a maximal feeling of joy (Deleuze 1990: 262). This ethics is therefore concerned with finding agreement, not by eliminating actual difference and privileging identity, but in the context of the actual diversity of bodies that express being in infinitely multiple ways. This acknowledgement of a permanent and primary ontological difference seems essential in postcolonial thinking about the social.

However, the question remains: what might this ethics of self-conduct augur for the other in my encounters? From a postcolonial perspective, it is imperative that encounters are *mutually* joyful: that each body is able to exercise its active power of existence and affective capacity; that one body is not destroyed or diminished by the other. If the conscientious relation of complex bodies, guided by active joy as outlined here, is to be practically useful in the context of postcolonialism, indigenous and non-indigenous communities must be capable of achieving a sociable quality of agreement and accord at the sites of their affective interactions. In Chapter 6, this postcolonial process of seeking agreement and identifying areas of affective compatibility through mutual understanding will be described in terms of the development of Spinozan 'common notions'. But first, it will be helpful to consider how different styles of desiring-subject emerge as different forms of satisfaction, reflected in the distinct emphases and values of different types of political society.

Subjective style and satisfaction: enjoyment and joy

On Deleuze and Guattari's view, the subject will not 'have' or 'reach' satisfaction, but itself emerges as a form of satisfaction: the subject styles a process of desiring-production to satisfy its emergence as a chosen actual form. In this final section of the present chapter, the issues of subjectivity, style, satisfaction and political society are examined more closely through analysis of Deleuze and Guattari's commentary on 'the imperialism of Oedipus' (1983). According to Robert Young, their argument in this work is useful for the critical analysis of colonialism because of the way in which 'philosophy, psychoanalysis, anthropology, geography, economics et al. are all brought together in one interactive economy and shown to be implicated in capitalism's colonizing operations' (1994: 19). In this way, they might be understood to be contributing to the earlier work by Fanon on subjectivity, psychiatric disorders and capitalist colonisation. Moreover, their analysis is significant for transformative political philosophy in general, in so far as they offer a critique of the psychoanalytic theory of normative subject-formation. Particularly in its Lacanian variant, this theory

Subjectivity

draws from Hegelian thought and the categories of dialectical negativity; Lacan's seminal text on the 'Mirror Phase' was written in 1936, directly following his participation in Kojève's seminar on Hegel and desire (see Lacan 1977). However, in their *Anti-Oedipus*, Deleuze and Guattari are not primarily interested in critiquing Hegelianism; instead, they are concerned with the ways in which the Oedipal subject, while produced through 'the old categories of the Negative', is complicit with the ideology of liberal individualism and works as the bulwark of the capitalist social system. They argue that the naturalised Oedipal model of individual integrity 'wards off' the revolutionary forces of desiring-production and the alternative possible forms of self and social organisation that might be materialised from an alternative coding of desire. While extended exploration of the connections between desire/lack, post-Hegelian communitarianism and post-Kantian liberalism will remain beyond the scope of this work, we might note that the normative model of the Oedipal psyche coincidentally represents, and normalises, the 'typical' subject of modern Western social practice, across both communitarian and liberal philosophies.

In Chapter 4, we saw that for Deleuze and Guattari, desire is not a property held by an individual subject, but is co-extensive with the entire social field. In fact, desire is 'desiring-production', the force of association that causes complex organisation to emerge and transform. In the context of social organisation, desire is always already implicated with power relations, since bodies associate according to the types of forces that define them. However, for Deleuze and Guattari (and Foucault), there are two types of power relation – micropolitical and macropolitical – each characterised by the particular quality of its relation to desire. Micropolitical relations remain open to desire: they are characteristically open to forming new associations with other bodies, which might then cause the existing association to transform. In comparison, macropolitical relations are characteristically resistant to change, and so are closed off from desire and the threat of destabilisation posed by the different associations that desire might induce the established structure to form. In this way, desire is both 'within' power structures (as an immanent cause of their formation) and also constitutes a permanent 'outside' which threatens to destructure and dissolve stable social and political orders. These political orders are revolutionary or progressive when they welcome the transformations that new assemblages of desire can bring, and they are reactive when they stifle or block the revolutionary and transformative force of desire.

Deleuze and Guattari's discussion of the Oedipal subject occurs in this context. They argue that Oedipus is an ideological limit that 'wards off' the transformative force of desiring-production by domesticating this true nature of desire and mystifying it as the incestuous familial desire of the Oedipal subject. The Oedipal complex thus justifies and necessitates the repression of desire for the benefit of society (imagine if everybody acted upon their unrepressed Oedipal desires), but properly conserves the *established* social order, since the actual object of repression is the transformative chaos of desiring-production, which Oedipus merely masks as incest: 'Strictly speaking, psychic repression is a means in the service of social repression. What it bears upon is also the object of social repression: desiring-production' (1983: 119).

According to Deleuze and Guattari, in all forms of social organisation, the 'prime function incumbent upon the socius has always been to codify the flows of desire, to inscribe them, to record them' (1983: 33). The universal function of the social body ('socius'), is to regulate alliances between bodies (for example through marriage) and thereby to establish filiations and lineages of descent that regulate and preserve economic patterns of production, circulation and accumulation and the broader social structures these engender. The fundamental aim of the socius is thus to 'ward off desire's potential for revolt and revolution' (1983: 120) by channelling social relations in established ways, limiting the types of alliances that can form, occluding the formation of new or different alliances between certain bodies already aligned, and by consolidating existing associations and supporting their perpetuation by encoding laws. The socius traps the free flow of association that unfettered desiring-production creates, establishing rules and limits that resist the free passage of desire and encourage the stability of the emergent social forms (1983: 139–45).

The capitalist social order, however, is unlike other forms of socius, in that it also works by *decoding* established flows and perpetually reorganising desire to create new objects for consumption and, correlatively, new perceptions of need (1983: 222–40). In capitalism, the socius is thus always drawn towards freeing up desiring-production and therefore towards its own limit and collapse. The capitalist social order responds to this problem by separating the family from society, thereby removing domestic reproduction from economic production (1983: 266). The capitalist socius then no longer directs itself towards the repression of the desiring-production that creates economic productivity, but instead focuses upon the repression of the reproductive sphere of the family and the desiring-production associated with familial reproduction. This repression bears particularly upon an alternative *interior* limit, created in the form of 'the Oedipal individual' (1983: 66, 154–66). Accordingly, the capitalist socius reduces its target of repression to the individual and his 'natural' Oedipal desires for incest, which arise from his ontological negativity, his essential alienation and his longing to regain lost ontological unity (with the mother/real) through identification (with the father/signifier) and socialisation (integration into the symbolic). However, in this act of reduction, desire itself is mystified: the vast realm of desiring-production as the creative force of all forms of actual being is compressed to incest, the 'dirty little secret' of the family.

> *It is in one and the same movement that the repressive social production is replaced by the repressing family, and that the latter offers a displaced image of desiring-production that represents the repressed as incestuous familial drives.* (1983: 119)

In fact, the true desire that masquerades as the threat of the incestual desires of the Oedipal family is still desiring-production – the threat to the established socius created by alternative alliances that would actualise alternative social forms. In normalising and repressing Oedipal desire, the capitalist socius actually represses relevant aspects of desiring-production (those that threaten the capitalist socius itself, such as homosexual relations that disavow the 'natural' form of the bourgeois family and so destabilise the 'separate spheres' ideology), even while the decoded flows of desiring-production are left free to invest the shifting structures of capitalist demand. According to Deleuze and Guattari, in the capitalist socius 'Oedipus is this displaced or internalised limit where desire lets itself be caught' (1983: 66). Psychoanalysis thus encloses all desiring-production within the circumscribed arena of the family, strangling it and 'triangulating' it in the form of the bourgeois family triad ('mommy-daddy-Me'): 'The political, cultural, world-historical and racial content is left behind, crushed in the Oedipal treadmill' (1983: 95).

This 'incurable familialism' (1983: 92) creates a false representation of desire, which both draws from and reinforces 'the old categories of the Negative' (Foucault 1983a: xiii). Deleuze and Guattari list 'lack, law and signifier' as the 'three errors concerning desire' at the heart of 'Oedipal encoding' (1983: 111). These are problematic because each involves the operation of a transcendent ideal that mystifies the true nature of causation in the real: rather than attending to the formative process of desiring-production that causes the emergence of Oedipus according to a specific coding of desire in relation to lack, psychoanalysis naturalises Oedipal desire/lack as an ontological given, as the only type of desire possible, and so pre-empts the direction of the subject's development, with the result that 'Oedipus is a "given" that is there from the very beginning' (1983: 3). In this way, 'Oedipus' is the 'subject of the signifier' that Lacan insists retroactively structures desire and causes subjectivity (Lacan 1977). Lacan's emphasis on the signifier as a cause of order corresponds with his notions of 'the symbolic' as the single, elementary structure that overlays all forms of social existence, and 'the real' as that which escapes signification and is unable to be symbolised. For Lacan, the symbolic order is the set of significations, posited through language, that structure the unconscious set of assumptions, conventions, desires and social meanings that give coherence to events in daily life. Access to the real and the realm of unconscious desire is therefore mediated by the symbolic order of signifiers, concepts and language. However, this access is never adequate, since there always remains a distance between signifier and meaning: a signifier never refers immediately to the meaning of the real it represents, but always to another signifier, in an endless chain of signification (see Lacan 1988b). In other words, signifiers are 'of' the symbolic realm, and can only ever refer to other signifiers in the symbolic realm, even though they purport to signify the unconscious real. The signifier has no true access to the real, since the real is that which cannot be symbolised or signified. Signification is therefore only ever ideal, and claims an adequacy of representation that is in truth only illusory.

Deleuze and Guattari's quarrel with Lacan therefore concerns Lacan's assumption that the symbolic causally structures desire and subjectivity, even while failing to capture the true nature of the real. The primary problem is that the symbolic realm is presented as a cause already given, and is expressed in relation to the generative negativity of the gap between reality and the ideal. Oedipus is lacking in the real, but exists as an ideal set of symbolic meanings that pre-exists and predetermines the 'realisation' of the Oedipal subject; the Oedipal signifier acts as an ideal point that causally anticipates normal identification and proper assimilation into the given symbolic order. Because the symbolic realm is presented by Lacan as that which causally structures desire and subjectivity, there is no real room for an emerging subject to diverge from developing in accordance with the existing symbolic order. Furthermore, the imposition

Subjectivity

of an already-given order of meaning upon an actual variety of subject-forming events reduces them to an Oedipal interpretation of experience, as occurs when the analysand exclaims: 'So *that's* what it was! So *that's* what this meant!' (1983: 66–7) According to Deleuze and Guattari, all subjective experience then becomes assimilated to a psychoanalytic interpretation: everything is made to signify the 'truth' of the Oedipal complex and desire in terms of original castration (lack) and incest. When the signifier is the cause of the subject, we witness the 'mystification of the unconscious' and the 'conversion of the unconscious to Oedipal forms and content' (1983: 175).

In this way, Lacan removes causation from the real. For Deleuze and Guattari, however, the causal force of desire is *absolutely real*: everything that exists is immediately produced through desiring-production in the real. Accordingly for them, the ideal is never a true *cause* of realisation, but is only ever an emergent *effect* of actualisation, brought about by relations of desire established in the real. It is in this sense that they seek to challenge the idea that Oedipus is a 'given'. The mistake made in the psychoanalytic conceptualisation of desire and the subject in terms of 'lack, law and signifier' is that the subject emerges as an effect, but takes itself for a cause. At the heart of the problem, then, is the misconception that the established regime of power (the law) causally structures desire and the subject (1983: 129).[9] Normal Oedipal subject-formation describes the process of the child's resigned acceptance of the fact of castration and the law of the father, his proper repression of incestuous desire, and his eventual identification with the father and entry into the symbolic order of the social milieu. The 'normal' subject thereby achieves identification with the established symbolic order – and with the Oedipal signifier, already waiting for the arrival of the subject. However, for Deleuze and Guattari, the established regime of power – of law and signification – is itself the *product* of desire (of desiring-production). Power does not simply impose an order on desire, but is in fact always already produced by desire.

In fact, these established orders of signification, which attempt to close off desire and repress it, to 'ward off desire's potential for revolt and revolution', to contain and domesticate the desiring-production that threatens to transform the established regime, could always be produced according to alternative rules for encoding desire. Deleuze and Guattari argue that the mode of subjectivity expressed as 'schizophrenic' and described in Oedipal analysis as 'abnormal', attests to such an alternative encoding of desiring-production. For Deleuze and

Guattari, the purpose of schizoanalysis is then to reveal the 'libidinal investments in our cultural and social milieu' (1983: 175) made by the normative model of subjectivity defined as Oedipus. Which alternative organisations of desire are repressed? Which established order is preserved by this particular repression of desire? With respect to Oedipus, they suggest: 'Oedipus is always colonisation pursued by other means, it is the interior colony, and . . . it is our ultimate colonial education' (1983: 170). Oedipus is an interior limit that captures and constrains the vast chaos of desiring-production by reducing it to a particular form that is presented as universal. Oedipus serves, for psychoanalytic theory, as an ontological model of the self. Oedipus is typical: individuals who deviate from his figure are perceived as psychotic or hysterical, as developmentally abnormal or badly Oedipalised. The invention of Oedipus is thus an event of *political* significance, since he effectively naturalises a particular concept of subjectivity, which is also the basis of modern social and political philosophy. Like all subjects, Oedipus is produced through desire and in relation to others. However, Oedipus is produced through a *particular* conception of desire that is presented as essential and universal: this is desire structured by lack and bound by particular encoding rules of familialism and individual containment. This concept of desire is necessary for the formation of the ontological model of selfhood that Oedipus embodies; Oedipus is foundational in legitimating the grand Western narratives of individual containment and teleological progress, desire and finite history, defining the trajectories of both capitalist imperialism and Enlightenment.

Taking desire/lack as a starting point results in an emphasis placed upon the achievement of identity; the subject emerges with the process of satisfaction, and satisfaction is here defined in terms of possession. When desire is connected with lack and satisfaction is connected with possession, relations with the other carry a constant undercurrent of conflict and hostility, since the difference represented by the other is a destabilising force that threatens to undo identity. The ontological generativity of desire/lack and the possessive form of satisfaction it engenders result in a particular form of appropriative subjectivity, and also in a particular kind of political society with a strong emphasis on rights-based justice, geared towards the protection of possessive satisfaction. While a more fully considered exploration of the relationship between desire, satisfaction and political society is called for, space limitations dictate that the short discussion that follows offers only a crude outline of this idea.

Subjectivity

As we have seen, Sartre, Fanon and others in the post-Hegelian tradition argue that through the act of recognition, the other confers upon me the subjectivity that I desire and lack, but also extracts my being from me, since the mediating act of recognition objectifies me and distances me from the immediacy of my self. In this way, the other 'steals my being', and I must seek its recovery in order to achieve my goal to be a self-directing agent, the foundation of my own being (Sartre 1996: 361ff.). Lacan similarly writes about the mediating social gaze and the subject's impossible desire for the *objet petit a* (1977: 67–105). More recently, Slavoj Žižek's (1993) analysis of the 'theft of enjoyment' resonates with these earlier ideas. Using Lacanian concepts to write about nascent nationalisms and ethnic conflict in the aftermath of the disintegration of communism in Eastern Europe, Žižek contends that national identity or identification is sustained by a community's belief in its particular 'way of life'. Here, 'way of life' means 'the way a community organises its feasts, its rituals of mating, its initiation ceremonies, in short all the details by which is made visible the unique way a community *organises its enjoyment*' (1993: 201). According to Žižek, then, at stake in ethnic tension is precisely the possession of this common enjoyment: the other is treated with fearful suspicion, as a body that wants to 'steal our enjoyment (by ruining our way of life)' (1993: 203). Satisfaction involves possessive enjoyment of an identifying 'way of life', which is however always perceived to be under threat of being appropriated (or annihilated), and must therefore be jealously guarded and protected from conniving others. However, Žižek points out this 'theft' is only ever an imagined threat, since for the Hegelian subject involved in a perpetual process of dialectical becoming, the lack of satisfaction or human fulfilment that jeopardises enjoyment of being is original: '[W]e never possessed what was allegedly stolen from us' (1993: 203).

The notion others can threaten being and its enjoyment is also central to the liberal tradition of social contract, but in this tradition the self is always-already given in full possession of her defining human qualities. The possibility that social participation might undermine these qualities is the underlying basis of human rights, which refer to natural properties understood to be inalienable in human identity. Rights protect me from the threat posed by others, who might possibly treat me in such a way that they stop me from enjoying aspects of my human being. Rights thereby affirm that there are certain aspects of my human being that must not be 'stolen' by others. A failure to recognise someone's human rights involves a failure to respect the inalienable humanity, hence dignity, of a person. Their enjoyment of their human being is 'thieved', leaving them diminished. This kind of analysis is particularly instructive in the context of the Stolen Generations of indigenous Australians, removed from their families and their cultural communities by interventionist and racist, post-colonial State policy. The Report of the Human Rights Commission to Government on the subject of the Stolen Generations is overtly presented in terms of human rights:

> To know who you are, where you are from and to whom you belong is a basic human entitlement. It is essential to the realisation of the 'dignity and worth of the human person' which underpins the Universal Declaration of Human Rights. (HREOC 1997: 17)

For the Stolen Generations, that which was stolen was, then, exactly the enjoyment of their human being, as it is experienced in the context of indigenous sociability, or cultural 'belonging'. It is, therefore, unsurprising that responses and recommendations flowing from the *Bringing Them Home* Report revolve around the need to 'restore identity' to indigenous individuals and communities, by renewing and strengthening family bonds, community and culture (HREOC 1997; Cornwall 2002).

While liberalism and communitarianism differ in their basic ontological commitments, they nonetheless share certain underlying values, including an emphasis on being or identity– either as a given set of defining human qualities, or as a goal to be pursued in common with others. Accordingly, the enjoyment of identity is privileged in both traditions, either as a right or as a benefit flowing from collective goods: in liberalism, individuals have the right to those inalienable qualities that define their human being; in communitarianism, individuals have a (qualified or mediated) right to enjoy the collective practices and goods that sustain both individual and collective forms of identity. A second point of connection between the two positions concerns an underlying ambivalence towards difference or others. In both traditions, benefits flow from the social connections the self forms in community with others, but those others simultaneously threaten one's enjoyment of being, potentially 'stealing' one's enjoyment of identity either by infringing upon one's inalienable integrity, or by 'stealing', monopolising or withholding the common goods the self requires for the purpose of identity-formation. Thus, in both traditions, an oppositional or annihilating attitude towards difference is

Subjectivity

produced by power relations and ultimately by the force of association described by desire in general, I have argued that a subject emerges properly *as* the exercise of experimentation and the practice of composition. Subjectivity involves the cultivation of a critical awareness of the particular and concrete *types* of desire that have been invested in self-formation as such, together with an ethical sensibility of the *types* of desires the individual practices, or should observe, in the immediate associations and relations that subsequently come to compose the power structures defining the social body, as a broad community of practice.

Underlying this view of subject-formation is the notion that individuals must have critical awareness in order to achieve subjectivity. This raises a problem of capacity: are individuals who lack critical awareness then understood to be inferior sorts of subject? In this chapter I have suggested that subjectivity is only ever partial. Subjects are never capable of a complete transparency or reflexivity, since we are always at least partially determined by the background context of 'unthought' discourses and structures that constitute us and into which we are born. This contextualising milieu is, in this sense, 'given'. Nonetheless, the collection of strata that organise social meaning, practice and identity is never uniform, fixed or final, but multiple and unstable, and therefore always has the possibility of being transformed through collective practice. Accordingly, individual capacities for critical reflexivity are themselves not given or normative, but are an expression of the forms of sociability that constitute and define individuality. Subjective capacity may therefore be enhanced when the embedding societies strive to maximise opportunities for established truths to be contested and transformed. A society that encourages the becoming of its established ways of being is a society that facilitates the development of the critical and ethical sensibilities of its subjects. Conversely, a society that stultifies critique and resists challenges to its existing way of life limits the capacities of its citizens to exercise their subjective agency of social transformation. However, just as subjectivity is ever partial, it is never completely stifled: there are always fissures and inconsistencies, disjunctions and paradoxes in our most stable beliefs and practices that enable us to locate and perform lines of flight:

> [T]here is always something that flows or flees . . . perhaps only a tiny trickle to begin with, leaked between the segments, escaping their centralisation, eluding their totalisation. (Deleuze and Guattari 1987: 216)

Once again, we come to the question of direction: how might subjects trace a deliberate line of flight, away from old colonial practices and assumptions and towards postcolonial performances of sociability? What kind of desire or association expresses a postcolonial relation of force? What is postcolonial?

Notes

1. A shortened version of this chapter appears as Bignall (2007b); the final two sections incorporate aspects of the essay published as Bignall (2010).
2. For work on Deleuze and Guattari's connections with complexity theory, see Bonta and Protevi (2004); also de Landa (2002).
3. A strand of feminist criticism is directed towards the abstract nature of this body, the body-without-organs and the strategy of becoming-woman, arguing that these concepts fail to address specifically female experiences of the body and subjectivity, and thus mask a politics of masculine normativity. By the end of this chapter, it should be apparent why I disagree with these criticisms: Deleuze and Guattari's abstract BwO only exists alongside a concrete body that actualises it. In considering the concrete female body and its construction as feminine, they would insist that this concrete form can only be properly understood with reference to a determining abstract and virtual BwO, which guarantees that actual conceptualisations of female experience and 'nature' could always be transformed and become-otherwise. For examples of feminist criticism, see Jardine (1985); Braidotti (1993); commentary by Gatens (1996); Goulimari (1999); and Fraser (1997).
4. In his early work *The Archaeology of Knowledge* [1969] (1972), Foucault still assumed a certain duality between discursive and non-discursive formations and hence retained an implicit commitment to the concepts of ideology and repression, which he then deconstructed in his later works, *Discipline and Punish* (1977) and *The Birth of the Clinic* (1973). In these later works, then, Foucault formulated his theory of power as normalisation and discipline, and this conceptualisation was subsequently refined in the volumes comprising the *History of Sexuality* with the idea that the disciplines not only have a normalising effect; they are also constitutive of reality. See Foucault (1980a, 1980b).
5. This is clear in the original French, where assemblage means both the action 'assembling' and the resulting structure or 'assemblage'. The use of 'assemblage' as a verb in English is, however, not common usage, which is perhaps why the complex interpretation this term requires is often reduced in readings of Deleuze and Guattari's work.

Subjectivity

6. See *Anti-Oedipus* (1987: 17, 20): '[T]he subject is produced as a mere residuum alongside the desiring-machines.'
7. Against Berlin's separation of positive and negative forms of liberty, MacCallum's triadic concept holds that any act of freedom contains both positive and negative elements: X is free from Y to do Z. For a definitive discussion of Berlin, MacCallum and others on 'freedom', see Gray (1990).
8. For a comparable discussion of complex and partial 'self to self' relations, see Velleman (1996). Here Velleman presents his view that 'self' does not refer to a single entity, but is a term used to express a reflexive mode of presentation in which one presents a part or aspect of oneself to oneself. Etienne Balibar (1997) also draws attention to Spinoza's concept of relational embodiment as a process of 'transindividuality' involving the partial meeting of bodies.
9. This is also where Deleuze and Guattari depart from Foucault, who maintains a primary place for power-relations. See Deleuze (1997b).
10. The justice/care debate has mainly been taken up by feminist philosophers, who argue that moral perspective is gendered, and that the abstract principles of Rawlsian liberal justice presuppose a masculine-identified moral perspective defined by an autonomous, rational, self-interested self. The polarisation and privileging of liberalism over communitarianism, and of 'justice' over 'care', is here seen as part of an unacknowledged masculinist political agenda. See Gilligan (1982); Frazer and Lacey (1993); Held (1984); Benhabib (1992).

6

What is 'Postcolonial'?

History today still designates only the set of conditions, however recent they may be, from which one *turns away* in order to become. (Deleuze and Guattari 1994: 96)

What difference does today introduce with respect to yesterday? (Foucault 1984a: 34)

A particular understanding of historical process as 'actualisation' arises from Deleuzian ontology. Actualisation contrasts with the dominant view of history as a dialectical process of progressive harmonisation caused by the generative *negativity* of desire/lack conceived in relation to a transcendent state of ideal perfection. While similarly driven by causal desire, actualisation is motivated by the immanent *positive* force of desiring-production, which involves bodies in an open-ended process of becoming. The purpose of the present chapter is now to ask: in the absence of a projected final harmony, what might be understood by the notion of 'the postcolonial' in history? In 1784, Immanuel Kant asked a similar question of *Aufklärung* (Enlightenment), and his response later assisted Michel Foucault in his attempts to conceptualise history as a process marked by rupture and discontinuity (1984a, 1986a). The first part of this chapter will consider Foucault's discussions of Kant on Enlightenment in some detail, in order to define 'the postcolonial' as a difference introduced to the process of history with the occurrence of events such as 'reconciliation'. I will propose that reconciliation does not *cause* this postcolonial difference, but is, among other events, an effect of a causal disposition towards forms of society that respect the principles of self-determination and peaceful co-existence, and that this causal disposition is a permanent virtuality, immanent to the historical process.

The following sections in this chapter will then argue the nature of the difference implied by the eruption of the postcolonial in history. In the second section, I will consider postcolonisation as process, as event and as practice, in terms of the concept of 'attitude' discussed by Foucault in his reading of Kant. Grounding my discussion in the concrete example of Australian society, I will consider how the 1992 High Court *Mabo* judgement on native title impacts upon the social imaginary, hinting at a rupture in the habitual attitude or disposition responsible for organising the habitual form of the relationship between indigenous and non-indigenous peoples in Australia. In the wake of *Mabo*, becoming-postcolonial requires not only the rejection of unsuitable, colonial attitudes of relation, but also a practised commitment to the institution of a 'common notion' of social engagement that recognises an alternative postcolonial attitude or disposition, here exemplified as 'listening with respect'. I will conclude by considering postcolonisation as a practical task involving the creation of mediating structures that affirm the continuing relationship between indigenous and non-indigenous societies, but also introduce a radical discontinuity in the historical and current nature of this relationship, creating the kind of difference discussed by Deleuze and Guattari as 'becoming-minor'.[1]

Enlightened progress and historical discontinuity

Much has been said about Foucault's apparent political reticence: his declaration about the death of the subject; his insistence that power pervades and prevails and that resistance is always already bound up by new forms of domination; his refusal to speak as an intellectual vanguard for revolution or to indicate and rationalise a particular direction or programme for transformative practice; his insistence that 'truth claims' about human social ideals and goals are never universally representative and value-neutral, but always infused by specific political interests. In Chapters 4 and 5, my discussion of Foucault and Deleuze on power, desire and subjectivity sought to dispel the misconception that their constructivist philosophies inevitably lead to political conservatism and the disablement of agency. Even so, their depictions of history as a non-linear process of rupture and discontinuity remain worrying, for on this view it would seem that cherished notions of progress and betterment, which suggest a process of continuous improvement throughout history, are rejected. Without a guiding notion of betterment, there seems to be little point in taking transformative action.

In his essay on Kant, the Enlightenment and the French Revolution, Foucault turns to Kant's remarks on 'the question of the teleology immanent in the very process of history' in order to draw attention to Kant's useful idea that certain events can be read as signs attesting to 'the existence of a cause, a permanent cause which throughout history has guided men in the way of progress' (Foucault 1986a: 88, 91–2).[2] Foucault's primary purpose is not to argue evidence of social progress, but rather to explicate a type of philosophical questioning evident in Kant, which does not seek to 'define the conditions under which a true knowledge is possible', but instead performs an alternative form of critical interrogation which addresses itself to the events taking place in the present moment (1986a: 96). Indeed, this is exactly the kind of critical practice that was discussed in Chapter 3 in relation to Deleuze, and which Foucault also champions. Foucault suggests that it is this mode of philosophical questioning that Kant also undertakes in 1784 writing about the Enlightenment, and subsequently in 1798, writing about the French Revolution.

In each case, Kant identifies these events as effects that testify to the existence of a cause of the 'constant progress of the human race' (Foucault 1986a: 91). This cause is not transcendent to an existing state of social being, in the form of a harmonious end predicted by a defined teleology. Rather, the cause is immanent, existing throughout history within the social fabric itself. Progress is compelled by the 'moral disposition' of humanity towards a 'faculty for betterment' (1986a: 94). This disposition describes a permanent tendency. It is an attitude of sociability, which is always present as a virtual (unformed) reality, and which becomes temporarily transparent and actual in precise historical events, such as the Enlightenment or the Revolution of 1794. This causal disposition can be discerned in the effects it produces; the events are effects that attest to the operation of the cause in action. The existence of the event establishes the reality of the effect, and thus also the existence of the cause. If this cause of human progress is to be identified as a historical constant, it must be possible to prove that it:

> has acted in the past, is acting in the present, and will act in the future ... We will then be sure that the cause which makes progress possible has not only been operative at a particular moment, but that it guarantees a general tendency of the whole human race to advance in the direction of progress. (Foucault 1986a: 92)

In short, then, in order to prove that there exists a permanent cause of progress in human society, we must be able to identify an event in the present that is a 'rememorative, demonstrative and prognostic' sign of a 'permanent progress embracing the human race in its totality' (1986a: 92).

What is 'Postcolonial'?

Predictably, Foucault indicates that for Kant, the Enlightenment and the Revolution are exactly the kinds of event that have this signifying function. However, the truly significant thing about these events evidencing progress is not the outcome of their success or failure in establishing a new and progressive social order, but rather the way in which each operates as spectacle, 'generally received by spectators who do not take part in it but watch it, witness it, and for better or worse, allow themselves to be swept along by it' (1986a: 93). The event itself is only indirectly a sign of progress; it is the surrounding public enthusiasm and the positive resonance of the event echoing in the social imaginary that has directive meaning and constitutes the indisputable sign of progress. This is so, because general public enthusiasm for the event is the sign affirming a particular social disposition of humanity, which Kant sees as manifesting itself

> in two permanent ways: the right of every people to provide itself with the political constitution which appears good to the people itself, and the lawful and moral principle of a constitution framed in such a way as to avoid, by its very principles, all possibility of offensive war. (Foucault 1986a: 93)

These two principles of self-determination and peaceful co-existence characterise the ideals and the subject of Enlightenment, and were indeed perhaps first posited with a measure of collective awareness by the thinkers and main participants of that movement. Enthusiasm for the ideals of the French Revolution a short time later once again attested to the existence of this disposition towards self-determination and social harmony, which was recalled from the memory of its previous enactment at the time of the upheaval of the Enlightenment, and demonstrated in that contemporary present by the event of the Revolution. Furthermore, the widespread enthusiasm for both events indelibly and broadly imprinted them upon the global social imaginary, such that they became firmly entrenched in human social memory, and can even now be predicted to be easily recalled 'at the occasion of each favourable circumstance' that might arise in the future (Foucault 1986a: 94).

In this way, the disposition that is attested to by such repetition of events of a socially transformative nature constitutes a permanent cause of progress, or 'enlightenment', in the history of human society. These types of events momentarily actualise, in a particular form, the virtual (hence formally undefined) disposition of societies towards forming autonomous and peaceful constitutions. Such events, occurring at various times throughout history, repeatedly attest to the constancy of this disposition, which gradually, sporadically and eventually attains an increasing solidity in the forms that actualise it. Each such event, even if it enjoys only temporary or marginal success, thereby 'attests to a permanent virtuality which cannot be ignored: it is the guarantee for future history of the continuity of progress' (Foucault 1986a: 95). Even when the actual forms fail, the disposition remains as a subterranean influence for future actualisations. In this way, Foucault identifies how Kant describes the permanent possibility of the progressive Enlightenment of society: it is the momentary achievement or actualisation, repeated time over time with increasing constancy and public awareness, of the moral disposition that exists as a permanent, virtual and immanent cause of progress. In our time, postcolonisation might be seen as an equivalent event taking place in our global present in various ways and locations, which again attests to the existence of this disposition. In this way, we might see the event of the postcolonial as part of a tradition that includes the French Revolution and many various struggles for independence and self-rule, as an event that 'completes and continues the process of *Aufklärung*' (Foucault 1986a: 94).

However, as Foucault himself famously insists, this kind of progress or process of betterment is not an inevitable feature of human history. History does not tread steadily towards a given harmonious end, and Foucault accordingly refuses to engage in speculative argument about the nature of ideal forms of society, or to list instructions for the achievement of a particular form of social concordance. For Foucault, there is no *final* cause to history, which indeed he argues is propelled solely by an immanent cause that he usually presents in terms of 'power-relations'. This immanent cause is by nature open, abstract and virtual, being simply the disposition of humans to form social connections. Although Foucault discusses, through Kant, *a concrete or particular example of this* cause of history in the form of a permanent disposition to a *particular kind of peaceful and autonomous sociability*, he does not claim that this is the *only* causal disposition. In fact, without any difficulty, we can identify other events in history – colonisation, war, fascism, terrorism – that testify to the existence of other, less 'enlightened' social dispositions, and we can easily prophesy the regression or descent of humanity towards forms of social chaos and annihilation. If this outcome is to be avoided, there is a need to cultivate collective awareness of the nature of the causal dispositions (racism, fear and hatred) indicated by these events; to see the repetition of such events in our present as warning signs that we have actualised a disposition to social discord; and to soundly reject soundly such dispositions as the chosen causes of our eventual, actual social forms. This challenge brings us, once again, to the point at which Foucault's (and Deleuze's) philosophy is perceived to become ambiguous: the issue of collective agency and common commitment to a purposeful transformation of history.

Chapter 5 discussed the process of directed actualisation that occurs when bodies 'take charge' of the formative force of desire, through experimentation and mindful action mediated by the constraints imposed by existing social practice. Social actors bring about particular actualisations of the present, in community with others and from within the constraints imposed by their given position within certain established structures. Through their chosen practices of relationship with others, these agents shape the general human disposition to be sociable into particular and defined forms of sociability. Social relations thereby take on characteristic forms and become institutionalised as generally established codes of conduct. In his discussion of Kant, Foucault affirms his own view that broad social structures or 'ways of belonging' emerge from local relations of power, but aligns this with a Kantian emphasis on subjective choice which is usually absent in Foucault's own work. Accordingly, in his first commentary on Kant on Enlightenment, Foucault explains that individuals are seen (by Kant) to have a constitutive role in the actualisation of emergent social structures, since they approach and position themselves in relation to each other and their wider society in terms of an 'attitude' of practice, which defines:

> a mode of relating to contemporary reality; a voluntary choice made by certain people; in the end, a way of thinking and feeling; a way too of acting and behaving that at one and the same time marks a relation of belonging and presents itself as a task. A bit, no doubt, like what the Greeks called an *ethos*. (Foucault 1984a: 39)

Historical discontinuities, marked by events such as the Enlightenment, can then be seen to signal epochal attitude shifts. These modify the modes of relations between individuals according to historically particular modes of social orientation, thereby compelling an accompanying shift in the actual social forms and structures that materialise these. Through Enlightenment, a society *enacts* its 'exit' from the pre-existing practices of being and belonging by a collective process of chosen action, which brings about a shift in its collective social behaviour. Thus, as Foucault writes elsewhere: 'the problem is no longer one of tradition, of tracing a line, but one of division, of limits; it is no longer one of lasting foundations, but one of transformations that serve as new foundations, the rebuilding of foundations' (1972: 5).

Throughout his work, Foucault consistently argues for this theory of historical discontinuity. In his early work on the 'archive' and 'archaeology', Foucault (1972) discusses historical discontinuity in terms of epistemic shifts and discursive rupture; in his later works on *Madness and Civilisation* (1961) and on *Discipline and Punish* (1977), historical discontinuity is evidenced in terms of successive shifts between pre-modern modes of social control and the new modern techniques of normalisation that replace them. Similarly, on Foucault's reading of Kant, the Enlightenment signifies a 'way out', in that it marks a release from the 'premodern' habits and attitudes of credulous faith and immature dependency upon an unquestioned external authority, and a corresponding shift towards a mature and critical modernity. In turn, 'ever since its formation [the attitude of modernity] has found itself struggling with attitudes of "countermodernity"' (Foucault 1984a: 39).[3] Indeed, as we have already seen in the previous chapter, according to constructivist philosophies like Foucault's and Deleuze's, the constitution of selves and societies takes place in terms of a contextualising milieu comprised of multiple and co-existing strata defining overlapping discourses, institutions and practices. The continuing historical dominance of a particular form of identification with certain culturally significant strata that collectively defines an attitude or 'ethos of belonging' is best interpreted as an exercise of social power or hegemonic normalisation upon the subject. This power can be challenged by the critical activity of the subject, exercised with respect to the existence of conflicting and minor modes of self-construction made possible by the multiplicity of strata circulating in the social milieu.[4] The contesting attitudes and dispositions work to undercut critically the founding assumptions of dominant attitudes and attendant material forms, at times resulting in a crisis event in which a new attitude momentarily or permanently succeeds in taking hold, such as occurred in the Revolt of May 1968 in Paris; or in the Freedom Rides for black civil rights in the south of the US in the 1960s; or in contemporary Australia, in the *Mabo* judgement of 1992. Such events signal the potential for a radical transformation of social imaginaries, attitudes and forms of belonging, in ways that respond to such events by re-imagining, reconstituting and restructuring forms of sociability and the structures that materialise them. When these shifts reconstitute society in ways that reflect the immanent organising principles of self-determination and peace, they contribute to the ongoing process of progressive Enlightenment. However, conceptualised as a discontinuous process of 'exit' driven by an immanent cause of enlightened social disposition, rather than by a teleological vision of social perfection, this 'progressive' process of history is disconnected from the historicism that has so problematically been implicated with imperial projects in the modern era. In this way, while he does not develop this in his own work, Foucault's philosophy of discontinuous history allows for a non-finite notion of progress, as he demonstrates through his reading of Kant on Enlightenment.

While Foucault's work is primarily concerned with historical shifts in the power structures and forms of domination that constitute subjects, his investigation of Kant on Enlightenment aligns a particular moment in Kant's thinking about the nature of history (the essay on *Aufklärung*) with Foucault's own theory of history, and simultaneously draws attention to an alternative emphasis possible within this view of history as discontinuous process. This is an emphasis placed on subjective agency and active choice in *bringing about* epochal shifts, which Kant identifies as 'attitudinal'. In his own work, Foucault traces the 'exit' from 'premodernity' brought about in Western society with the creation of new modern techniques of discipline that bear upon and constitute the subject. He nonetheless explains that for Kant, the 'exit' from premodernity is made possible, not (only) by the implementation of the new techniques of knowing and of social control that Foucault primarily attends to, but by the practice of a new mode of subjectivity, a new 'modern' attitude of critical reasoning and personal responsibility, which is asserted against the previous ways of 'thinking and feeling, acting and behaving'. While the emphasis on enlightened progress, subjective choice and agency is properly Kant's and not Foucault's, I think Foucault is here pointing to the existence of a concept of directed progress that is consistent with his own philosophical emphasis on discontinuity and difference. Nonetheless, Foucault specifically interprets Kant on Enlightenment in order to insist that this particular concept of progress is not itself the *cause* of teleological history, but the contingent *effect* of an immanent and virtual cause that is repetitively attested to on significant occasions throughout history and is described by Kant as an enlightened 'attitude' or 'ethos'; progress is therefore not inevitable, only permanently possible. Progress of the 'enlightened' sort takes place only to the extent that it is chosen and practised through mindfully orchestrated relations of a particular kind of sociable engagement. Progress accordingly requires the exercise of subjective choice to participate in the sorts of relations that can actualise a common ethos of enlightened society and the institutions that support such an ethos. Progress thus also requires an exercise of public commitment, calling for a degree of common faith and fidelity to the practice of the chosen attitude, which neither Foucault nor Deleuze devotes significant energy to developing. Subsequent sections of this chapter will turn to the task of defining suitable content for an attitude or sociable disposition towards the 'enlightened' social form potentially actualised through a common commitment to postcolonialism.

Listening respect

With the 1992 decision of the Australian High Court, the *Mabo* case introduced a discontinuity, a difference, into the contemporary Australian social-scape (see Patton 1995, 1996a). It decisively rejected the racist notion of *terra nullius* pervading the colonial social imaginary, and opened up new potential for constituting society on a different and postcolonial basis of relationship. *Terra nullius* was introduced with colonisation as a principle of sociability, which enabled the colonial establishment of a 'single and clearly ordered system of institutions and laws' (Tully 1995: 84). The emergence of these social structures took place through the practice of an attitude which itself embodied the assumptions of *terra nullius* and reproduced them in the form of colonial social relations. *Terra nullius* is then a colonial attitude, which Irene Watson refers to as a 'demon spirit', a *muldarbi* (1998: 4; see Patton 1999; Svirsky 2010). Characterised by its 'erasure of the Indigenous being', and its 'ability through force to domina[te] all that is different or fails to conform to those who hold power' (Watson 1998: 14), this *muldarbi* certainly does not position individuals according to forms of sociability that might be thought of as 'enlightened' or 'postcolonial'.

In her historical fiction, *The Secret River*, Kate Grenville (2005) vividly depicts the brutal effects caused by the *muldarbi* attitude that informed and shaped the social practices of early settlers and indigenous locals in the Hawkesbury River area of New South Wales. Primarily a story about identity, belonging and relationship to land,

What is 'Postcolonial'?

The Secret River traces the journey of a convict, William Thornhill, who is sent with his family from a life of extreme poverty and hardship in London slums, to a new beginning in New South Wales. Thornhill is defined by his generalised lack – of property, of freedom, of class privilege, of choice. His only claims are to his life, his wife and family, and his labour power. However, the exploiting class extracts his labour from him for an unfair price that does not permit him to support his family. Driven to a necessary thievery by the harshness of the British class system and the unendurable poverty it produces, Thornhill finds that his subsequent arrest threatens to separate him from his life and family, leaving him with truly nothing.

His indenture as a convict sentenced to exile with his family in Australia is therefore a perverse blessing, preserving his life, his relationship with his family and his capacity for work. And upon being granted his ticket of leave after a few years, Thornhill is, perhaps for the first time, presented with a situation of real opportunity and choice: in the face of his hitherto defining lack, the reader sympathetically understands the overwhelming seduction presented in the promise of land. Here, Thornhill finally has a chance to grasp at something, to become propertied – a landowner – to erase his ontological emptiness and frustration through an act of appropriation. The reader empathises as Thornhill covets, and eventually claims, a hundred acres of fertile land along the Hawkesbury River. And, like Thornhill, the reader is apprehensive when the indigenous inhabitants first make their appearance in the text, and sensitive to the threat these aboriginal people might pose to Thornhill's new identity as a free propertied settler, making a new life for himself and his family. If *they* belong here, if the land already belongs to *them*, Thornhill's already fragile belonging is suddenly invalidated. The presence of the aborigines threatens to snatch away his claim to this land, to *his* land, leaving him once again with nothing. Unlike Thornhill, however, the reader is doubly apprehensive because the threat of harm is perceived as mutual: the colonising Thornhill threatens the indigenous way of life, just as the indigenous presence and prior occupancy threatens Thornhill and his dreams of self-fulfilment.

Like Thornhill, the reader is immediately and viscerally shocked and repulsed by the way some of Thornhill's neighbours have reacted towards this indigenous presence and the threat of ownership it insinuates. Enslaving, torturing, raping, murdering: these are not initially seen as valid choices of response or modes of interaction by Thornhill. In fact, influenced by the example of his wife,

Sal, Thornhill appears 'tolerant', though still wary, of the presence of the natives, and begins an almost amicable rapport with them, including a rudimentary form of trade. Communication between the Thornhills and the natives remains barred, however, by the *muldarbi* assumptions the Thornhills make about indigenous people, and accordingly, by the attitude of relation they are disposed to practise towards the aboriginal people living on the land with them. Repeatedly, the Thornhills fail to listen to the information freely and generously given by the aborigines: lessons about food sources, about the land, and about indigenous people and their ways. This information is received suspiciously or dismissed outright, the assumption being that such information is culturally inferior, primitive or wrong. Even names of indigenous people are received by the Thornhills in a spirit of ingratitude and denial, and their use of aboriginal language is clumsily clipped and anglicised, made more palatable, but simultaneously refused on 'its own terms and as it speaks to us' (Tully 1995: 23). Only privately can Thornhill admit to a tenuous admiration or respect for indigenous ways – and never can he translate this secret learning into practice, for this would surely permit a cultural exchange that the very procurement of land, on the basis of *civil nullius*, had forbidden.

Once chosen, this colonial attitude of relation involving the denial and annihilation of aboriginal authority and knowledge followed its inevitably nasty trajectory. Faced with the extermination of their customs, their names, their food sources and their living places, the indigenous people resisted by reclaiming spaces for living, by continuing their traditional activities such as burning and assembling for ceremonies, by gathering food on their traditional lands (even when this food was now planted by the settlers), and at times by retaliating against colonial violence with violence. And this indigenous resistance and retaliation was met with increased violence and recalcitrance, the mutual discord finally culminating in the genocide of the indigenous community. The *muldarbi* disposition towards the 'erasure of indigenous being' was thereby made actual in the most horrific and final of ways. The original potential for an enriching cultural exchange posited by the meeting of indigenous and non-indigenous peoples was left unrealised, aborted by the stifling *muldarbi* attitude that was born from colonial desire for appropriation, and the concurrent fear of loss – the fear of the other as the threatening force that steals one's being.

If postcolonisation requires the practical rejection of *terra nullius* and the due recognition of cultural difference, then post-colonial society must responsibly reject the colonial attitude, the *muldarbi* that is the principle of *terra nullius* embodied in colonial social practice. Furthermore, it would seem that postcolonial reconciliation requires the public substitution of an alternative, postcolonial attitude, which does situate individuals in a relation of belonging suited to the task of constituting a postcolonial sociability that caters to the demands of mutual cultural recognition. Reconciliation therefore suggests an opportunity to begin 'a national mind shift' (Dodson 2000: 265), a 'new mode of relating to contemporary reality' (Foucault 1984a), enabling social actors to live according to a postcolonial attitude or ethos. The question remains: what kind of practice would attest to and actualise this postcolonial attitude? What is postcolonial?

James Tully also wonders about the character of this 'critical attitude or *spirit* in which justice can be rendered to the demands for cultural recognition' (1995: 1). He invites his readers to think about Bill Reid's sculpture *The Spirit of Haida Gwaii* as an 'ecumenical symbol for the mutual recognition and affirmation of all cultures that respect other cultures and the earth' (1995: 21).[5] The sculpture is clearly a representation of the capacity indigenous cultures have for survival and revival through hybridisation. It is also read here as a symbol of

> a post-imperial dialogue on the just constitution of culturally diverse societies . . . in which the participants are recognized and speak in their own languages and customary ways. They do not wish either to be silenced or to be recognized and constrained to speak within the institutions and traditions of interpretation of the imperial constitutions that have been imposed over them. (Tully 1995: 24)

Tully believes that the appropriate attitude in which to approach both the sculpture itself, and the 'post-imperial dialogue' it symbolises, is firstly described by a willingness to listen to its culturally diverse spirits. Moreover, this diversity is heard, not by

> recognizing it as something already familiar to us and in terms drawn from our own traditions and forms of thought. This imperial attitude is to be abjured. Rather, recognition involves acknowledging it in its own terms and traditions, as it wants to be and as it speaks to us. (1995: 23)

Leaving aside, for the moment, the problem that indigenous 'terms and traditions' have been seriously damaged by colonisation, and indigenous voices have in some cases been irreparably shattered, for Tully a postcolonial attitude or stance is identified partly as a refusal of the 'empire of uniformity' that characterises modern nationalism as the exclusion or assimilation of cultural diversity to a dominant, normative culture. Indeed, as Tully insists, the creation of an appropriately 'post-imperial' attitude or spirit requires a:

> world reversal, from a habitual imperial stance, where one's own customary forms of reflection set the terms of the discussion, to a genuinely intercultural popular sovereignty where each listens to the voices of the others in their own terms. (1995: 24)

This suggests a shift away from colonial processes and practices of capture, imposition of homogeneity, and exclusion of contesting difference, towards the postcolonial recognition of multiplicity in its variable forms of expression. In so far as Irene Watson's depiction of the *muldarbi terra nullius* describes these characteristically colonial activities, reconciliation suggests the practice of an oppositional attitude, which might be characterised in terms of a 'listening respect', or *miwi-ellin*. This is a Ngarrindjeri phrase explained to me by Victor Wilson: *miwi* means spirit, and *ellin* means 'something like respect in listening and talking . . . the old fellas used it . . . you don't really hear it any more'.[6] The approach suggested by this alternative, postcolonial attitude is one of openness and empathy, requiring of the participants a 'civic ability to see their association from multiple viewpoints' (Tully 1995: 25). It also involves a willingness to question, contest and renegotiate one's own established viewpoint and customary assumptions, with the result that one's identity and the association itself *becomes*, in an 'endless series of contracts and agreements, reached by periodical intercultural dialogue' (Tully 1995: 26).

While postcolonial theory is conventionally concerned with the conditions under which subaltern speech is impossible or becomes possible, a renewed emphasis on the ethics of listening places significant responsibility for postcolonial transformation back onto the settler classes, who have historically neglected their cultural and social obligations to acknowledge the other, on the other's own terms of discourse. Thus, subaltern speech is impossible in so far as it remains unheard or 'insensible' because it is interpreted from an inflexible viewpoint, or with a stubborn ear that is determined to remain deaf. Like Zarathustra, subaltern speech has 'not the mouth for these ears' (Nietzsche 1976: 128). Writing about the hesitant process of postcolonial reconciliation in Australia, Patrick Dodson cautions: 'Unless the dialogue between us is premised on the concept of "the listening heart" then our relationship will remain out of balance and our endeavours will be doomed' (2007: 29). While emphasis on subaltern agency and the revitalisation of speech-forms silenced by colonialism is important in the process of postcolonisation, a similar emphasis on settler agency responsible for cultivating a 'listening heart' is equally important.

For Deleuze, the task of 'making inaudible forces audible' is common to many contemporary domains of engagement, and he cites music, biology and philosophy as examples of disciplines which are beginning to seek ways of joining 'heterogenous, multiple, non-coincident' forces, without imposing 'a common measure' of unification upon those forces. He writes:

> We are all faced with somewhat similar tasks. In philosophy, classical philosophy presents itself with a kind of rudimentary substance of thought, a type of flow that one then attempts to submit to concepts or categories. Yet philosophers are increasingly seeking to elaborate a very complex material of thought to make sensible forces that are not thinkable in themselves... There is no absolute ear; the problem is to have an impossible one – making audible forces that are not audible in themselves. In philosophy, it is the question of an impossible thought; making thinkable through a very complex material of thought forces that are unthinkable. (2007: 160)

Transposed to the realm of post-colonial politics and the process of postcolonisation, this task involves the expression of an 'impossible' unity; elaborating a very complex social fabric, in order to make room for the positive expression of the complexly mixed social identifications and cultural perspectives that comprise postcolonial society, but have traditionally been reduced to a simple and singular form based on colonial interests, interpretations and representations.

The combination of 'subaltern speech' and 'impossible ear' provides the basis for a postcolonial politics and ethics of association grounded in 'listening respect'. Unlike a Derridean 'politics of friendship' where the bond with the other is haunted by the negativity of aporia and the possibility of mourning, which disturbs the self-identity of the desiring subject (Derrida 2005), a Deleuzian 'politics of friendship' concerns a positive experimentation with the associative force of desire. This results in a deterritorialisation of both self and the other, as relational bodies experiment with new combinations of interaction, in order to increase the joyful experience of their association. John Protevi comments:

> When bodies join in the mutual experimental deterritorialisation that is love, we find Deleuze and Guattari's most adventurous concept: the

living, changing, multiplying virtual, the unfolding of the plane of consistency. Love is complexity producing novelty, the very process of life. (2003: 191)

In this way, Protevi notes, Deleuze and Guattari move beyond the practice of deconstruction resulting from 'awareness of the breakdown of consciousness as experience of aporia', and move towards an experimental constructivism which is not simply critical of an existing reality, but also a political exercise of desire, of friendship or love, resulting in a material transformation of this reality (2003: 192). As an example of the practice of this kind of critical/constructive politics of association, Leela Gandhi (2006) points to the experimental and transgressive couplings evidencing 'fin-de-siècle' radicalism aimed at countering colonial social codes of exclusion and segregation. A mindful 'politics of friendship' practised in intimate relations between individuals and in the affective combinations of collective bodies can be a radical force of social critique and transformation, bearing upon the established macropolitical practices and discourses of a society.

According with Foucault's attention to the Kantian conceptualisation of 'attitude', the friendly stance suggested here is firmly grounded in the relational practices of a community. In fact, as argued in Chapter 4, the orientation of a body towards others is qualitatively defined by the nature of its desire. A postcolonial attitude of 'listening respect' is an attitude of desire or association that immediately disposes bodies to act and interact in ways that correspond to their broader desire for a particular kind of social engagement appropriate to a postcolonial way of life. Accordingly, society becomes postcolonial as actors 'practise the spirit they embody' (Tully 1995: 27). The skeleton of an outline to the question 'What is postcolonial?' is here beginning to emerge. Postcolonialism can be thought of as an attitude, or more precisely, the practice of an attitude of listening respect, *miwi-ellin*. This practice is asserted as a critical alternative to the *muldarbi* attitude of *terra nullius* and its associated practices and material structures that constitute colonialism. The performance of this attitude is a choice and a task undertaken by individuals in community with others. It is an attitude of friendly relation or sociability, which becomes sensible only in terms of collective participation. Because the social imaginary is 'constitutive of, not merely reflective of, the forms of sociability in which we live' (Gatens and Lloyd 1999: 143, 140–3), the interrelationships between individual attitudes and collective practices, agency and sociability deny any simple separation of the individual from the community, or any clear opposition between individual and collective freedoms. This means that widely practised individual performances of a postcolonial ethos become actualised as the collective phenomenon of postcolonial society: the institutions, structures and modes of discourse and thought that make possible the *public* performance of a postcolonial ethos and, in turn, provide the context for the ongoing constitution of postcolonial subjectivity. However, as the effect of a relational practice, the actualisation of postcolonial society calls not only for a mindfully exercised subjective choice that puts into practice the form of desire expressed as 'listening respect', but also a common commitment to creating the mutual understandings and the social conditions that reflect, develop, reinforce and support the idea and the attitude of postcoloniality. At a most foundational level, these conditions include the cultivation of cultural intimacy and the conscientious striving towards 'common notions' that provide a joyful basis for mutual agreement. The effort to find mutual understanding and agreement at the complex sites of affective engagement between bodies or communities is a necessary platform for the negotiated development of mediating institutions capable of expressing and 'hearing' diverse cultural and political perspectives.

Cultural intimacy and common notions

Throughout *Multitude*, Hardt and Negri (2004) make reference to a notion of the 'common', which is the emergent product of the activities and labours of the multitude, and simultaneously the contextualising conditions in which all production takes place. While this notion of the 'common' articulates 'the democracy of the multitude as a theoretical possibility', this remains abstract in their discussion, although in the closing pages of the book they signal the need for a 'political standpoint' able to organise the decision-making power of the multitude in a common project they define as 'love' (2004: esp. xi–xvii, 348–9). In the discussion that follows, I will suggest that a 'common notion' *of the postcolonial* is one such 'political standpoint', which then opens onto the concrete task of performing non-imperial interpersonal ethics as well as the strategic material transformation necessary for the expression of postcolonialism as a collective social ethos, that remains implicit but abstract in Negri's and Hardt's terminology of the common, the multitude and love. As we will see, this role of common notions in grounding a perspective for collective social practices guided by an ethics of joy both rests upon and expands the Deleuzian conception of partial subjects and complex encounters, presented in Chapter 5.

From a postcolonial perspective, it is imperative that encounters are *mutually* joyful: that each body is able to exercise its active power of existence and affective capacity; that one body is not destroyed or diminished by the other. If an ethics of complex bodies guided by active joy is to be practically useful in the context of postcolonialism, indigenous and non-indigenous communities must be capable of achieving a sociable quality of agreement and accord at the sites of their affective interactions. This process of seeking agreement and identifying areas of affective compatibility through mutual understanding can be described in terms of the development of 'common notions', which Deleuze explains 'internally determine the mind to understand the agreements of things, as well as their differences and oppositions' (1990: 276).

A common notion is an 'idea of a similarity of composition in existing modes' (Deleuze 1990: 275), and so involves reaching an understanding about which aspects of bodies are compatible and can combine in agreeable ways. In this way, 'a common notion is always the idea of something positive', however the process of finding common notions nonetheless 'begins with bodies very disparate from one another and very opposed to one another' (Deleuze 1990: 285, 281). Indeed, the colonial meeting of indigenous and non-indigenous peoples created a collision of 'very disparate' bodies, which being merely thrown together by geographical and historical circumstance, did not initially actively seek or desire engagement. As Kate Grenville (2005) illustrates in her tale of colonial settlement, each considered the other largely in terms of their opposing ways of being and of doing things; the historical beginnings of the encounter between indigenous and non-indigenous bodies were marked by cultural misunderstanding and mutual incomprehension spawning conflict and disagreement, and at this point in time, it is hard to see where postcolonial compatibility might be forged.

However, over time, post-colonial communities have come to understand each other better, and through the 'slow learning of what agrees with our nature, the slow effort of discovering our joys' (Deleuze 1990: 262), we have begun to identify aspects of our respective bodily compositions that have a similarity and so might form the basis of agreement in our relation with each other. Both indigenous peoples and settler communities are beginning to understand that we often now share a sense of belonging to the land itself (although this sense of belonging might be experienced in culturally different ways), which has at times been recognised in the legislative forms of native and shared title, and in cultural forms of artistic expression including dance, music and art. These last have been vital sites of positive interaction since the earliest days of colonial settlement (Clendinnen 2003), often mutually recognised as sites of shared appreciation, understanding and creative joy.

These instances of joyful encounter occasioning shared understandings of compatible views and practices represent 'common notions'. While initially arising from passive encounters and inadequate ideas rather than from interactions we have deliberately and actively contrived, common notions represent the point at which a common body becomes capable of an active agency of relation and self-assemblage. When joyful affects are produced in us by fortuitous passive encounters, such as occurred when the British arrivals to Australia danced merrily with indigenous welcoming parties on the sands of Botany Bay and Sydney Cove in 1788 (Clendinnen 2003: 8ff.), 'we can form an idea of what is common to some external body and our own', since 'when we encounter a body that agrees with our own, when we experience a joyful passive affection, we are induced to form the idea of what is common to that body and our own' (Deleuze 1990: 279, 281). From this passive joy, then, emerges an understanding of the way a particular aspect of the other's body combines successfully with ours, which is then the basis for an adequate idea, according to which we can begin to shape our encounters in the future. Since it describes that which participating bodies understand to be 'common' in their union, the joyful experience of common notions is necessarily mutual and shared, and so common notions also describe an ontological agreement that might be thought of as a prerequisite for postcolonialism: 'if it be true that two opposed bodies have something in common, one can never . . . be opposed to the other or bad for the other through what it has in common with it' (Deleuze 1990: 281).

However, most significantly, Deleuze's creative interpretation of Spinozan embodiment and the resultant theory of subjectivity elaborated in Chapter 5 allows that the development of common notions as the basis for postcolonial sociability does *not* require us to disavow significant differences between bodies and eliminate sites of disagreement, in favour of a smooth and bland social harmony which simply privileges acts of co-identification. For Deleuze emphasises that bodies meet 'bit by bit' and while their meeting should be guided by common notions, these do not describe how bodies are compatible in their entirety. Rather, common notions describe an emergent understanding of how disparate bodies can join in partial and selective ways at particular sites of affectivity that encourage joyful experiences of the relationship, while avoiding conducting the relation in a way that causes sadness to either body. In this way, 'even in the case of a body that does not agree with our own, and affects us with sadness, we can form an idea of what is common to that body and our own' (Deleuze 1990: 286; also Deleuze and Guattari 1983: 258). A body affected by sadness will come to understand that the particular aspect of the union causing the sad affect is incompatible with its nature. Thus, even in disagreement we can find joy, since 'an active joy always follows from what we understand' (Deleuze 1990: 287). In so far as we understand bodily disagreement to be the cause of sadness, this ceases to be a passion, instead enabling the formation of an adequate idea of our own body and that of the other, and an awareness of how the nature of their respective compositions prohibits their successful combination.

For example, indigenous and non-indigenous peoples have very different understandings about land ownership and use, but these different understandings might be 'combined' via the construction of mediating concepts such as native title, which occupy a space between the two systems of common and indigenous law (Pearson 1997a; see also Patton 2000: 128–31). Deleuze and Guattari name this process 'unnatural participation', by which they mean that even when bodies do not by nature agree, the formation of 'common notions' allows a mutual becoming and a unity that 'expresses them both' (1983: 258). However, the indigenous practice of punitive spearing in preference to incarceration (which is perceived by many indigenous people to be inhumane) is arguably incommensurable with non-indigenous views on bodily integrity and criminal justice; likewise, indigenous systems of kinship, social responsibility and collective care for country based on skin-groups and interconnected systems of belonging enshrined in the laws of the Dreaming, are arguably incompatible with non-indigenous legal traditions based on notions of individual autonomy and transferable property rights. The two systems embody 'conflicting imaginaries' (Gatens 2008).

In reaching an understanding about the incompatibility of such perspectives and practices, it becomes apparent that their combination or unification can only be achieved by the subordination of one viewpoint to the other and the imposition of one set of bodily features on another, thus destroying the composition defining that other body, and so causing sadness. The alternative to this imposition of a sad relation is to resist the attempt to combine incompatible aspects of bodies, for example by instead enabling both indigenous and non-indigenous systems of justice to exist and be self-determining, comprising separate judicial and punitive forms that apply as necessary and relevant, according to the nature of the crime and the identity of the criminal body involved. The challenge we face is to engage each other in ways that will maximise our mutually joyful affects, and minimise disagreeable combinations that reduce the complexity of our co-existence and affect one or both of us with sadness. Bodies meet 'bit by bit': they might joyfully combine where possible, and might seek to reach agreement through persuasive argumentation, but where agreement is not possible, they should avoid coercing an unhappy fit through assimilation, elimination or subordination. Developing adequate understanding of both agreement and disagreement in the various facets of a relationship allows bodies to relate to one another in ways that find joy and avoid unhappy conflict.

I therefore would like to suggest that 'the postcolonial' can usefully be described as a Spinozist 'common notion'. This may be thought of as the point where a post-colonial community engages in the necessary cultural intimacy and the 'listening respect' that allows it to develop a collective awareness of the ways in which the elemental bodies that make it up can be combined without domination and coercion, in partial and selective ways according to their identification of compatible sites of agreement. Conversely, postcolonial sociability is facilitated by a collective awareness of the ways in which interacting communities disagree and should not be forced to unite. The notion of the postcolonial gestures towards a historically different quality of relationship between formerly colonising and colonised bodies, beginning a new kind of sociability that enables their joyful 'compossibility'. This emphasises their capacity to co-exist in a complex national body that maintains the power of each participating body to persevere in being, and which enhances each body in virtue of its participation in the association.

This practice of relation departs or 'exits' from colonial and postcolonial practices and concepts of interaction, which have historically involved the clumsy imposition of one entire body upon another, creating an overall incompatible or sad association marked by the loss of indigenous traditions and their institutionalised disadvantage, as well as by the closed insularity of the colonial culture that steadfastly resisted learning anything from the indigenous knowledge it supplanted. There is no realistic option of ending the association that was born with colonisation: in post-colonial nations, indigenous and non-indigenous bodies occupy the same territory; each experiences a significant sense of belonging. In fact, this sense of belonging or situation is something we now have in common. The challenge we face is to develop compatible ways of *belonging together*, which refrain from destroying the potentially joyful complexity of our association by compelling incompatible and uncomfortable unifications at the sites where we disagree, and which instead will positively enrich both communities as we selectively gain from each other's traditions, forming new and more complex practices of interaction and belonging. Postcolonial reconciliation involves both indigenous and non-indigenous bodies in a process of becoming-compatible by joining in affirming and selective ways, drawing from a 'common notion' of the postcolonial, itself guided by an ethic of joy bringing 'compossibility'.

In fact, concrete examples of the postcolonial as a 'common notion' of compatible engagement already exist in the form of 'mediating' concepts and practices, such as native and shared title, which 'stand midway between the traditional owners on the one hand and non-indigenous institutions on the other' (Webber 2000: 86). The elaboration of similar concepts, institutions and practices that can successfully mediate the diverse scope of the interface between indigenous and non-indigenous ways of being, making them 'compossible', constitutes the practical dimension of postcolonisation, which globally, has scarcely begun.

Becoming-minor and mediation

As a movement that ends colonial ways of being and begins postcolonial social practice, postcolonisation offers a moment of discontinuity; it recommends a 'way out' of the conventions and habits of practice characteristic of past colonial histories. Postcolonial difference can be conceptualised as the creation of new styles of social assemblage – conducted within a contextualising cultural milieu also enabling new modes of subject-formation – and as a chosen practice of a postcolonial attitude which social agents are responsible for performing (see Burney 2000). This particular attitude can be exemplified as a 'respectful listening' to others, which in practice requires mutual cultural intimacy and enables a kind of social organisation reflecting the peaceful co-existence of self-determining societies that engage in affirmative acts of mutual recognition. In this way, 'the postcolonial' may be considered alongside those events identified by Kant as a contemporary moment of developing collective awareness that attests to the existence of a permanent virtual and immanent, causal disposition towards progressive Enlightenment. However, postcolonialism requires not only that our immediate social attitudes and relations be mindfully transformed, but also that the interface between indigenous and non-indigenous legal and political institutions be revised to allow the genuine expression of mutual recognition and respect. As Dale Turner writes:

> If we want a relationship of peaceful coexistence with Aboriginal peoples, then we must change our attitudes about them and their cultures. How to move this imperative into the public space, especially into our legal and political practices, is a serious challenge . . . one with both philosophical and practical dimensions. (2001: 322)

In Deleuzian parlance, postcolonisation begins a 'bloc' of becoming-minor that operates between settler and colonised communities and prompts the transformation of all aspects of their relationship, at each of the mediating sites of their affective engagement (Deleuze and Guattari 1987: 232ff.). Here, 'minor' does not refer to 'minority groups' identified in terms of number or degrees of political representation, but rather is a qualitative term indicating a position 'which deviates from the majority or standard which is the bearer of the dominant social code . . . [and which] provides an element capable of deterritorialising the dominant social codes' (Patton 2000: 7). Becoming-minor is the creative process that 'runs between' established positions, and which significantly 'involves the subjection of the standard [majority] to a process of continuous variation or deterritorialisation' (Patton 2000: 48). For Deleuze and Guattari (1987: 238), 'every becoming is a bloc of coexistence' and as a process of becoming-minor, postcolonisation offers both indigenous and non-indigenous peoples an opportunity to redefine their modes of co-existence in ways that contest and transform post-colonial culture, social structures and the colonial identifications, norms and assumptions these continue to rely upon.

In this way, postcolonialism is the 'minor', 'uncommon' or 'untimely' relationship between bodies, which exists as a virtual alternative to our current forms of social arrangement and so contests and transforms the established colonial and post-colonial forms of subjectivity, sociability and culture, and which becomes actual through practice and repetition. As part of this cultural becoming, postcolonialism draws attention to the relational aspects of selfhood, both on the level of interaction between individuals, and also on the more abstract level of cultural interaction between the collective entities of 'non-indigenous' and 'indigenous' communities. As a process of becoming-minor, postcolonial reconciliation necessarily refuses the impulse to coerce a unified national identity that encompasses all possible differences. In fact, postcolonialism properly calls for the construction of that which Henry Giroux refers to as:

> a notion of border identity that challenges any essentialized notion of subjectivity while simultaneously demonstrating that the self as a historical and cultural formation is shaped in complex, related, and multiple ways through their interaction with numerous and diverse communities. (Giroux 1993: 10)

Interactive relations not only enable identification; they simultaneously promise the permanent possibility of creating and transforming identity when the alliances that constitute these interstitial spaces between bodies undergo a critical shift. In these creative spaces mediating the interface where identities meet, new modes of social existence and practice can arise, through the mutual becomings produced by the encounter. For Tully, the direction of this creative practice of intersubjective becoming is the role to be played by the 'mediator' in a politics of mutual cultural recognition. This mediating character embodies the 'spirit' or 'attitude' towards others that is appropriate, even necessary, for postcolonial practices. The mediator is a figure who is able to put into practice the process of reflexive becoming through ethical associations with others, and thus who is able to 'show others how to act appropriately within the complex politics of cultural recognition' (Tully 1995: 211–12). However, as Dale Turner (2001) points out, the 'mediator' position may require various approaches, depending on the complexity of the mediator's identification with the identities she combines. In other words, the variety of subject positions and identifications produced in the legacy of colonial history suggests different agencies of response are required in bringing about the postcolonial 'becoming' of the existing relationship; furthermore, these different, possibly conflicting terms of response must be successfully negotiated and mediated in a non-imperial way, finding complex forms of agreement based upon mutual recognition.

What is 'Postcolonial'?

As we have seen, for Deleuze a body is at one and the same time an individual and a collective, being any stable form comprised of elemental parts joined in consistent relations of force. Accordingly, becoming-minor is a process that takes place between all types of relative bodies as they come into contact with one another and create new hybrid forms through their engagement: selves, philosophies, languages, cultures, systems of law and governance can all be subjected to a process of flight and affective reconfiguration as their constituting elements recombine to form new complex assemblages with other bodies. Postcolonial engagements thus call for forms of mutual cultural recognition that are able to register and moderate the complex and uneven interaction of indigenous and settler worlds and worldviews at their multiple sites of conjunction.

In some respects, a movement towards this type of cultural recognition was begun in Australia in 1992, at the time of the High Court's decision with respect to the *Mabo* case. In refuting *terra nullius* in terms of indigenous land ownership, the *Mabo* judgement provided an indirect challenge to the perceived legitimacy of the British colonial assertion of sovereignty over Australian territories (Reynolds 1996; Nettheim 1993).[7] In recognising the prior existence and continuation of native title, the court recognised the prior existence and continuation of indigenous custom and law as a source of native title, and of indigenous polities as sources of indigenous law. For this reason, it has been suggested that *Mabo* impacts upon certain assumptions underlying Australian constitutionalism (Webber 2000; see also Djerrkura 1999). In recognising, albeit covertly, the continuing relevance of indigenous legal and political traditions, *Mabo* underscores the need to restructure the relationship between the co-existing indigenous and non-indigenous societies in a way that respects their partially autonomous legal, political and cultural systems. Acknowledging the partial autonomy of these orders affirms the mutual influence of their interaction in the period since the British invasion. Further, by acknowledging that autonomy is partial and relative, indigenous and non-indigenous Australians admit that their respective and distinctive traditions must operate within the context of continuing interaction between their communities. The constitutional significance of *Mabo* is precisely that it foregrounds the opportunity to reinterpret this relationship on a different foundation from that previously provided by *terra nullius* and its attendant framework of assumptions and institutional supports. This is the primary impulse behind calls for a treaty document between indigenous and non-indigenous peoples. *Mabo* clearly reiterates the need for a negotiated settlement of the terms of their continuing relationship, as well as the constitutional protection of the rights and responsibilities outlined by the agreement.[8] Gatjil Djerrkura suggests that constitutional reform should refrain from developing an 'extensive catalogue of Indigenous rights for inclusion in the Constitution' (1999: 12). Instead, the emphasis should be upon the creation of open-ended principles which define a relationship capable of recognising the possible 'multiple futures' self-determining communities might decide for themselves in the mediated context of their continuing traditions and their respectful interaction with other communities.[9]

In *Strange Multiplicity*, Tully outlines open-ended principles enabling this kind of politics of mutual cultural recognition. He acknowledges that particular demands for cultural recognition may clash violently when they are asserted against each other in a 'cacophony of heterogenous claims' (1995: 5). However, his primary aim is to identify a common form to the politics of cultural recognition, by articulating 'disregarded resemblances' and shared objectives across diverse political and cultural groupings. Accordingly, he asserts that diverse demands by various cultural groups have a common inspiration: '[W]hat they share is a longing for self rule: to rule themselves in accord with their customs and ways' (1995: 6). This commonality unites otherwise disparate cultural and political groupings in terms of a common political goal of self-determination. The nature of this goal also enables Tully to situate the politics of cultural recognition as a latest phase within the anti-imperialist trajectory (see also Djerrkura 1999: 8). The demand for cultural recognition is part of an enduring struggle for liberty from cultural domination, assimilation and exclusion; the self-conscious creation of public institutions that foster mutual cultural recognition enables 'the expression of a genuinely post-imperial age' (Tully 1995: 17). Furthermore, institutional expression of mutual cultural recognition actualises the social disposition towards the provision of 'a political constitution which appears good to the people itself' and which 'avoids all possibility of offensive war', identified by Kant in the context of Enlightenment.

Tully proposes three principles of non-imperial association: recognition, consent and continuity. While I cannot hope to do justice to a proper consideration of these here, I want to suggest that the Deleuzian ontology we have traversed offers potential for expanded interpretation of these principles, promising new scope for their expression in a postcolonial context. Of his three principles, Tully identifies 'recognition' as the most 'difficult' to realise. He cites many reasons why cultural recognition has frequently been denied in Western political practice, including 'the pursuit of property and the splendour of empire, the misunderstanding and fear of others different from oneself', and the very 'language' of constitutionalism, which privileges identity and uniformity (1995: 198). Similarly here, in Chapters 1 and 2, I made the argument that 'recognition' is a concept that has often been problematically conceived in Western philosophy because it is grounded in a particular ontology of desire, identity and difference, each intimately bonded with a causal and generative ontological negativity. According to this ontology, the recognition the other affords me is both satisfying and threatening: I rely upon the other to substantiate me and alleviate my ontological emptiness and alienation, but the other embodies a difference that contests the fullness and adequacy of my identity and so also threatens to undo me, or else to 'recognise' me in a way that I do not like.

Deleuzian ontology offers an alternative view of desire, relational selfhood and satisfaction, which corresponds with an alternative form of recognition. I recognise others exactly as I recognise myself; we are complex bodies that have been creatively produced through the positive generative force of desiring-production and the constructive process of different/ciation. Because we are each identified in terms of the affections that result from our relations, I recognise others in terms of the affects our relationship produces, and so I look for the agreements I may potentially form with them; at the same time, I interpret the other in terms of the ways in which we obviously disagree and will not happily combine. However, because my identity is determined by the ways in which I combine with the other, and my identity expands and becomes more complex and joyful as I develop more complex relations and actively chosen affections, the other is not naturally threatening to me but instead primarily offers me an opportunity to assemble myself in increasingly complex, compatible and joyful ways. In recognising that my relations with others are always partial, that we combine in selective ways and can sensibly avoid imposing upon each other at the sites where our bodily compositions disagree, my recognition of the complex composition embodied in the form of the other is the basis for a politics of joyful assemblage and an ethics of care. It benefits me to understand the other in order to recognise properly the complexity of the other and so learn how we might successfully unite compatible aspects of our bodies for mutual benefit, and conversely, to realise when our combination in particular respects will cause discomfort or despair and is best avoided. I can only understand the other well by practising a listening respect and learning. In this way, the Deleuzian ontology of actualisation and complex identification through selective association might be mobilised as a response to the 'real complexity' of the post-colonial world, which Duncan Ivison insists must be a starting point for postcolonial political philosophy:

> More complex and multilayered forms of political identification and association need to be developed in order to cope with the real complexity ... [of the social world] ... Hybrid political institutions and associations – both domestic and international – are needed to accommodate increasingly hybrid people. (Ivison 2002: 48)

Tully's second constitutional principle of 'consent' is, of course, well established in liberal political theory as a principle of the legitimacy of political institutions, and Ivison's discussion in *Postcolonial Liberalism* is centrally focused upon this concept. For Ivison, the complexity of post-colonial polities and the political reality of conflict and disagreement that contests identity and uniformity entails that genuine consensus is practically impossible to reach; accordingly, he proposes the need to think in terms of a 'discursive *modus vivendi*' in order to find provisional 'agreements that do not overidealize consensus' (2002: 73). While it is not clear, and I think it is quite doubtful, that the Deleuzian ontology of complex relation and affective individuality presented here can easily be incorporated into liberalism (even if this is a radically transformed liberalism), there is certainly room in this ontology of association for a principle of consent that is generally consistent with Ivison's rendition of consensus in *Postcolonial Liberalism* and with Tully's in *Strange Multiplicity*, as forms of provisional and partial agreement solicited through negotiation.

At heart, liberal consent involves a 'liberty to engage in self-rule' (Tully 1995: 184); to decide the terms of one's political identifications and the circumstances in which one's freedoms might be curtailed for the common benefit. However, as Ivison notes, if liberalism is to avoid the charge of 'atomism' it must acknowledge that selves are 'permeable' and 'mediated' by their social context (Ivison 2002: 50–2); for Ivison, Tully and others, the liberty of consent then properly involves rationalising negotiated forms of agreement regarding norms and rules of engagement that emerge from collective practices in particular circumstances. According to the Deleuzian ontology of complex selfhood defined through association, liberty is similarly found in one's capacity for active decision-making in one's chosen practices of assemblage and composition. If liberty is a 'right', then it is on this view a 'right' to form the assemblages one chooses; that is, as much as is possible from within the constraints of one's limited understanding of oneself and others, and one's complex relations of determination with and by others, one will rightfully seek to associate freely with other bodies in ways that enable joyful combinations and avoid harmful ones. However, as we have seen, my liberty of self-determination does not properly involve me deciding which social bodies to associate with and which to avoid altogether (since these bodies are always already encountered as the contextualising social milieu that a self is constituted in and by), but rather which *partial aspects* of another body encountered in my environment I understand can be actively selected for association with me, on the basis of their suitability for creating a more complex and joyful composition that adds to us both, or rejected on the basis that the combination that results will be detrimental to one or both bodies.

As eternal principles observing fixed and inalienable qualities of human nature and dignity, established notions of 'human rights' clearly do not accord with this Deleuzian ontology since, as we have seen, Deleuze conceptualises bodies as multi-faceted, internally unstable, conflicted and complex assemblages characterised by their mutating affective relations with other bodies. While it remains beyond the scope of this work to develop properly a Deleuzian perspective on rights or political society, it is important to note that his approving comments on jurisprudence as the ongoing creation or modification of legal principles on a case by case basis, 'make it clear that Deleuze is not opposed to rights as such but only to the idea that there exists a definitive set of human rights grounded in some rights-bearing feature of human nature' (Patton 2005a: 405; see Lefebvre 2005, 2008). For Deleuze, 'there are no "rights of man," only "rights of life", and so, life unfolds case by case' (Deleuze and Parnet 2003). This perspective on rights corresponds to his ontology, which as we have seen, considers bodies to be 'infinite multiplicities' enmeshed in affective relations of power, which are multi-levelled and shift according to changing engagements with other bodies in a social milieu, thus taking form according to the internal composition of a body at a particular time. Because affective relations are variable and contextual, and power is simultaneously a force of composition and of decomposition affecting participating bodies at multiple sites of engagement, the 'rightful' limits to the impact of one body's powers upon another can only be decided according to the context of the situation in which their meeting occurs. In this way, 'Our ability to resist control, or our submission to it, has to be assessed at the level of our every move' (Deleuze 1995: 176).

For Deleuze and Guattari, as well as for Foucault, fluid micropolitical relations between bodies act as scaffolding for the emergence of more rigid macropolitical structures and conventions such as rights and political institutions servicing public debate and distributive justice (Deleuze and Guattari 1983: 213–28; Guattari 1984; Foucault 1990: 93; see also Connolly 1999, 2008; Patton 2004, 2005b; Lefebvre 2008; Golder and Fitzpatrick 2009). According to the logic of 'becoming', 'emergence' or 'actualisation', careful forms of sociability practised at the micropolitical level are conducive to the development of macrostructures that institutionalise and entrench these norms within political society as formal guiding principles for just and ethical action. On this view, a right is best seen as a 'political invention [requiring] a whole lot of micropolitical preparation' (Connolly 2008: 234). Rights, as established principles of engagement, then act back upon the relations acted out at the micropolitical level, guiding and protecting bodies in their fluid and immediate relations of practice. The complex interplay between micropolitical and macropolitical levels of society constitutes the intricate movement that Deleuze names 'folding'. This 'folding' is important because careful sociability and 'listening respect' are not guaranteed at the micropolitical level, and bodies frequently find themselves immobilised and constrained by macropolitical structures that may have emerged from original benevolence; care and attentiveness alone is insufficient as a basis for satisfying relations and protection from political abuse. Agreed principles of justice are additionally needed to regulate micropolitical engagements between bodies; to formally safeguard participating bodies from wholesale destruction and protect the *mutuality* of their affectivity and becoming. Furthermore, institutions of public reason and deliberation are required for the incremental development of 'common notions' that might define an emergent understanding of 'rights' and 'norms' as necessary principles for guiding the negotiations and mediations between relative bodies engaged in relations of power, as they work towards reaching consent and agreement about the ways in which their complex interaction might proceed with a maximum mutual benefit and minimum harm.

However, bodies must rightfully consent not only to the associations they might form, but also to the ways in which these associations can prompt new kinds of affection or ways of being affected resulting in radical bodily transformations. This principle of just relationship between bodies is recognised in Tully's third principle of 'continuity', which acknowledges one's bodily right to preserve an existing form of identity without destruction resulting from an association imposed upon this body by another. In the context of our reading of Deleuzian affective embodiment, the need to preserve a 'sense of self' that can provide an anchor for the reasoned development of common notions and protect a body from radical debilitation and collapse during its processes of becoming informs a normative dimension to Deleuze's perspective on bodily assemblage and transformation. This is discernible in comments made throughout his work, stemming from his early reading of Spinoza where he writes: 'All a body can do (its power) is also its "natural right"' (Deleuze 1990: 257). By this he means that any particular body has a 'natural right' actively to form associations that will allow it both to persevere in select aspects of its being *and* to enhance its affective power, according to its *conatus*. In so far as the development of common notions is central to this emergent rational activity of self-formation that gradually develops from one's passive affections, it follows that some core structure or consistency is also rightfully required to persist through the body's transformations, in order for it to be able to form adequate ideas and common notions by coherently 'thinking the body' and the nature of the relations it forms with others. Accordingly, the nature of the body as an affective assemblage also 'constitutes what can be called *a right to desire*' (Deleuze and Parnet 1987: 147): all bodies have the right to exercise discretion and preference in forming and transforming the situations and associations that constitute their identity, and this activity is normatively guided by the development of adequate ideas of selfhood, common notions of relationship, and the experience of joy. Clearly, the colonial seizure of territory and the forcible removal of indigenous peoples from their traditional lands and children from their communities, forbidding the continuity of their associations with family and territory, with their religious practices and their own languages, demonstrates a comprehensive failure to respect this 'right to desire'.

As a result of this past injustice and the imposition of a sad and oppressive relationship that resulted in the discontinuity of indigenous enjoyment because of the forced destruction and debilitation of collective indigenous bodies, indigenous and non-indigenous communities must now find ways to meet in a contemporary situation that is deeply scarred by the history of colonisation. Indigenous 'terms and traditions' have been seriously damaged by colonisation, and indigenous voices have in some cases been irreparably silenced. We do not currently meet on equal footing, since one community has emerged from the experience of colonisation diminished, fragmented, curtailed and controlled, while the other enjoys a legacy of historical privilege incorporating a relative freedom to act at will without cultural temperance or due accountability. In assessing the 'rightful limits' to our current affective impact upon one another, we must first assess our differing abilities to 'resist control' in light of the history that has brought us to our current state of engagement; we must look at how the scars have been etched over time, and with the benefit of hindsight we might come to appreciate the depth and nature of the injury, and the scope and nature of the redress that is required if indigenous communities are to redevelop a cohesive (though not fixed or essential) sense of self. This primary 'sense of self' is required if we are to connect with and affect one another on a more equal basis, properly sharing in the postcolonial production of common notions according to which our bodies are able actively to meet 'bit by bit' in ways that partially transform them both, bringing mutual joy and avoiding debilitating sadness and destruction. Hindsight allows an appreciation of how our historical engagements might have been more careful and more respectful, in turn allowing a vision of how things might alternatively have taken place and form, in turn allowing better understanding of the present in terms of its wounds and its potential for healing, prompting redress for the painful wrongs of the past and shaping postcolonial transformation for the future:

> Inquiry into our confused beginnings suggests that the possibility of a decent co-existence between unlike groups must begin from the critical scrutiny of our own assumptions and values as they come under challenge. We might then be able to make informed decisions as to which uncomfortable differences we are prepared to tolerate and which we are not, rather than to attempt the wholesale reformation of what we identify as the defects of the other. A lasting tolerance builds slowly out of accretions of delicate accommodations made through time; and it comes, if it comes at all, as slow as honey. (Clendinnen 2003: 288)

While this may be so, in post-colonial law, considerable consternation arises with respect to the notion of 'continuity' in the face of colonial disruption. It is unclear whether certain rights can be understood to continue through discontinuous historical epochs when the bases or sources of those rights – identified with indigenous traditions and territories – have been radically disrupted. In Australia, the Supreme Court's judgements in the cases of *Mabo* and *Wik* affirmed that antecedent native title rights survive the imposition of British sovereignty. Furthermore, the court acknowledged the existence and survival of indigenous systems of law and governance as the source of native title. This would seem to rely upon a version of historical process that allowed for the continuity of these rights and structures. How is legislative continuity able to be reconciled with Foucault's and Deleuze's privileging of historical *discontinuity*, both philosophically and practically?

One possible response to this problem is implicit in Deleuze's and Foucault's models of history, which as we have seen, distinguish between virtual reality as an open, continuous and permanent presence, and actual reality as discrete, contingent and discontinuous manifestations of this permanent virtuality. On this view, it is possible to identify, for example, indigenous interests in land as having a permanent, though virtual existence, which may or may not be actually recognised by others and protected in the form of native title rights. The failure to recognise these interests in actual legal practice does not, however, diminish or extinguish their continuing existence as a real, though currently virtual, fact. Furthermore, if, as Kant asserts, there is evidence for a permanent human disposition towards social arrangements that are peaceful and self-determining, the permanence of this disposition derives from its virtuality and its indetermination in fact. The disposition towards peaceful self-determination exists as a virtual foundation for all societies, however it refrains from specifying the actual forms in which this tendency might be realised. Indeed, as Foucault appreciates, the virtual disposition cannot be specified in terms of actual forms, because this would contradict the principle of self-determination that the virtual disposition comprises. The permanence of this disposition grounds a historical continuity, while the contingency of the actual forms in which the disposition becomes realised is a source of the potential for historical discontinuity.

Accordingly, claims about antecedent and continuing native title and self-determination rights are claims that, at the time of colonisation, indigenous communities were self-determining, with legal traditions connected to their social interactions and their occupation of specific territories. While colonisation introduced (and imposed) a radical discontinuity in actual forms of affective identification when indigenous peoples began entirely new ways of interacting with non-indigenous peoples, their cultures and their institutions, the virtual disposition of indigenous peoples to be self-determining remains. Similarly, we might now expect postcolonisation to introduce a radical discontinuity into our current actual social forms and habits of interaction, but hopefully this difference will be one that better actualises the permanent virtual disposition to self-determination and mutual cultural recognition that, according to Kant, suggests a continuous, immanent cause of social progress.

However, a Deleuzian principle of continuity will not recognise an associated right with respect to an unchanging bodily identity stemming from pre-contact existence and continuing unchanging (even if unacknowledged) through colonisation. For Deleuze, identity constantly shifts and transforms because a body is defined by the affective relations into which it enters. Thus, Deleuzian 'rights' concerning continuity will not stem from fixed forms of identity and associated traditions, but from agreed emergent rules of association that set limits to the kinds of transformations a body can be made to endure. In fact, the complex nature of this sort of continuity is acknowledged in much current understanding about the mediated nature and content of indigenous title, which in effect works as a 'recognition concept' between the two systems of Indigenous and non-Indigenous law (Pearson 1997a). Jeremy Webber writes:

> The content of indigenous title is not simply a carry-forward of what was before; the very content of indigenous title has been marked by its encounter with non-indigenous society. This is true not just in the cataclysmic sense that some indigenous rights have been extinguished. Rather, the very content of the rights has been transformed through a process of translation and re-expression (2000: 64).

In other words, although in its *Mabo* decision the Australian High Court acknowledged that the laws and customs of indigenous societies are the creative source of native title, recognition by the common law is necessary for this title to have a continuing relevance in contemporary decisions about land use and ownership. In this way, native title mediates the two bodies of law in Australia, and in the process of their association via this mediating concept, both bodies are transformed as they participate in the 'becoming-minor' of Australian jurisprudence following the *Mabo* decision. In the case of indigenous law, the expression of a fundamental interest in the land as 'title rights' meaningfully arose only in the context of colonisation, which introduced the need for the protection of those interests from an encroaching and appropriating external body (McNeill 1997; Pearson 1997a). The rules of land use hitherto regulated by indigenous laws of social interaction, custom and co-existence were not prepared for the messy reality of invasion, were not conceptualised as rights against infringement, and did not have the appropriate structure for accommodating international relations of the sort introduced with colonisation. Native title, then, while having its source in indigenous law, is not 'of' indigenous law. Neither is it 'of' the common law, which upon the recognition and affirmation of antecedent native title in the *Mabo* and *Wik* decisions was forced to abandon certain primary assumptions about its own nature and integrity. Webber explains:

> *Mabo* involved a reconsideration of the feudal foundations of Australian land law, with the radical title of the Crown being taken henceforth as a national attribute of sovereignty and an abstract postulate of the doctrine of tenures, rather than an irrebuttable presumption that absolute beneficial ownership had been held, at some historical moment, by the Crown ... The common law thereby made room for a kind of title that had its roots outside the system, in the pre-contact legal orders of the indigenous peoples. (2000: 69)

Furthermore, the *Mabo* decision additionally forced the common law to accommodate a shift in its usual understanding about the nature of property entitlement, since native title is held in common by an indigenous community, rather than being the preserve of individual owners. However, as Webber again points out:

> [T]he 'collective' nature of indigenous title is an implicit recognition of the political and legal autonomy of indigenous societies, not a description of the actual form of landholding practised within them. The tenure is 'collective' because the common law treats the land as the province of the community concerned; any internal allocation is left to the community. (2000: 71)

This once again emphasises that the significance of the *Mabo* decision lies in its recognition that Australian society is comprised of coexisting, partially autonomous societies, each with its own system of government and law, which interact in complex, selective and partial ways. In recognising both the existence of these discrete bodies and the fact of their relationship and co-existence, the *Mabo* decision makes apparent the pressing need better to define the complex terms of the relationship, and to create concepts and structures that will properly allow for both autonomy and interdependence in the administration of the continuing interaction between the societies. In this way, native title is only one of a range of 'mediating concepts' that will be required as indigenous and non-indigenous bodies globally seek to define the terms of their cohabitation. Much is yet to be invented, including mediating structures of 'shared sovereignty', which necessarily depart from traditional indigenous notions of government, but also depart from traditional Western notions of indivisible authority invested in a singe power (Patton 1996a). A mediating concept of this sort requires the sound dismissal of the notion of unified national identity, with the acknowledgement that there are many co-existing narratives of nationhood that we assemble in context-dependent circumstances in order to define contemporary experiences of collective existence. In short:

> [I]nstitutions have to be developed to provide for the effective management of the indigenous/non-indigenous divide – institutions that can hold indigenous resources, while relating to the broader society in a manner that non-indigenous law can accommodate; structures that can protect indigenous interests in lands that are subject to joint indigenous/non-indigenous use. (Webber 2000: 85)

In fact, some mediating institutional structures already exist, for example in the form of the Land Councils that have been created to deal with native title claims. These structures 'stand midway between the traditional owners on the one hand and non-indigenous institutions on the other' (Webber 2000: 86). They require a departure from traditional indigenous forms of authority with respect to land use, since the Council members are drawn from a collection of indigenous communities, and therefore decisions made about a particular territory will include input from indigenous individuals who are not the traditional owners of that territory. Nonetheless, through the Councils, indigenous peoples collectively regain control of their lands, and in a way that also partly accommodates the reality of dislocation and dispossession following colonisation. Land Councils are thus examples of mediating structures that can effectively accommodate specifically indigenous interests, such as native title, by creating an institutional form of their expression and recognition that is accommodated within the structures and norms of liberal democracy.

However, a postcolonial 'politics of becoming' may well extend beyond the creation of structures that take form easily within the existing and dominant modes of government and systems of political thought imported with colonialism, because mediation takes place according to the partial and complex engagements of bodies, which calls for 'a negotiated and always contestable set of entry, exit and reversal points between liberal and indigenous normative orders' (Ivison 2002: 162). It is beyond the scope of this project to evaluate the relationship between liberalism and colonialism and to decide whether a transformed liberalism can feasibly accommodate claims for cultural recognition, as Ivison and others assert that it can. While I agree with Bhikhu Parekh when he notes that liberalism becomes illiberal when the 'determining principle' is 'arbitrarily imposed by a narrowly defined liberalism' (1995: 97), and while I am certainly sympathetic to the construction of a more expansive and postcolonial liberalism such as that described by Ivison, I worry that liberalism remains grounded in an ontology that associates difference with a negativity it seeks to limit (see Coole on Kant 2000: 13–43); and so I suspect that, like the dialectical philosophy explored here in Chapters 1 and 2, liberalism tends to reinforce imperial assumptions and attitudes at the heart of existence.

Accordingly, I have here taken an alternative view that the conventional liberal principles of consent, recognition and continuity that support self-determination can be better expressed in postcolonialism, not only with respect to a clearly socialist ontology of relational selves and constitutive communities, but also one which also allows a positive role for difference, which in postcolonial philosophy surely should not be seen primarily as a force of conflict to be eliminated, curtailed or managed. In this work, I have argued that the positive ontological perspective on difference described in the work of Deleuze might be usefully put to work in the context of developing a postcolonial political philosophy that actively welcomes relations with the other, rather than foregrounding and normalising a naturalised social ontology of conflict and disagreement (cf. Ivison 2002: 73). On my view, the creation of mediating structures will most sensibly produce the 'becoming-minor' of the majoritarian (liberal) basis of contemporary post-colonial ways of living and of thinking, as conventional patterns of existence and habits of thought are mindfully transformed through the new affective relations that develop through new styles and forms of contact. Mediating structures can provide a degree of historical continuity, recognising and affirming the ongoing interests and values of the respective communities, and in some instances conventional principles of relationship, including liberal principles, will be retained. However, postcolonial processes of mediating transformation will simultaneously introduce a significant discontinuity into colonial and post-colonial history, as they begin a process of negotiation, adjudication and creative accommodation in the way these principles are defined, supplemented by new ideas, and reassembled into entirely new bodies of postcolonial thought and practice. With the creation of mediating structures and 'middle' ways of thinking and understanding, postcolonial society engages in 'both ways' learning (Ivison 2002: 1), which both affirms the continuing relationship between indigenous and non-indigenous peoples and also radically alters the nature and the philosophical basis of this relationship as it has historically been conceived. Postcolonial mediation of this sort accordingly recognises the 'right to desire' and the 'right to bodily continuity' that I have suggested are implicit within the Deleuzian philosophy of affective embodiment.

While a theory of rights and a supporting concept of democratic political society remains undeveloped in Deleuze's work, there is arguably room to develop aspects of his thought towards a more comprehensive notion of rights as emergent 'common notions', which can enable and safeguard the active processes of self-development and joyful practice that are characteristically destroyed by acts of colonisation. Without doubt, Deleuzian philosophy also offers concepts of selfhood and sociability that are useful in the context of creating non-imperial styles of thought and practice. Because his intellectual lineage situates him in a minor philosophical tradition that he incorporates and also creatively transforms in his own oeuvre, many of Deleuze's concerns and concepts are not restricted by the dominant emphases and the entrenched terms of debate of much Western political theory, and at least in some respects, can be made to accord with recent attempts made by Tully, Ivison and others to 'postcolonise' liberalism; although in my view the kind of ontological scaffolding required in order for societies to welcome this postcolonial 'becoming' transforms liberal philosophy beyond recognition as such. In this respect, Deleuze's work might be seen to offer Western theory an exit from its habitual terms of reference, which often cause it to remain fettered to problematic notions of identity and difference, and limit its effectiveness in assisting the birth of new forms of postcolonial society. In this chapter I have argued that Deleuze's concept of embodiment as a process of complex affective assemblage enables an understanding of relational selfhood that gives rise to an ethic of joyful sociability based on material practices

What is 'Postcolonial'?

of self-awareness, listening respect and attentiveness to the other. In this way, Deleuzian philosophy supports forms of social practice that potentially guide us towards the joyful experience promised by a common notion of the postcolonial. In beginning to outline some content that might usefully inform this common notion of postcolonialism, I have appealed to an idea central to the tradition of Enlightenment; that we ought to alter mindfully our relationships in a way that actualises the universal disposition to social accord, mutual recognition and self-determination. This disposition has always been available to us, but we must struggle to enact it in our chosen practices, both individual and collective, by maintaining an attitude of relation in which each acknowledges that the other has something to say, and listens respectfully to the other.

Notes

1. Aspects of this chapter draw from ideas first expressed in Bignall and Galliford (2003) and incorporate parts of the chapter published as Bignall (2010).
2. This is Kant's argument, not Foucault's; however I believe that Foucault is here reading Kant in order to point to a concept of progress that is consistent with his own theory of history as discontinuity. Nonetheless, he insists that this kind of progress is not the only cause of history, and is not inevitable, only permanently possible, as we will see below.
3. This agonism is Nietzschean, not Hegelian: it is neither dialectical nor teleological. For a general discussion of Foucault and agonism, see Pickett (1996).
4. In this particular sense, 'attitude' is a profoundly political conceptual tool, contrary to the argument put forward by John Fielder (1996).
5. Tully (1995: 17–18) describes the sculpture as

> a black bronze canoe, over nineteen feet in length, eleven feet wide, and twelve feet high, containing thirteen passengers, *sghaana* (spirits or myth creatures) from Haida mythology . . . *Xuuwaji*, the bear mother who is part human and bear father sit facing each other at the bow with their two cubs between them. *Tsaang*, the beaver, is paddling menacingly amidships, *qqaaxhadajaat*, the mysterious, intercultural dogfish woman, paddles just behind him and *Qaganjaat*, the shy but beautiful mouse woman is tucked in the stern. *Ghuuts*, the ferociously playful wolf, sinks his fangs in the eagle's wing and *Ghuut*, the eagle, seems to be attacking the bear's paw in retaliation. *Hlkkyaan qqusttaan*, the frog, who symbolizes the ability to cross boundaries (*xhaaidla*) between worlds, is, appropriately enough, partially in and out of the boat. Further down in

the canoe, the ancient reluctant conscript, brought on board from Carl Sandburg's poem, 'Old Timers', paddles stoically (up to a point). *Xuuya*, the legendary raven – the master of tricks, transformations and multiple identities – steers the canoe as her or his whim dictates. Finally, in the centre of this motley crew, holding the speaker's staff in his right hand, stands *Kilstlaai*, the chief or exemplar, whose identity, due to his kinship to the raven (often called *Nangkilstlas*, the One who gives orders) is uncertain.

The name of the sculpture means 'the spirit of the home of the people'.

6. Victor Wilson/Simone Bignall, Personal Correspondence, 5/11/01. Victor Wilson is a Ngarrindjeri elder and a prominent political figure in regional and national indigenous communities.
7. The challenge is 'indirect' or 'covert', because the Australian court allegedly cannot challenge an act of State from which it derives its own authority.
8. In recent Australian history, calls for the negotiation of a treaty include the establishment of the tent embassy in 1972, the 1979 proposal put forward by the National Aboriginal Congress for the negotiation of a Makarrata, Kevin Gilbert's 1987 draft proposal, the 1988 Barunga Statement presented to Prime Minister Bob Hawke, and the proposals put forward by the Council for Aboriginal Reconciliation.
9. Here, Djerrkura (1999: 8) cites Lois O'Donaghue's remark on self-determination, made in 1993 at a session of the United Nations Working Group on Indigenous Peoples: 'There is not a single future to which we must conform, there are multiple futures'.

Conclusion: Postcolonial Agency

Thought is a freedom in relation to what one does, the motion by which one detaches oneself from it, establishes it as an object, and reflects on it as a problem. (Foucault 1984d: 388)

The task of philosophy when it creates concepts, entities, is always to extract an event from things and beings, to set up the new event from things and beings, always to give them a new event: space, time, matter, thought, the possible as events. (Deleuze and Guattari 1994: 33)

This work began with the idea that ontology shapes agency. I argued that the generative or causal force of negativity that is central to the movement of the dialectic and commonly underpins other philosophies of transformation including critical theory and deconstruction, is problematically associated with difference and desire. This association results in a representation of difference in essentially negative terms, and an imperial or possessive inclination of self to other. Grounded in the causal negativity of difference, critique is then associated with a politics of negation, which ambiguously positions bearers of difference as the active agents of change, but simultaneously as the problematic negativity that desire seeks to eliminate or transform. This foundational attitude towards difference, and the conceptualisation of difference in negative terms, is worrying when viewed from the perspective of postcolonial political philosophy. Furthermore, when responsibility for transformative action rests with the negating class, the active critical potential and the accountability of the dominant class is elided, with the result that the apathy of the privileged is excused, or else that efforts actually made by the dominant settler class to assist the process of postcolonial transformation are inadequately recognised and poorly supported. In my view, there is little motivation for settler classes to engage in postcolonial transformation when this is not presented as a common task responsibly shared by all within the postcolony.

A broader problem, also associated with the ontological negativity of difference and desire, relates to the dialectical philosophy of process, which informs the dominant Western view of progressive history-making. When history is understood to be driven by the causal negativity of difference and desire, each conceptualised in relation to the transcendent ideal of mutual recognition, a problem for postcolonialism emerges because the process remains fettered to a form of agency grounded in an imperial disposition, generating social forms that reproduce relations of power structured by the impulse of mastery, and by relations of desire aimed at the appropriation of the missing object of enjoyment. To break with post-colonial sociability, postcolonialism requires the introduction of a genuine historical discontinuity rather than a progressive process of continuous reconciliation. The historical discontinuity potentially defining the postcolonial calls for the inauguration of new kinds of difference, and a qualitative difference in the kind of sociability that is practised.

As a solution to the problem of generative ontological negativity and the processes of agency and history it drives, an alternative ontological perspective was sought by turning to the work of Deleuze and Guattari. Their positive conceptualisation of causal difference and creative desire offers an alternative view of ontological process, as actualisation driven by an immanent virtual positivity. This ontology gives rise to a theory of complex relational embodiment enabling multifaceted, interactive and affective forms of subjectivity, which was in turn suggested to be a suitable basis for a theory of postcolonial agency and postcolonial philosophies of transformative action. It was also argued that the productive ontology of actualisation or virtual different/ciation corresponds with a theory of historical discontinuity, also evident in the work of Foucault. The final chapter proposed some of the characteristics of sociability emerging from the chosen practice of an attitude of 'listening respect' that might be appropriately thought to define the historical discontinuity introduced with postcolonialism.

In the process of arguing for the suitability of Deleuze's positive ontology of different/ciation as a useful basis for postcolonial practice, this work coincidently engaged with the prevailing criticism that Deleuzian philosophy leads to an impoverished politics and a disabled ethics. I have argued that taking the actual as an object of critique does not lead to a disdain for the actual: Deleuze certainly privileges and celebrates virtuality as a causal source of diverse processes of actualisation, and virtual difference also ensures the permanent possibility of the transformation of any given actual form; but the virtual exists only in relation to the actual forms that embody it

Conclusion: Postcolonial Agency

in a concrete instance. Deleuze's political philosophy of virtual creativity only makes sense as a materially engaged practice employed in the here and now of the real world. I also outlined a concept of unity evident in Deleuze's work, which I suggested organises communities of practice at the level of the *virtual* conditions defining the emergence of a problematic actual, rather than at the level of an (alternative) imaginary *actual* describing an ideal solution. In this way, I sketched the possibility that Deleuzian political thought helps us imagine the complex forms of collective unity described by Richard Day (2001:38) as 'a multiplicity of coming communities, working together and in disparateness to simultaneously ward off corporate, national and state identifications and to nurture new forms of creative commonality'.

Finally, by developing Deleuze and Guattari's concept of individual agents as complex assemblages of desire, power and enunciation, I argued that subjectivity involves the act or performance of complex assemblage of self and world. For Deleuze and Guattari, the reasoned activity of assemblage entails there must always be a subject who thinks, and that accordingly, for such subjects, it is possible to provide guidelines for action. In this sense, elements of their work provide for a pragmatic and context sensitive ethics. However, for Deleuze and Guattari, there are no universally binding principles of conduct; instead, ethics 'concerns the way in which this world . . . will be enfolded: the constitution of a mode of existence as an ethos or way of expressing the world' (Goodchild 1997: 44; Deleuze 1989: 171–3). An existential ethos is shaped in 'this world'; that is, in one's concrete situations of engagement. For Deleuze (1995: 100), ethics therefore describe a 'set of optional rules that assess what we do, what we say, in relation to the ways of existing involved. We say this, do that: what way of existing does it involve?' The 'optional' character of Deleuzian ethics raises important questions about motivation and commitment, which are left unanswered in Deleuze's work. Why should one prefer postcolonialism over post-colonialism? In the absence of universal reasons for action, what basis can there be for a common fidelity to a chosen path of 'expressing the world'? Such questions are voiced with increasing urgency in contemporary social philosophy, as thought grapples with the material reality of global conflict, imperialism, strife, terror, poverty and the problem of apathy.

One inspired response to this situation is given in Simon Critchley's (2007) work on ethics and commitment. Critchley begins with the idea that philosophy responds to the generative negativity that is the failure and disappointment thrown up by the 'present time defined by the state of war' in which global humanity finds itself (2007: 8). In this morass of contemporary conflict, we suffer a 'motivational deficit' and a 'moral deficit', each connected to the 'felt inadequacy' that evidences 'the lack at the heart of democratic life'. The problem is that existing structures of liberal democracy have apparently failed to provide an alternative to the active nihilism of terrorism; they seem unable to stop us from plunging into 'violent injustice', and cannot alleviate the threatening suspicion that social participation is meaningless (2007: 6, 8). Critchley seeks a solution to this situation by reinvigorating the possibility of subjective conscience and commitment to ethical action, which he does by connecting Badiou's notion of 'fidelity' to Levinas' notion of the subjective 'trauma' prompted by the experience of the 'unfulfillable demand' of the alienated other in relation to the self. The unfulfillable demand is the source of splitting and felt inadequacy within the subject; Critchley argues that this experience of subjective trauma in the face of the other's demand – the experience of internal splitting and division – is itself the experience of 'conscience', and the affect of internalised trauma accordingly becomes the ground for political action. On Critchley's view, accepting the ontological negativity of the divided self as a ground for political action logically tends towards a deepening of democratic engagement. When the ethical subject is 'defined by commitment or fidelity to an unfulfillable demand', politics cannot then be confined to order and consensus, but is rather the 'manifestation of dissensus, the cultivation of an anarchic multiplicity' that involves a 'continual questioning from below of any attempt to impose order from above' (2007: 13).

While I am certainly sympathetic to the political outcome Critchley arrives at, reading his work from a postcolonial perspective reveals, once again, that a starting point of given negativity – strife, conflict, lack, inadequacy – prompts problematic subtextual representations of self and other, which to me, seem likely to compromise the quality of the social engagement that is possible. In this case, beginning with the infinite demand of the other and the basic failure of the self to cope with this demand positions the other as essentially deprived and needy; the other is a force that acts upon me to make me feel bad. This hardly seems like a good starting point for postcolonial sociability. Furthermore, I worry that the notion of ethical conscience arising from internalised trauma assumes too much subjective goodwill in relation to the other. The suggestion made is that my experience of the infinite demand of the other, and of my own inadequacy in relation to this unfulfillable demand, will weigh upon me and will affectively prompt my 'felt' conscience and commit me to ethical action. But what if I don't *care* enough about the ontological alienation of the other, or about my ontological alienation from the other, to feel a consequential inadequacy at the heart of my self? What if I am hostile to the very fact of the other's demands upon me, or resentful of the trauma he causes me to experience at the heart of my being? What if the other can't 'speak' those demands in a way that I conventionally understand, or if I haven't made the effort to 'listen' well enough even to hear that infinite demands are being made?

In this work, I have argued that a more appropriate starting point for postcolonial engagement is found by looking for examples of positive experience; by identifying examples of social connection that are felt to be joyful, rather than those that emphasise the productive negativity of 'felt inadequacy' and strife. This is not to say that most human societies aren't predominantly characterised by conflict, war, trauma, alienation and exploitation: quite obviously, they are. However, within this majoritarian muddle of violence and hostility, there also exist minor modes of positive social engagement, quotidian acts of kindness, and exemplary practices of genuine care and concern that join participating bodies in the mutual experience of joy. Starting with this positive experience of relationship, these moments of 'felt adequacy' actually occurring in 'this world', enables selves and communities to begin to understand how they can combine well with others; from the positive experience of mutual accord, they can start to identify affective sites of combination that will work well as the location of a complex form of union with the other. This developing understanding is rewarded by the gradual emergence of a common notion, an active understanding about 'good' forms of engagement, which may then guide bodies in the formation of preferred connections that are actively forged, and so increasingly gratifying to experience.

However, common notions do not automatically lead to increasingly joyful forms of sociability: understanding must be put into action; thought must be put into practice. This translation involves not only a necessary decision to act, but also a committed effort to care about the kinds of assemblage that one participates in and an act of choice regarding how to proceed with the association: what attitude of desire is called for, based upon the understanding that has been developed about joyful sociability and respective bodily natures? If this choice is made carefully and intently, the reward is the experience of an increased joy that is felt with the actualisation of a mutually enhancing complex union. Here, ethical commitment is best understood as a subjective fidelity, both individual and collective, to the labour of creating the conditions that enable the active experience of joy, practised firstly with respect to the concrete task of developing a thorough understanding of the self, the other, and the complex ways in which they affect each other as co-existing multiplicities. This can only be done by practising a 'listening respect' that enables a proper learning about the other. The motive for doing so is the reward offered by the complex understanding that is reached with the development of common notions, since this understanding is the basis for the experience of increased joy in future relationships. A second call for commitment emerges with the formation of the common notion; this is a call to put the collective understanding of self and other into careful practices of association, by making the effort to desire – to connect and associate – in ways that deliberately cultivate the actualisation of new and joyful forms of shared unity. The motive for doing so is the reward promised by the resulting experience of a joyful relation with the other, which being born of shared understanding and active intention, is an active joy that is all the more exquisite to experience.

In this work, I have connected the experience and the ethics of joy to the idea of postcolonialism. I have argued that a postcolonial attitude of 'listening respect' provides a basis for thinking about the kinds of desire and the virtual dispositions that are appropriate for the actualisation of complex forms of joyful mutuality that embody the principles of peaceful co-existence and self-determination. Respectful listening practised between relative bodies enables knowledge of the affective capacities and compatibilities of self and other, providing the basis for contingently made ethical choices about the kinds of action and interaction that may create mutually beneficial forms of complex assemblage. Guided by the joyful experience of genuine mediation, together with a practised fidelity to the ongoing performance of the forms of desire that are understood to be appropriate in actualising such forms of mediated co-existence, these contextually informed ethical choices lead to an emergent collective ethos of postcolonialism. Embodied in the various concrete actualisations that proceed from chosen practices of postcolonial desire, which is based in listening respect and carefully selected from the

Conclusion: Postcolonial Agency

infinite possible forms virtual desire can take, this ethos is characterised by the sociable principles of mutuality, recognition, consent and continuity that underpin the possibility of joy. Joyful sociability is necessarily postcolonial; postcolonial sociability describes a normatively preferred range of situated engagements because it rewards participating bodies with the positive experience of joy.

This work has created a concept of agency that I hope may be of help in bringing the virtual idea of the postcolonial present into actual eventuality. Thought is a constructive practice in which concepts are created as events and so made actual, but as a form of 'conceptual being', the event of theory in certain respects remains virtual. Philosophy, or concepts, must be combined with performance in acts of practice, in order to produce the complex *material* event of the actual. Accordingly, until the ideas presented here are taken up as tools in actual practices of relation and movements of transformation, the event of the alternative postcolonial present conceptualised here will remain practically virtual. The concepts described here – of postcolonial agency, transformative practices of positive joyful engagement and a postcolonial ethos of 'listening respect' – are best understood as transitive steps on the path to a becoming-postcolonial. This becoming takes shape only as we make the decision to activate these ideas as practical tools and inject them into our daily practices of being. The performance of postcoloniality involves making a choice to relate in careful and partial ways guided by common awareness of social compatibility and a knowledge about how it is possible to avoid discord by joining with others in mutually enhancing modes of engagement; this is a practice that I have argued might be best thought of as a 'politics of friendship' based on principles of complex recognition, consent and continuity. Conscientiously adopted as a collective task informed by a common notion of enlightened progress, postcolonisation invites individuals and communities to assemble according to relational practices of desire and power that have been actively selected because they allow a 'respectful listening' to complex expressions of difference. Emergent institutions of postcolonial sociability provide the basis for communities to evaluate and affirm these differences through carefully designed structures of negotiation and interaction. As a virtual form of sociability made actual through a labour of creation and choice, this practice promises the active composition of a complex postcolonial collective and the reward of joy.

Bibliography

Adorno, T. (1973), *Negative Dialectics*, London: Routledge and Kegan Paul.

Agamben, G. (1993), *The Coming Community*, trans. M. Hardt, Minneapolis: University of Minnesota Press.

Ahluwalia, P. (2010), *Out of Africa: Post-structuralism's Colonial Roots*, London and New York: Routledge.

Ahmad, A. (1987), 'Jameson's Rhetoric of Otherness and the "National Allegory"', *Social Text* 17: 3–25.

Ahmad, A. (1992), *In Theory: Classes, Nations, Literatures*, London and New York: Verso.

Ahmad, A. (1995), 'The Politics of Literary Postcoloniality', *Race and Class* 36(3): 1–20.

Alfred, T. (1999), *Peace, Power, Righteousness: An Indigenous Manifesto*, Ontario: Oxford University Press.

Altman J. and M. Hinkson (2007), *Coercive Reconciliation*, Melbourne: Arena.

Armstrong, A. (1997), 'Some Reflections on Deleuze's Spinoza: Composition and Agency', K. Ansell-Pearson (ed.), in *Deleuze and Philosophy: The Difference Engineer*, New York: Routledge, pp. 44–57.

Aronson, R. (1980), *Jean-Paul Sartre: Philosophy in the World*, London: New Left Books.

Ashcroft, B., G. Griffiths and H. Tiffin (1995), *The Postcolonial Studies Reader*, London and New York: Routledge.

Atkinson, J. (2007), 'Indigenous Approaches to Child Abuse', in J. Altman and M. Hinkson (eds), *Coercive Reconciliation*, Melbourne: Arena, pp. 151–63.

Attwood, B. (2000), 'The Burden of the Past in the Present', in M. Grattan (ed.), *Reconciliation*, Melbourne: Black Inc., pp. 254–9.

Bacchi, C. (1996), *The Politics of Affirmative Action: 'Women', Equality and Category Politics*, London: SAGE.

Balibar, E. (1995), 'Ambiguous Universality', *differences* 7(1): 47–74.

Balibar, E. (1997), *Spinoza: from Individuality to Transindividuality*, Delft: Eburon.

Barrett, M. (1991), *The Politics of Truth*, Oxford: Polity.

Bartlett, R. (1993), *The Mabo Decision*, Sydney: Butterworths.

Bibliography

Bartlett, R. (1996), 'Dispossession by the Native Title Tribunal', *WA Law Review* 26: 108–37.

Behrendt, L. (2007), 'The Emergency We Had To Have', in J. Altman and M. Hinkson (eds), *Coercive Reconciliation*, Melbourne: Arena, pp. 15–21.

Benhabib, S. (1992), 'The Generalized and the Concrete Other', in *Situating the Self*, London: Polity Press, pp. 148–77.

Berlin, I. (1999), 'Two Concepts of Liberty', in G. Sher and B. Brody (eds), *Social and Political Philosophy: Contemporary Readings*, Orlando: Harcourt Brace, pp. 624–36.

Bernasconi, R. (1996), 'Casting the Slough: Fanon's New Humanism for a New Humanity', in L. R. Gordon et al. (eds), *Fanon: A Critical Reader*, Oxford and Cambridge: Blackwell, pp. 113–22.

Bhabha, H. (1987), 'Interrogating Identity', in L. Appignanesi (ed.), *The Real Me*, London: ICA Documents, pp. 5–11.

Bhabha, H. (1994), *The Location of Culture*, London: Routledge.

Bhabha, H. (2000), 'On Minorities: Cultural Rights', *Radical Philosophy* 100: 3–6.

Bignall, S. (2007a), 'Indigenous Peoples and a Deleuzian Theory of Practice', in A. Hickey-Moody and P. Malins (eds), *Deleuzian Encounters: Studies in Contemporary Social Issues*, Sydney: Palgrave Macmillan, pp. 197–212.

Bignall, S. (2007b), 'A Superior Empiricism: The Subject and Experimentation', *Pli* 18: 204–21.

Bignall, S. (2008), 'Postcolonial Agency and Poststructuralist Thought: Deleuze and Foucault on Desire and Power', *Angelaki* 13(1): 127–49.

Bignall, S. (2010), 'Affect and Assemblage: Ethics beyond Enjoyment', in S. Bignall and P. Patton (eds), *Deleuze and the Postcolonial*, Edinburgh: Edinburgh University Press, pp. 78–102.

Bignall, S. and M. Galliford (2003), 'Reconciling Replicas: The Second Coming of the *Duyfken*', *Cultural Studies Review* 9(2): 37–68.

Bignall, S. and P. Patton (2010), *Deleuze and the Postcolonial*, Edinburgh: Edinburgh University Press.

Bonta, M. and J. Protevi, (2004), *Deleuze and Geophilosophy: A Guide and Glossary*, Edinburgh: Edinburgh University Press.

Boundas, C. (1996), 'Deleuze-Bergson: An Ontology of the Virtual', in P. Patton (eds.), *Deleuze: A Critical Reader*, Oxford: Blackwell, pp. 81–107.

Bourdieu, P. (1977), *Outline of a Theory of Practice*, trans. R. Nice, New York: Cambridge University Press.

Bourdieu, P. (1990), *Logic of Practice*, trans. R. Nice, Oxford: Polity Press.

Braidotti, R. (1993), 'Discontinuing Becomings: Deleuze on the Becoming-Woman of Philosophy', *Journal of the British Society of Phenomenology* 24(1): 44–55.

Brennan, T. (1990), 'The National Longing for Form', in H. Bhabha (ed.), *Nation and Narration*, London: Routledge, pp. 44–70.

Brown, W. (1998), 'Genealogical Politics', in J. Moss (ed.), *The Later Foucault* London and New Delhi: SAGE, pp. 33–50.

Burney, L. (2000), 'Not Just a Challenge, an Opportunity', in M. Grattan (ed.), *Reconciliation*, Melbourne: Black Inc., pp. 65–74.

Butler, J. (1987), *Subjects of Desire*, New York: Columbia University Press.

Butler, J. (1996), 'Universality in Culture', in J. Cohen (ed.), *For Love of Country*, Boston: Beacon Press, pp. 45–52.

CAR (1994a), *First Report: Walking Together*, Canberra: Commonwealth of Australia.

CAR (1994b), *Addressing Disadvantage: Key Issues Paper No. 5*, Canberra: Commonwealth of Australia.

CAR (1997), *Second Report: Weaving the Threads – Progress towards Reconciliation*, Canberra: Commonwealth of Australia.

CAR (2001), *Final Report: Reconciliation – Australia's Challenge*, Canberra: Commonwealth of Australia.

CERD, (2000), *Response to Australia*, Geneva: United Nations Press.

Chakrabarty, D. (2000), *Provincialising Europe*, New Jersey: Princeton University Press.

Charney, E. (1999), 'Cultural Interpretation and Universal Human Rights', *Political Theory* 27(6): 840–7.

Chesterman, J. and B. Galligan (1997), *Citizens Without Rights*, Cambridge: Cambridge University Press.

Chow, R. (1988), *Ethics after Idealism*, Bloomington and Indianapolis: Indiana University Press.

Cixous, H., with C. Clement (1986), *The Newly Born Woman*, trans. Betsy Wing, Manchester: Manchester University Press.

Clendinnen, I. (2003), *Dancing with Strangers*, Melbourne: Text Publishing.

Clifford, M. (2001), *Savage Identities: Political Genealogy after Foucault*, New York and London: Routledge.

Colebrook, C. (1999), 'A Grammar of Becoming', in E. Grosz (ed.), *Becomings*, Ithaca and London: Cornell University, pp. 117–41.

Connolly, W. (1998), 'Beyond Good and Evil: The Ethical Sensibility of Michel Foucault', in J. Moss (ed.), *The Later Foucault*, London and New Delhi: SAGE, pp. 108–29.

Connolly, W. E. (1999), *Why I Am Not a Secularist*, Minneapolis: University of Minnesota Press.

Connolly, W. E. (2008), 'An Ethos of Engagement', in S. Chambers and T. Carver (eds), *William Connolly: Democracy, Pluralism and Political Theory*, London: Routledge, pp. 231–53.

Connor, M. (2005), *The Invention of Terra Nullius: Historical and Legal Fictions on the Foundation of Australia*, Sydney: Macleay Press.

Bibliography

Coole, D. (2000), *Negativity and Politics: Dionysus and Dialectics from Kant to Poststructuralism*, London and New York: Routledge.

Coole, D. (2005), 'Rethinking Agency: A Phenomenological Approach to Embodiment and Agentic Capacities', *Political Studies* 53: 124–42.

Cornwall, A. (2002), *Restoring Identity: Final Report of the Moving Forward Consultation Project*, Sydney: Public Interest Advocacy Centre.

Critchley, S. (2007), *Infinitely Demanding: Ethics of Commitment, Politics of Resistance*, London and New York: Verso.

Davis, M. (2007) 'Arguing over Indigenous Rights: Australia and the United Nations', in J. Altman and M. Hinkson (eds), *Coercive Reconciliation*, Melbourne: Arena, pp. 97–111.

Day, R. (2001), 'Ethics, Affinity and the Coming Communities', *Philosophy and Social Criticism* 27(1): 21–38.

de Certeau, M. (2002), *The Practice of Everyday Life*, trans. S. Rendall, San Diego: University of California Press.

de Landa, M. (2002) *Intensive Science and Virtual Philosophy*, London: Continuum.

Deleuze, G. (1969), *Logique du sens*, Paris: Les Éditions de Minuit.

Deleuze, G. (1983), *Nietzsche and Philosophy*, trans. H. Tomlinson, London: Athlone Press.

Deleuze, G. (1986), *Foucault*, trans. S. Hand, Minneapolis: Minnesota University Press.

Deleuze, G. (1988a), *Le Pli: Leibniz et le Baroque*, Paris: Les Éditions de Minuit.

Deleuze, G. (1988b), *Spinoza: Practical Philosophy*, trans. R. Hurley, San Francisco: CityLights.

Deleuze, G. (1989), *Cinema 2: The Time-Image*, London: Athlone.

Deleuze, G. (1990), *Expressionism in Philosophy: Spinoza*, trans. M. Joughin, New York: Zone Books.

Deleuze, G. (1991a), *Empiricism and Subjectivity*, trans C. Boundas, New York: Columbia University Press.

Deleuze, G. (1991b), *Bergsonism*, trans. H. Tomlinson and B. Habberjam, New York: Zone Books.

Deleuze, G. (1994), *Difference and Repetition*, trans. P. Patton, London: Athlone Press.

Deleuze, G. (1995), *Negotiations*, trans. M. Joughin, New York: Columbia University Press.

Deleuze, G. (1997a), 'Immanence: A Life . . .', *Theory, Culture and Society* 14(2): 4–5.

Deleuze, G. (1997b), 'Desire and Pleasure', trans. Dan Smith, in A. Davidson (ed.), *Foucault and his Interlocutors*, Chicago: University of Chicago Press, pp. 183–92.

Deleuze, G. (1999), 'Bergson's Conception of Difference', trans. M. MacMahon, in J. Mullarkey (ed.), *The New Bergson*, Manchester:

Manchester University Press, pp. 42–65; original (1956), 'La conception de la différence chez Bergson', *Les Études Bergsoniennes* IV: 77–112.

Deleuze, G. (2007), *Two Regimes of Madness: Texts and Interviews 1975–1995*, trans. A. Hodges and M. Taormina, rev'd edn, New York: Semiotext(e).

Deleuze, G. and M. Foucault (1977), 'Intellectuals and Power', in D. Bouchard (ed.), *Foucault, Language, Counter-memory, Practice*, trans. D. Bouchard and S. Simon, Ithaca: Cornell University Press, pp. 205–17.

Deleuze, G. and F. Guattari (1983), *Anti-Oedipus: Capitalism and Schizophrenia*, trans. R. Hurley, M. Seem and H. Lane, Minneapolis: University of Minnesota Press.

Deleuze, G. and F. Guattari (1987), *A Thousand Plateaus*, trans. B. Massumi, Minneapolis: Minnesota University Press.

Deleuze, G. and F. Guattari (1994), *What Is Philosophy?*, trans. G. Burchell and H. Tomlinson, London and New York: Verso.

Deleuze, G. and C. Parnet (1987), *Dialogues*, trans. H. Tomlinson and B. Habberjam, New York: Columbia University Press.

Deleuze, G. and C. Parnet (2003), *L'Abécédaire de Gilles Deleuze avec Claire Parnet*, CD-Rom: Vidéo Éditions Montparnasse.

Derrida, J. (1974), *Of Grammatology*, trans. G. Spivak, Baltimore: John Hopkins University Press.

Derrida, J. (2005), *The Politics of Friendship*, London and New York: Verso.

Diprose, R. and R. Ferrell (eds) (1991), *Cartographies: Poststructuralism and the Mapping of Bodies and Spaces*, Sydney: Allen and Unwin.

Dirlik, A. (1990), 'Culturalism as Hegemonic Ideology and Liberating Practice' in A. R. JanMohammed and D. Lloyd (eds), *The Nature and Context of Minority Discourse*, New York: Oxford University Press, 394–431.

Djerrkura, G. (1999), 'Indigenous Peoples, Constitutions and Treaties', Paper presented at *A Dialogue on Indigenous Rights in the Commonwealth*, Institute of Commonwealth Studies, London.

Dodson, M. (1994), 'The End in the Beginning: Re(de)finding Aboriginality', Speech for the Wentworth Lecture, Australian Institute of Aboriginal and Torres Strait Islander Studies, Canberra.

Dodson, M. (1998), 'Linking International Standards with Contemporary Concerns of Aboriginal and Torres Strait Islander Peoples', in S. Pritchard (ed.), *Indigenous Peoples, the United Nations and Human Rights*, Sydney: Federation Press, pp. 18–29.

Dodson, P. (2000), 'Lingiari: Until the Chains are Broken', in M. Grattan (ed.), *Reconciliation*, Melbourne: Black Inc., pp. 265–6.

Dodson, P. (2007), 'Whatever Happened to Reconciliation?', in J. Altman and M. Hinkson (ed.), *Coercive Reconciliation*, Melbourne: Arena, pp. 21–31.

Bibliography

Dumm, T. L. (1996), *Michel Foucault and the Politics of Freedom*, London and New Delhi: SAGE.

During, S. (1995), 'Postmodernism or Post-colonialism Today', in B. Ashcroft et al. (eds), *The Post-colonial Studies Reader*, London and New York: Routledge, pp. 125–30.

Eveline, J. (1993), 'The Politics of Advantage', *Political Theory Newsletter* 5: 53–67

Fanon, F. (1952), *Peau noire, masques blancs*, Paris: Éditions du Seuil.

Fanon, F. (1961), *Les damnés de la terre*, Paris: François Marpero.

Fanon, F. (1967a), *Black Skin, White Masks*, trans. C. M. Markmann, New York: Grove Press.

Fanon, F. (1967b), *The Wretched of the Earth*, trans. C. Farrington, Harmondsworth: Penguin.

Fielder, J. (1996), 'Postcoloniality and Mudrooroo Narogin's Ideology of Aboriginality', *Span* 32: 43–54.

Foucault, M. (1961), *Madness and Civilization: A History of Insanity in the Age of Reason*, trans. A. Sheridan, London: Tavistock.

Foucault, M. (1972), *The Archaeology of Knowledge*, trans. A. Sheridan, London: Tavistock.

Foucault, M. (1973), *The Birth of the Clinic*, trans. A. Sheridan, London: Tavistock.

Foucault, M. (1977), *Discipline and Punish*, trans. A. Sheridan, London: Allen Lane.

Foucault, M. (1980a), 'Truth and Power', in C. Gordon (ed.), *Power/Knowledge*, Brighton: Harvester, pp. 109–33.

Foucault, M. (1980b), 'Power, Right, Truth', in C. Gordon (ed.), *Power/Knowledge*, Brighton: Harvester, pp. 92–108.

Foucault, M. (1983a), 'Preface', in G. Deleuze and F. Guattari, *Anti-Oedipus: Capitalism and Schizophrenia*, trans. R. Hurley, M. Seem and H. Lane, Minneapolis: University of Minnesota, pp. xi–xiv.

Foucault, M. (1983b), 'The Subject and Power', Afterword in H. Dreyfus and P. Rabinow (eds), *Michel Foucault: Beyond Structuralism and Hermeneutics*, 2nd edn, Chicago: University of Chicago Press.

Foucault, M. (1984a), 'What is Enlightenment?', in P. Rabinow (ed.), *The Foucault Reader*, London: Penguin, pp. 32–50.

Foucault, M. (1984b), 'Nietzsche, Genealogy, History', in P. Rabinow (ed.), *The Foucault Reader*, London: Penguin, pp. 76–101.

Foucault, M. (1984c), 'Space, Knowledge and Power', in P. Rabinow (ed.), *The Foucault Reader*, London: Penguin, pp. 239–57.

Foucault, M. (1984d), 'Polemics, Politics and Problematizations', in P. Rabinow (ed.), *The Foucault Reader*, London: Penguin, pp. 381–390.

Foucault, M. (1986a), 'Kant on Enlightenment and Revolution', trans. C. Gordon, *Economy and Society* 15(1): 88–96.

Foucault, M. (1986b), *The Care of the Self: History of Sexuality, Vol. 3*, trans. R. Hurley, New York: Random House.

Foucault, M. (1986c), 'Of Other Spaces', *Diacritics* (Spring): 24–36.

Foucault, M. (1988), 'The Ethic of Care for the Self as a Practice of Freedom', in J. Bernauer and D. Rasmussen, *The Final Foucault* (eds), Boston MA: MIT Press, pp. 1–20.

Foucault, M. (1990), *The Will to Knowledge: History of Sexuality. Vol.1: An Introduction*, trans. R. Hurley, London: Penguin.

Foucault, M. (1991), 'Governmentality', in G. Burchell, C. Gordon and P. Miller (eds), *The Foucault Effect: Studies in Governmentality*, Chicago: Chicago University Press, pp. 87–104.

Fox, N. F. (2003), *The New Sartre*, London and New York: Continuum.

Fraser, M. (1997), 'Feminism, Foucault and Deleuze', *Theory, Culture and Society* 14(3): 23–37.

Fraser, N. (1981), 'Foucault on Modern Power: Empirical Insights and Normative Confusions', *Praxis International* 3: 272–87.

Frazer, E. and N. Lacey (1993), *The Politics of Community*, Hertfordshire: Harvester Wheatsheaf.

Fuery, P. (1995), *Theories of Desire*, Melbourne: Melbourne University Press.

Gandhi, L. (1998), *Postcolonial Theory: A Critical Introduction*, Sydney: Allen and Unwin.

Gandhi, L. (2006), *Affective Communities: Anticolonial Thought, Fin-de-Siècle Radicalism, and the Politics of Friendship*, Durham and London: Duke University Press.

Gatens, M. (1993), 'Through a Spinozist Lens: Ethology, Difference, Power', in P. Patton (ed.), *Deleuze: A Critical Reader*, Oxford and Cambridge: Blackwell, pp. 162–87.

Gatens, M. (1996), *Imaginary Bodies: Ethics, Power and Corporeality*, London and New York: Routledge.

Gatens, M. (2008), 'Conflicting Imaginaries in Australian Multiculturalism: Women's Rights, Group Rights and Aboriginal Customary Law' in G. B. Levey (ed.), *Australian Multiculturalism*, New York: Berhgan Books, pp. 151–71.

Gatens, M. and G. Lloyd (1999), *Collective Imaginings: Spinoza, Past and Present*, London and New York: Routledge.

Gilbert, K. (1977), *Living Black*, Melbourne: Penguin.

Gilbert, S. (1995), 'A Postcolonial Experience of Aboriginal Identity', *Cultural Studies* 9(1): 145–9.

Gilligan, C. (1982), *In a Different Voice: Psychological Theory and Women's Moral Development*, Cambridge: Harvard University Press.

Giroux, H. (1993), 'Living Dangerously: Identity Politics and the New Cultural Racism – Towards a Critical Pedagogy of Representation', *Cultural Studies* 7(1): 1–27.

Bibliography

Golder, B. and P. Fitzpatrick (2009), *Foucault's Law*, London and New York: Routledge.

Goodall, H. (1996), *Invasion to Embassy*, Sydney: Allen and Unwin/Black Books.

Goodchild, P. (1996), *Deleuze and Guattari: An Introduction to the Politics of Desire*, London and New Delhi: SAGE.

Goodchild, P. (1997), 'Deleuzean Ethics', *Theory, Culture and Society* 14(2): 39–50.

Goulimari, P. (1999), 'A Minoritarian Feminism: Things to Do with Deleuze and Guattari', *Hypatia* 14(2): 97–120.

Gray, T. (1990), *Freedom*, Hampshire: Macmillan.

Grenville, K. (2005), *The Secret River*, Melbourne: Text Publishing Company.

Grosz, E. (1995), *Space, Time and Perversion*, Sydney: Allen and Unwin.

Grosz, E. (1999), 'Thinking The New: Of Futures Yet Unthought', in E. Grosz (ed.), *Becomings*, Ithaca and London: Cornell University, pp. 15–29.

Guattari, F. (1984), *Molecular Revolution: Psychiatry and Politics*, trans. R. Sheed, New York: Penguin.

Guattari, F. (1996), 'Microphysics of Power/Micropolitics of Desire', in G. Genosko (ed.), *The Guattari Reader*, London: Blackwell, pp. 172–81.

Hall, S. (1987), 'Minimal Selves', in L. Appignanesi (ed.), *The Real Me*, London: ICA Documents, pp. 44–6.

Hall, S. (1996), 'When was "The Post-Colonial"? Thinking at the Limit,' in I. Chambers and L. Urti (eds), *The Postcolonial Question: Common Skies, Divided Horizons*, London and New York: Routledge, pp. 242–60.

Hallward, P. (2001), *Absolutely Postcolonial: Writing between the Singular and the Specific*, Manchester: Manchester University Press.

Hallward, P. (2006), *Out of this World*, London and New York: Verso.

Hardt, M. (1993), *Gilles Deleuze: An Apprenticeship in Philosophy*, Minneapolis: University of Minnesota Press.

Hardt, M. (1995), 'Spinoza's Democracy: The Passions of Social Assemblages', in A. Callari and S. Cullenberg (eds), *Marxism in the Postmodern Age: Confronting the New World Order*, London and New York: Guildford Press, pp. 24–33.

Hardt, M. and A. Negri (2000), *Empire*, Cambridge: Harvard University Press.

Hardt, M. and A. Negri (2004), *Multitude*, London: Penguin.

Hegel, G. W. F. (1900), *The Philosophy of History*, trans. J. Sibree, London and New York: Colonial Press.

Hegel, G. W. F. (1969), *Science of Logic*, trans. A. Miller, New Jersey: Humanities Press.

Hegel, G. W. F. (1977), *Phenomenology of Spirit*, trans. A. V. Miller, ed. J. N. Findlay, Oxford: Clarendon Press.

Held, V. (1984), *Rights and Goods*, Chicago: University of Chicago Press.
Hindess, B. (1998), 'Politics and Liberation', in J. Moss (ed.), *The Later Foucault*, London and New Delhi: SAGE, pp. 50–64.
Howells, C. (2000), 'Sartre: Desiring the Impossible', in H. J. Silverman (ed.), *Philosophy and Desire*, London and New York: Routledge, pp. 85–96.
HREOC (1997), *Bringing Them Home: Report on the National Inquiry into the Stolen Generations*, Canberra: Human Rights and Equal Opportunities Commission.
Huddart, D. (2006), *Homi K. Bhabha*, London and New York: Routledge.
Huggins, J. (1990), 'Response', in S. Janson and S. McIntyre (eds), *Through White Eyes*, Sydney: Allen and Unwin, pp. 168–9.
Ivison, D. (2002), *Postcolonial Liberalism*, Cambridge: Cambridge University Press.
James, R. (1997), 'Rousseau's Knot: The Entanglement of Liberal Democracy and Racism', in B. Morris and G. Cowlishaw (eds), *Race Matters: Indigenous Australians and 'Our' Society*, Canberra: Aboriginal Studies Press, pp. 53–77.
JanMohamed, A. R. (1985), 'The Economy of Manichean Allegory: The Function of Racial Difference in Colonialist Literature', *Critical Inquiry* 12(1): 59–87.
Jardine, A. (1985), *Gynesis: Configurations of Woman and Modernity*, Ithaca: Cornell University Press.
Jordan, D. (1984), 'The Social Construction of Identity: The Aboriginal Problem', *Australian Journal of Education* 28: 274–90.
Kaplan, C. (1996), *Questions of Travel: Postmodern Discourses of Displacement*, Durham: Duke University Press.
Kauffman, S. (1993), *The Origins of Order: Self-Organisation and Selection in Evolution*, Oxford: Oxford University Press.
Kawash, S. (1999), 'Terrorists and Vampires: Fanon's Spectral Violence of Decolonisation', in A. Alessandrini (ed.), *Frantz Fanon: Critical Perspectives*, London and New York: Routledge, pp. 235–58.
Keating, P. (2000), 'The Redfern Park Speech', in M. Grattan (ed.), *Reconciliation*, Melbourne: Black Inc., pp. 60–4.
Kojève, A. (1980), *Introduction to the Reading of Hegel*, trans. J. H. Nichols, ed. A. Bloom, Ithaca: Cornell University Press.
Kojève, A. (1996), 'Desire and Work in the Master and 'Slave'', in J. O'Neill (ed.), *Hegel's Dialectic of Desire and Recognition: Texts and Commentary*, New York: SUNY, pp. 49–85.
Kristeva, J. (1982), *Powers of Horror: An Essay on Abjection*, New York: Columbia University Press.
Kristeva, J. (1990), *Strangers to Ourselves*, trans. L. S. Roudiez, New York: Columbia University Press.
Kristeva, J. (2000), *Crisis of the European Subject*, trans. S. Fairfield, New York: Other Press.

Bibliography

Kruks, S. (1996), 'Fanon, Sartre and Identity Politics', in C. Gordon et al. (eds), *Fanon: A Critical Reader*, Oxford and Cambridge: Blackwell, pp. 122–34.

Kukathas, C. (2003), *The Liberal Archipelago: A Theory of Freedom and Diversity*, New York: Oxford University Press.

Kymlicka, W. (1995), *Multicultural Citizenship*, Oxford: Oxford University Press.

Lacan, J. (1977) *Écrits: A Selection*, trans. A. Sheridan, London: Tavistock.

Lacan, J. (1988a), *Seminar Book II: The Ego In Freud's Papers*, trans. S. Tomaselli, Cambridge: Cambridge University Press.

Lacan, J. (1988b), 'Seminar on the Purloined Letter', trans. J. Mehlman, in J. Muller and W. Richardson (eds), *The Purloined Poe: Lacan, Derrida and Psychoanalytic Reading*, Baltimore: John Hopkins University Press, pp. 28–54.

Lacan, J. (1993), *Seminar: Book III on the Psychoses 1955–6*, trans. R. Grigg, ed. J.-A. Miller, London: Routledge.

Laclau, E. (1990), *New Reflections on the Revolution of Our Time*, London: Verso.

Laclau, E. and C. Mouffe (1985), *Hegemony and Socialist Strategy*, London: Verso.

Langton, M. (1993), *'Well, I heard it on the radio and I saw it on the television . . .'* Sydney: Australian Film Commission.

Langton, M. (1994), 'Aboriginal Art and Film: The Politics of Representation', *Race and Class* 35(4): 89–106.

Lash, S. (1984), 'Genealogy and the Body: Foucault/Deleuze/Nietzsche', *Theory, Culture and Society* 2(2): 1–17.

Lattas, A. (1987), 'Savagery and Civilisation', *Social Analysis* 21: 39–58.

Lattas, A. (1991), 'Nationalism, Aesthetic Redemption and Aboriginality', *TAJA* 2(3): 307–23.

Lazarus, N. (1999), 'Disavowing Decolonisation', in A. Alessandrini (ed.), *Frantz Fanon: Critical Perspectives*, London and New York: Routledge, pp. 161–94.

Lefebvre, A. (2005), 'A New Image of Law: Deleuze and Jurisprudence', *Telos* 130: 103–26.

Lefebvre, A. (2008), *The Image of Law: Deleuze, Bergson, Spinoza*, Stanford: Stanford University Press.

Mansell, M. (1992), 'The Court Gives an Inch But Takes Another Mile', *Aboriginal Law Bulletin* 2(57): 172–6.

Mansell, M. (2007), 'The Political Vulnerability of the Unrepresented' in J. Altman and M. Hinkson (eds), *Coercive Reconciliation*, Melbourne: Arena, pp. 73–85.

Marcuse, H. (1960), *Reason and Revolution*, Boston: Beacon Press.

May, T. (1991), 'The Politics of Life in the Thought of Gilles Deleuze', *SubStance* 66: 24–35.

McBride, W. (1991), *Sartre's Political Theory*, Bloomington: Indiana University Press.

McCarney, J. (2000), *Hegel on History*, London and New York: Routledge.

McConaghy, C. (2000), 'The Web and Today's Colonialism', *Australian Aboriginal Studies* 1(2): 48–56.

McKay, B. (1999), *Unmasking Whiteness: Race Relations and Reconciliation*, Nathan: Griffith University.

McNeill, K. (1997), 'The Meaning of Aboriginal Title', in M. Aesch (ed.), *Aboriginal and Treaty Rights in Canada*, Ontario: UBC Press, pp. 138–50.

Mengue, P. (2008) 'People and Fabulation' in I. Buchanan and N. Thoburn (eds), *Deleuze and Politics*, Edinburgh: Edinburgh University Press, pp. 218–40.

Miller, C. L. (1993), 'The Post-Identitarian Predicament in the Footnotes of *A Thousand Plateaus*: Nomadology, Anthropology and Authority', *Diacritics* 23(3): 6–35.

Miller, D. (1995), *On Nationality*, Oxford: Oxford University Press.

Molnar, H. (1995), 'Indigenous Media Development in Australia: A Product of Struggle and Opposition', *Cultural Studies* 9(1): 169–90.

Mouffe, C. (1993), *The Return of the Political*, London: Verso.

Mudrooroo (1995), 'White Forms, Aboriginal Content', in B. Ashcroft et al. (eds), *The Postcolonial Studies Reader*, London and New York: Routledge, pp. 228–32.

Negri, A. (1991), *The Savage Anomaly*, trans. M. Hardt, Minneapolis: University of Minnesota Press.

Nettheim, G. (1993), '"The Consent of the Natives": Mabo and Indigenous Political Rights', *Sydney Law Review* 15(2): 223–46.

Nicoll, F. (1998), 'Blacklash: Reconciliation After *Wik*', *Meanjin* 57(1): 167–83.

Nietzsche, F. (1976), 'Thus Spoke Zarathustra', trans. W. Kauffman, in W. Kauffman (ed.), *The Portable Nietzsche*, London: Penguin, pp. 103–440.

Nietzsche, F. (1992), *Ecce Homo: How One Become What One Is*, trans. R. J. Hollingdale, 2nd edn, Harmondsworth: Penguin.

Olkowski, D. (1999), *Gilles Deleuze and the Ruin of Representation*, Berkeley: University of California Press.

Oxenham, D. (1999), *A Dialogue on Indigenous Identity: Warts 'n' All*, Curtin Indigenous Research Centre: Gunada Press.

Parekh, B. (1995), 'Liberalism and Colonialism: A Critique of Locke and Mill', in S. Pieterse and B. Parekh (eds), *The Decolonisation of Imagination*, Sydney: Zed Books, pp. 81–98.

Parry, B. (1987), 'Problems in Current Theories of Colonial Discourse', *Oxford Literary Review* 9: 27–58.

Bibliography

Parry, B. (1994a), 'Resistance Theory/Theorising Resistance or Two Cheers For Nativism', in F. Barker, P. Hulme and M. Iverson (eds), *Colonial Discourse/Postcolonial Theory*, Manchester: Manchester University Press, pp. 172–96.

Parry, B. (1994b), 'Signs of Our Times. Discussion of Homi Bhabha's *The Location of Culture*', *Third Text* 28(29): 5–24.

Parry, B. (2004), *Postcolonial Studies: A Materialist Critique*, London and New York: Routledge.

Patton, P. (1984), 'Conceptual Politics and the War-Machine in *Mille Plateaux*', *SubStance* 44(45): 61–80.

Patton, P. (1995), 'Post-Structuralism and the Mabo Debate' in M. Wilson and A. Yeatman (eds), *Justice and Identity: Antipodean Practices*, Sydney: Allen and Unwin, pp. 153–71.

Patton, P. (1996a), 'Sovereignty, Law and Difference in Australia: After the Mabo Case', *Alternatives* 21: 149–70.

Patton, P. (1996b), 'Concept and Event', *Man and World* 29: 315–26.

Patton, P. (1998), 'Foucault's Subject of Power', in J. Moss (ed.), *The Later Foucault*, London and New Delhi: SAGE, pp. 64–78.

Patton, P. (1999), 'Justifying Aboriginal Rights: A Philosophical Perspective', in T. Smith (ed.), *First Peoples, Second Chance*, Canberra: The Australian Academy of the Humanities, pp. 61–81.

Patton, P. (2000), *Deleuze and the Political*, London and New York: Routledge.

Patton, P. (2004), 'Power and Right in Nietzsche and Foucault', *International Studies in Philosophy* xxxvi (3): 43–61.

Patton, P. (2005a), 'Deleuze and Democracy', *Contemporary Political Theory* 4: 400–13.

Patton, P. (2005b) 'Deleuze and Democratic Politics', in L. Tønder and L. Thomassen (eds), *Radical Democracy: Politics between Abundance and Lack*, Manchester and New York: Manchester University Press, pp. 50–67.

Patton, P. (2010), *Deleuzian Concepts: Philosophy, Colonization, Politics*, Stanford: Stanford University Press.

Pearson, N. (1997a), 'The Concept of Native Title at Common Law', in Galarrwuy Yunupingu (ed.), *Our Land Is Our Life: Land Rights – Past, Present, Future*, Brisbane: University of Queensland Press, pp. 150–62.

Pearson, N. (1997b), '*Mabo*: Towards Respecting Equality and Difference', in G. Cowlishaw and B. Morris (eds), *Race Matters: Indigenous Australians and 'Our' Society*, Canberra: Aboriginal Studies Press, pp. 209–19.

Pickett, B. (1996), 'Foucault and the Politics of Resistance', *Polity* 28(4): 445–67.

Poole, R. (2000), 'Justice or Appropriation: Indigenous Claims and Liberal Theory', *Radical Philosophy* 101: 5–17.

Pritchard, S. (1998), *Indigenous Peoples, The United Nations and Human Rights*, Sydney: Federation Press.
Protevi, J. (2003). 'Love', in P. Patton and J. Protevi (eds), *Between Derrida and Deleuze*, London and New York: Continuum, pp. 183–95.
Rajchman, J. (2000), *The Deleuze Connections*, Cambridge: MIT Press.
Rawls, J. (1971), *A Theory of Justice*, Cambridge: Harvard University Press.
Raz, J. (2009), *Between Authority and Interpretation: On the Theory of Law and Practical Reason*, New York: Oxford University Press.
Reynolds, H. (1988), *The Law of the Land*, Melbourne: Penguin.
Reynolds, H. (1996), *Aboriginal Sovereignty*, Sydney: Allen and Unwin.
Reynolds, H. (2000), 'A Crossroads of Conscience', in M. Grattan (ed.), *Reconciliation*, Melbourne: Black Inc., pp. 53–60.
Reynolds, H. (2006), 'A New Historical Landscape: Response to Connor', *The Monthly* 11: 50–3.
Said, E. (1978), *Orientalism: Western Conceptions of the Orient*, London: Penguin.
Said E. (1986), 'The Imagination of Power', in D. Hoy (ed.), *Foucault: A Critical Reader*, Oxford and Cambridge: Blackwell, pp. 149–57.
Sandel, M. (1984), 'The Procedural Republic and the Unencumbered Self', Political Theory 12(1): 81–96.
Sartre, J.-P. (1943), *L'Être et le néant*, Paris: Gallimard.
Sartre, J.-P. (1948), *Anti-Semite and Jew*, trans. G. Becker, New York: Schocken Books.
Sartre, J.-P. (1960), *Critique de la raison dialectique*, Paris: Gallimard.
Sartre, J.-P. (1967), 'Preface', in F. Fanon, *The Wretched of the Earth*, trans. C. Farrington, Middlesex: Penguin, pp. 7–26.
Sartre, J.-P (1976a), *Black Orpheus*, trans. S. W. Allen, Paris: Présence Africaine.
Sartre, J.-P. (1976b), *Critique of Dialectical Reason*, trans. A. Sheridan, New Jersey: Humanities Press.
Sartre, J.-P. (1983), *Cahiers pour une morale*, Paris: Gallimard.
Sartre, J.-P. (1996), *Being and Nothingness*, trans. H. Carby, London: Routledge.
Sartre, J.-P. (2001), *Colonialism and Neocolonialism*, trans. A. Haddour, S. Brewer and T. McWilliams: London and New York: Routledge.
Schatzki, T., K. Cetina and E. von Savigny (eds) (2001), *The Practice Turn in Contemporary Theory*, London and New York: Routledge.
Schrift, A. D. (1995), 'Putting Nietzsche to Work: The Case of Gilles Deleuze', in P. Sedgewick (ed.), *Nietzsche: A Critical Reader*, Oxford and Cambridge: Blackwell, pp. 250–76.
Schrift, A. D. (2000), 'Deleuze, Nietzsche, Spinoza: An Other Discourse of Desire', in H. J. Silverman (ed.), *Philosophy and Desire*, New York and London: Routledge, pp. 173–86.

Bibliography

Silverman, H. J. (2000), 'Twentieth Century Desire and the Histories of Philosophy', in H. J. Silverman (ed.), *Philosophy and Desire*, London and New York: Routledge, pp. 1–17.

Simons, M. (2003), *The Meeting of the Waters: The Hindmarsh Island Affair*, Sydney: Hodder.

Smith, C. and G. Ward (2000), 'Globalisation, Decolonisation and Indigenous Australia', *Australian Aboriginal Studies* 1(2): 3–11.

Soja, E. (1989), *Postmodern Geographies: The Reassertion of Space in Critical Social Theory*, London and New York: Verso.

Spivak, G. C. (1985), 'Can the Subaltern Speak?', *Wedge* 7(8): 120–30; reprinted in C. Nelson and A. Grossberg (eds) (1988), *Marxism and the Interpretation of Culture*, London: Macmillan, pp. 271–313.

Spivak, G. C. (1986), 'Displacement and the Discourse of Woman', in M. Krupnick (ed.), *Displacement: Derrida and After*, Bloomington: Indiana University Press.

Spivak, G. C. (1999), *A Critique of Postcolonial Reason: Towards a History of the Vanishing Present*, Cambridge: Harvard University Press.

Stavrakakis, Y. (1999), *Lacan and the Political*, London and New York: Routledge.

Stoler, A. L. (1995), *Race and the Education of Desire: Foucault's History of Sexuality and the Colonial Order of Things*, Durham: Duke University Press.

Svirsky, M. (2010), 'The production of *Terra Nullius* and the Zionist-Palestinian Conflict, in S. Bignall and P. Patton (eds), *Deleuze and the Postcolonial*, Edinburgh, Edinburgh University Press, pp. 200–250.

Tamir, Y. (1993), *Liberal Nationalism*, New York: Princeton University Press.

Taylor, C. (1985a), *Atomism and the Primacy of Rights: Philosophical Papers II*, Cambridge: Cambridge University Press.

Taylor, C. (1985b), *Human Agency and Language: Philosophical Papers I*, Cambridge, Cambridge University Press.

Taylor, C. (1989), *Sources of the Self*, Cambridge, Cambridge University Press.

Tully, J. (1995), *Strange Multiplicity: Constitutionalism in an Age of Diversity*, Cambridge: Cambridge University Press.

Tully, J. (2000), 'The Struggles of Indigenous Peoples for and of Freedom', in D. Ivison, P. Patton and W. Sanders (eds), *Political Theory and the Rights of Indigenous Peoples*, Cambridge: Cambridge University Press, pp. 36–59.

Turner, D. (2001), 'Vision: Towards an Understanding of Aboriginal Sovereignty' in R. Beiner and W. Norman (eds), *Canadian Political Philosophy*, Oxford: Oxford University Press, pp. 318–34.

Turner, L. (1996), 'On the Difference between the Hegelian and Fanonian Dialectic of Lordship and Bondage', in L. Gordon, T. D. Sharpley Whiting

and R. T. White (eds), *Fanon: A Critical Reader*, Oxford and Cambridge: Blackwell, pp. 134–55.
Velleman, J. D. (1996), 'Self to Self', *Philosophical Review* 105: 39–76.
Walzer, M. (1986), 'The Politics of Michel Foucault', in D. Hoy (ed.), *Foucault: A Critical Reader*, Oxford: Blackwell, pp. 51–69.
Walzer, M. (1990), 'Nation and Universe', in Grethe B. Peterson (ed.), *The Tanner Lectures on Human Values* XI, Salt Lake City: Utah University Press, pp. 509–56.
Watson, I. (1998), 'Naked Peoples: Rules and Regulations', *Law/Text/Culture* 4(1): 1–17.
Webber, J. (2000), 'Beyond Regret: Mabo's Implications for Australian Constitutionalism', in D. Ivison, P. Patton and W. Sanders (eds), *Political Theory and the Rights of Indigenous Peoples*, Cambridge: Cambridge University Press, pp. 60–89.
Wuthnow, J. (2002), 'Deleuze in the Postcolonial: On Nomads and Indigenous Politics', *Feminist Theory* 3(2): 183–200.
Young, I. M. (1990), *Justice and the Politics of Difference*, Princeton: Princeton University Press.
Young, R. (1990), *White Mythologies: Writing History and the West*, London and New York: Routledge.
Young, R. (1994), 'Colonialism and the Desiring-Machine', in T. D'haen and H. Bertrens (eds), *Liminal Postmodernisms*, Amsterdam and Atlanta: Rodopi Press, pp. 11–34.
Young, R. (1995), *Colonial Desire: Hybridity in Theory, Culture and Race*, London: Routledge.
Young, R. (2001), 'Sartre: the "African Philosopher"', in J.-P. Sartre, *Colonialism and Neocolonialism*, London and New York: Routledge, pp. vii–xxiv.
Žižek, S. (1989), *The Sublime Object of Ideology*, London: Verso.
Žižek, S. (1993), *Tarrying with the Negative*, Durham: Duke University Press.

Index

aboriginality, 79–92, 98(n.11), 115, 120, 124; *see also* blackness; Negritude
active/reactive, 50, 132–4, 143, 148, 167, 177
actualisation/realisation, 9, 34, 101–3, 107–8, 110, 126, 145, 181
adequate ideas, 171–2, 209–11, 221
Adorno, T., 45, 51
advantage, 110, 119–21
affectivity, 45, 139, 149, 151, 170–6, 186, 206–28, 232–6
agreement, 6, 10, 20, 125, 134, 150–1, 164, 172, 175–6, 204, 207–12, 214, 216–8, 220, 222; *see also* consensus; consent
Ahmad, A., 18, 71, 97(n.7), 122
Alfred, T., 18, 138
ambivalence, 47, 66, 72–6, 88, 94, 119, 184, 187
America, 84, 89, 145
Anti-Oedipus, 145, 147, 176–82, 191
assemblage, 14–16, 103, 109–10, 113, 122–3, 127(n.4), 146–8, 155–6, 159–60, 162, 164–9, 170–2, 177, 190(n.5), 209, 212, 215, 217, 219, 221, 233, 235–6
assimilation
  of difference, 7, 18, 23, 30, 35–6, 43–6, 48, 57–8, 69, 73–4, 85, 87, 95, 185, 204, 211, 216
  policy, 20, 24, 87, 204, 211, 216
attitude, 2, 7, 8, 11, 12, 20, 22, 25, 42–8, 57–8, 79, 115, 122, 169, 187, 192–4, 197–207, 212–14, 227, 229, 229(n.4), 231–2, 235–6
Australia, 9, 10, 18, 30, 62, 77–93, 98, 120, 126, 145, 184–6, 193, 198, 200–1, 204, 209, 215, 223–5, 230(n.7), 230(n.8)
authenticity, 21, 47–8, 54, 63, 74, 84–5, 88–9
autonomy, 49, 191(n.10), 195–6, 210, 215, 225–6

Bacchi, C., 82
Balibar, E., 123–5, 174, 191(n.8)
Barrett, M., 51
becoming-minor, 163, 193, 198, 212–15, 224, 227
Being and Nothingness, 44, 47, 49–50, 58(n.5), 58(n.6)
Bergson, H., 9, 102–3, 109
Berlin, I., 167, 188, 191(n.7)
Bhabha, H., 2, 18, 44, 62, 65, 71–4, 75, 97(n.1), 135
binary struggle, 2, 72; *see also* oppositional politics
blackness, 53, 63–70; *see also* aboriginality; Negritude
bloc of becoming, 104, 213
body without organs (BwO), 155–7, 160–4, 167–8, 190(n.3)
Bringing Them Home, 184, 186
Butler, J., 19, 36–9, 41, 43, 123–5

capitalism, 39, 75, 78, 117, 176–9, 188

care, 142, 170, 186–8, 191(n.10), 210, 217, 220, 235
  of the self, 140–2, 150
Césaire, A., 63
chaos, 103–8, 110, 116–17, 147, 156–8, 161, 164, 178, 182, 196
choice, 11, 40, 42–8, 71–2, 145, 153, 168, 175, 186–8, 197, 199–201, 206–7, 235–7
civilisation, 77, 79, 110, 147, 170
'civil nullius', 77–9, 202
Cixous, H., 67
coding, 67, 178–82
cohesion, 85, 112, 122–4, 222
colonial discourse, 64, 71–3, 77, 135
common commitment, 25, 122–7, 193, 197, 200, 207, 233–4, 236
common notions, 151–3, 176, 193, 207–12, 220–2, 228–9, 235–7
communitarianism, 5–6, 8, 33, 66, 87, 177, 184–5, 187, 191(n.10)
complexity theory, 127(n.3), 190(n.2)
compossibility, 150, 152, 211–12
conatus, 127(n.4), 148–50, 172, 221
concept creation, 14–17
conceptual personae, 17–18
conflict, 5, 7, 39, 47, 50, 54, 56, 59(n.7), 69, 90–1, 100, 102, 110, 117, 126, 134, 169, 182–3, 185, 208, 210, 227, 233–5
consensus, 6, 77, 126, 218, 234
consent, 42, 216–20, 227, 237
constitutionalism, 10, 79, 215–18
continuity, 166, 174, 196, 216, 221–4, 227–8, 237
Coole, D., 8, 12, 18–19, 31, 39, 51
cosmopolitanism, 85–7, 185; see also globalisation
Council for Aboriginal Reconciliation (CAR), 80–2, 87, 98(n.10), 120
counter-actualisation, 16, 113–14, 117, 142; see also deterritorialisation

counter-discourse, 60, 94–5
Critchley, S., 233–4
critical theory, 7, 18, 51, 76, 96, 118, 138, 231
culturalism, 61, 66

death of the subject, 162, 193
decolonisation, 1, 4, 19, 24, 70–1, 84–5, 95
deconstruction, 54, 60–1, 66, 70–2, 74–6, 89, 96, 206, 231
Deleuze, G., 9–10, 14–24, 55, 74, 97, 100–27, 131–81, 188–200, 205–10, 213, 215, 219–28, 232–3
democracy, 109, 126, 207, 226, 228, 234
Derrida, J., 25, 54, 55, 71, 96, 205
desire
  and lack, 8, 18, 23, 29, 34–6, 40, 41, 43–4, 49, 54, 57, 93–5, 100, 144–5
  materialism of, 145–6
  sexual, 44, 46, 73
  to be, 8, 41–2, 45–7, 52, 57, 69, 71, 146
  typology of, 14–15, 146, 148, 150–2, 177–8, 180, 186–9
desiring-production, 9, 22, 55, 105, 131, 144–7, 150, 152–3, 165, 176–82, 188, 192, 217
destruction, 35–6, 68, 89, 116, 118, 164, 172–3, 175–6, 186–8, 208, 211–12, 220–2, 228
deterritorialisation, 16, 117–20, 137, 142, 160, 166, 205, 213
  relative/absolute 117–18
Djerrkura, G., 216, 230(n.9)
diagram, 151, 160, 163–4
different/ciation, 24, 97, 106–16, 124, 158, 217, 232
disadvantage, 9, 23–4, 31, 77–83, 88, 98(n.10), 109, 110, 115, 119–21, 145–6, 187, 211

Index

Discipline and Punish, 131, 190(n.4), 198
discontinuity, 3–4, 9, 11, 95, 109, 192–3, 197–200, 212, 221, 223–4, 228, 232; *see also* exit
dispositions, 10–12, 140, 148, 153, 187, 192–200, 202, 213, 216, 223–4, 229, 232, 236; *see also* attitude; listening respect; *muldarbi*
dispossession, 80–3, 98(n.12), 226
Dodson, M., 18, 79, 83
Dodson, P., 80, 83, 204
domination, 2, 4, 21, 38–9, 61, 65, 67, 94, 96, 118, 120–1, 132–8, 140–2, 187–8, 193, 199, 216
Draft Declaration of Indigenous Rights, 86
dreaming, 92–3, 210

emanation, 103, 105, 107–8, 121
Empire, 1–2
encounter with the other, 46, 77, 11, 149–51, 169–76, 187–8, 208–9, 214, 219, 224
enjoyment, 8, 25, 80–1, 85, 90–1, 99(n.14), 119, 121, 153, 156, 176, 183–8, 196, 221–2, 232
Enlightenment, 11, 30, 61, 182, 192–9, 213, 216, 229
epistemology, 1, 11, 21, 32, 75, 95, 198
equality, 4, 65, 85, 87, 91, 109, 119–20, 186
eternal return, 167
ethology, 149–51
ethos, 4, 10–12, 20, 156, 169, 197–200, 203, 207, 233, 236–7
Eurocentrism 21, 61, 63, 78, 95
Eveline, J., 119–20
evil, 127, 173, 188
exit, 3, 192, 197–9, 212, 227–8
experimentation, 106, 160–9, 189, 197, 205–6

fabulation, 124–6
familialism, 179–82
Fanon, F., 18, 22, 29–30, 36, 40–1, 44, 56, 58, 62–70, 71, 85, 88, 90, 94, 97(n.1), 97(n.2), 176, 183
feminism, 61, 69, 97(n.6), 119, 114, 190(n.3), 191(n.10)
fixture, 41, 63, 74, 104, 107, 110, 112, 119, 122, 136–7, 146, 159, 219, 224
fold, 155–6, 168–9, 220
force relations, 10, 25, 104, 127(n.2), 132–3, 135–6, 147, 157, 164, 168, 215
Foucault, M., 4, 9, 10–11, 19, 21, 55, 71, 74, 127(n.2), 131, 135–50, 153(n.2), 154(n.4), 155, 157, 177, 190(n.4), 191(n.9), 192–200, 206, 220, 223, 229(n.2), 229(n.3), 232
Fox, N. F., 50
Frankfurt School, 51
Fraser, N., 139
freedom, 13, 40, 42, 44–9, 68–9, 109, 115, 118, 139, 141–2, 167–9, 191(n.7), 198, 201, 207, 216, 218–19, 222, 231
Freedom Rides, 98(n.12), 198
friendship, 4, 20, 25, 50, 142, 205–6, 237
futures, 2, 3, 21, 25, 106, 122, 124, 127, 140, 151–2, 194–6, 209, 216, 222, 230(n.9), 236
  future people, 21, 114, 124
  preferred future, 9, 11, 13, 123, 127, 134, 151, 153, 167, 235, 237

Gandhi, L., 25, 61, 97(n.4), 97(n.6), 206
Gatens, M., 149, 171, 190(n.3)
gaze, 45–6, 49, 63, 73, 79, 169, 183, 187

gender, 65, 74, 191(n.10)
genealogy, 45, 132, 134, 143, 150
geology, 156–8
Giroux, H., 214
globalisation, 2, 75, 88, 123
governmentality, 141
grammar, 105, 117, 127(n.3), 148, 158
Grenville, K., 18, 200, 208
Guattari, F., 10, 14–15, 17, 55, 102–4, 116–17, 122–5, 131, 136, 143–5, 147–8, 150–3, 155–68, 170, 176–82, 188, 190(n.2), 190(n.3), 190(n.5), 191(n.9), 193, 205–6, 210, 213, 220, 232–3

Hallward, P., 10, 21–2, 115–18, 122
Hardt, M., 1–2, 124, 127(n.4), 153(n.3), 207
harmony, 4, 30, 39–40, 54, 84, 91–2, 102, 117, 126, 134, 192, 195, 209
Hegel, G. W. F., 6–7, 22–4, 29, 31–42, 45, 48–51, 55–7, 58(n.2), 58(n.3), 58(n.4), 58(n.5), 60, 62–3, 70, 93, 95–6, 101, 134, 144, 177
Hindmarsh Island, 250
historicism, 61, 68, 199
  'not yet' of history, 2, 21, 68, 91, 123–4
History of Sexuality, 121, 131, 136, 140, 190(n.4)
hostility, 50–1, 90, 182, 235; see also conflict
human rights, 6–7, 85–7, 98(n.13), 117, 124, 138, 183–7, 219
hybridity, 19–20, 53, 72, 203, 215, 218

idealism, 8, 95, 145
illusions, 8, 31, 52, 54, 61, 101, 111–12, 119, 124, 186

immanent causation, 9–12, 25, 55–6, 91, 100, 105–6, 127, 132, 147–8, 151, 177, 196, 199, 213, 224
impartial justice, 85, 87
inclusion, 5, 82, 123, 187, 216
incorporeal transformation, 168; *see also* body without organs
individualism, 49, 51, 86, 117
intimacy, 206–7, 211, 213; *see also* sexual desire
invisibility, 67, 78–9, 83
Ivison, D., 18, 26(n.1), 86, 218, 227–8

Jews, 44, 47–8, 63, 65
joy, 25, 50, 127(n.4), 149–53, 156, 169, 172–3, 175–6, 186–8, 205, 207–12, 217, 219, 221, 222, 228–9, 235–7
  as motivation, 236
jurisprudence, 80, 87, 219, 224

Kant, I., 5, 8, 10–11, 51, 60, 96, 144, 177, 192–9, 206, 213, 216, 223–4, 227, 229(n.2)
knowledge, 55, 73, 87, 89, 92–3, 95, 106, 135, 143, 146, 156, 172, 194, 202, 212, 236
Kojève, A., 22–3, 30, 32, 35–7, 40–2, 45, 48, 50–1, 56–7, 58(n.3), 58(n.4), 58(n.5), 69–70, 177
Kristeva, J., 54

Lacan, J., 22, 35, 36, 51–5, 71, 125, 144, 176–7, 180–1, 183
Laclau, E., 53, 126
lack, 7–9, 18, 23, 25, 29, 31, 34–5, 41–4, 49, 51–7, 72, 76–81, 91, 93, 100, 108, 144–6, 152–3, 169, 177–83, 187–8, 192, 201, 234
land, 39, 77, 82–3, 88, 98(n.12), 186, 200–2, 209, 210, 215, 221–6

Index

Langton, M., 92
Lash, S., 142
law, 77, 79, 82, 85, 92, 98(n.13), 117, 136, 143, 179, 181, 195, 200, 210, 222–6
  indigenous, 79, 82, 87, 210, 215, 223–6
Lazarus, N., 62
legislation ,188, 209, 223; see also policy
liberalism, 5–6, 8, 26(n.1), 85–7, 177, 183–5, 187, 191(n.10), 218, 226–8, 234
liberation, 16, 61, 63, 65, 67, 71
  of desire, 147, 150–1
line of flight, 163, 189–90
listening, 19, 202–5, 235
listening respect (*miwi-ellin*), 12, 22, 25, 200, 204–7, 211, 218, 220, 229, 232, 236–7
love, 50, 54, 186, 205–6, 207

Mabo, 79–80, 193, 198, 200, 215–16, 223–5
machinism, 147–8, 157–60, 191(n.6)
macropolitics/micropolitics, 20, 124, 135–43, 177, 206, 220
Mansell, M., 88
Marxism, 7, 8, 36, 39, 41, 49, 51–2, 56, 58(n.6), 59(n.7), 61–2, 64, 66, 69, 70–1, 75–6, 94–6, 97(n.7), 117, 144
mastery, 39, 69, 93–6, 131, 138, 167, 232
  master/slave, 33, 67, 69
memory, 195
milieu, 103–4, 158–63, 167, 170–1, 173, 175, 181–2, 189, 198, 212, 219
mimicry, 73–4, 95
mind, 160, 171–2, 208
minoritarian, 39, 61, 90, 124, 213
miscegenation, 73
molar/molecular, 136, 147, 154(n.4)

motivation, 3, 7–8, 14, 30, 46, 49–50, 54, 56, 60, 76, 94, 96, 100, 144, 166, 192, 231, 233–6
Mouffe, C., 53, 126
Mudrooroo, 92
muldarbi, 200, 202–6
Multitude, 1–2, 124–5, 207
mutuality, 3, 47–8, 149–50, 173, 176, 186–7, 208–9, 211, 220, 236–7

nationalism, 61–2, 66, 71, 75–6, 87–8, 97(n.7), 98(n.11), 183, 185, 203
native title, 5, 79–80, 84–7, 98(n.9), 193, 210, 215, 223–6
Native Title Tribunal, 88
negation, 7–9, 19, 23–5, 29–40, 48–58, 59(n.7), 61–3, 66, 69–71, 76, 89–94, 96, 100–1, 108, 113, 133–4, 231
  double negation, 7, 23, 35, 92
Negri, A., 1–2, 124, 153(n.3), 207
Negritude, 63–8
network of power, 103, 135, 141
Nietzsche, F., 9, 19, 55, 127(n.2), 131–4, 140, 145, 148–9, 167, 229(n.3)
norms, 139, 141–2, 150, 175, 177, 189, 204, 213, 218, 220–1, 226–7, 237

Oedipus, 156, 176–82, 188
Of Grammatology, 71
ontology, 2, 5–10, 12, 25, 29, 32–3, 37, 54–5, 61, 66, 94, 101–8, 122, 131–2, 148–9, 192, 216–19, 227, 231–2
oppositional politics, 2, 19, 23, 60–1, 66–7, 70–2, 76, 87, 90, 93, 95, 114–15, 117, 119, 121, 204
oppression, 21, 38, 47–8, 64, 66–7, 71, 75, 89–90, 92, 96, 167, 221
Orientalism, 72, 135

Parekh, B., 227
Parry, B., 18, 71, 75, 97(n.1), 122
part-subjects, 166–7, 174–5, 213–15
passions, 149, 165, 172, 175, 210; *see also* affectivity
Patton, P., 18, 79
peace, 127, 186, 192, 195–6, 199, 213, 223, 236
Pearson, N., 90
Phenomenology of Spirit, 6, 37, 58(n.3)
plane of composition, 104–6, 117, 122, 164
plane of consistency, 160–1, 206
plane of immanence, 103, 105–6, 125–6, 155–6, 161, 164
Plato, 35, 144–5
policy, 9, 24, 82–3, 88, 98(n.13), 184
positive philosophy, 3, 9, 10, 23–4, 54–5, 80, 91, 97, 100–1, 103, 108, 111, 113–14, 118–20, 145, 152, 192, 227, 232, 235
  critique of presence, 31, 44, 55, 118–20
Postcolonial Liberalism, 218
postcolonial temporality, 2–3, 20
power relations, 9, 25, 30, 82, 136–44, 148–9, 155, 167, 177, 188–9, 191(n.9), 196–7, 219–20, 232
privilege, 4–5, 21, 75, 110, 114, 121, 187, 201, 222, 231; *see also* advantage
problem
  of aboriginality, 77–83, 88
  constitution, 17–22
progress, 6–7, 30, 36, 56, 61, 67, 76, 90, 93, 95, 182, 193–6, 199–200, 224, 229(n.2), 237
protection of interests, 10, 86, 98(n.13), 110, 138, 175, 182–3, 185, 187–8, 216, 220–1, 223, 225–6; *see also* human rights

psychoanalysis, 7, 18, 49, 51, 53, 64, 71, 76, 146, 176–82

racism, 40–1, 63–4, 66, 78–9, 81, 184, 196, 200
Rawls, J., 5, 191(n.10)
real
  Lacanian, 53, 55, 179–81
  real/ideal, 54, 145
reason, 11, 32–3, 87, 199, 220–1, 233
recognition, 29–30, 36–40, 44–9, 51, 53, 55, 57–8, 58(n.6), 59(n.7), 62–70, 76, 79–80, 83–5, 87, 89, 91–2, 94–5, 119, 134, 151, 169–70, 183, 185, 203–4, 213–17, 223–9, 232, 237
  misrecognition, 38, 47, 53, 57, 78, 83, 184, 221
reconciliation
  postcolonial, 2–3, 4, 9–10, 11–12, 14, 19, 20, 24, 30–1, 62, 77, 80–4, 90–1, 100, 114, 120, 126, 139, 145–6, 192, 203–4, 212, 214
  dialectical, 8, 30, 39, 50, 56; *see also* universals
redress of past injustice, 4, 81, 120, 170, 222
resistance, 1–2, 4, 14, 21, 24, 31, 38, 58(n.6), 60–2, 70–93, 94, 98(n.12), 111–21, 122–4, 126, 135, 137–44, 147, 193, 202
responsibility, 4, 8, 10, 12, 20–1, 24, 26, 40, 42–3, 81, 83, 113, 139, 185, 188, 199, 203, 210, 212, 216
settler, 4, 19, 83, 120, 204–5, 231
Reynolds, H., 18

sado-masochism, 45–8, 57
sadness, 149, 172, 175, 210–11, 221–2
Said, E., 18, 44, 71–2

Index

Sandel, M., 9
Sartre, J.-P., 22, 29–30, 35–6, 40–51, 54, 57–8, 58(n.5), 58(n.6), 58(n.7), 63, 65, 67, 69, 144, 169, 183
satisfaction
  dialectical/imperial, 8, 23, 25, 35–6, 37–8, 40, 43, 49, 54, 95, 131, 153, 182–3, 185, 187
  joyful, 150, 186, 188, 217
  strategic, 153, 156, 173, 176, 182
savages, 87, 143
Secret River, 200–1
self-determination, 44, 57, 64, 167–8, 171, 192, 195, 199, 211, 213, 216, 219, 223–4, 227, 229, 230(n.9), 236
self-evidence, 16, 121, 137
Senghor, L., 63
settlers, 4–5, 9, 19, 77, 90–1, 120–1, 200–2, 204–5, 209, 213, 215, 231
social imaginary, 193, 195, 200, 206
socius, 178–9
solidarity, 50, 88, 122
sovereignty, 1–2, 77, 98(n.13), 136, 138, 204, 215, 223, 225–6
Spinoza, B., 9, 12, 19, 102, 127(n.4), 131, 145, 148–52, 155(n.3), 171–4, 176, 186, 191(n.8), 209, 221
Spirit of Haida Gwaii, 203, 229(n.5)
Spivak, G., 18, 21–2, 71, 74–5, 93, 96
state, 83, 98(n.13), 136, 145, 185–7
  state-form, 137, 139
Stavrakakis, Y., 51
Stoler, L., 97(n.5), 143
Strange Multiplicity, 216, 218
strata, 103, 116, 136–7, 139, 157–69, 189, 198

style, 155–6, 165, 167–9, 176, 212, 227–8
subaltern speech, 21–2, 74–5, 204–5

Taylor, C., 9
teleology, 7, 30, 40, 42, 56, 61, 68, 91, 100, 182, 193–4, 199, 229(n.3)
terra nullius, 77–80, 98(n.8), 200, 202–4, 206, 215
theft of enjoyment, 45, 48, 99(n.14), 170, 183–7
third world literature, 71
Thousand Plateaus, 156, 160
traditions
  indigenous, 16, 19–20, 64, 88–9, 121, 174, 202–3, 210–11, 215, 221–6
  western, 5, 9, 19, 24–5, 35, 55, 70, 102, 144–5, 169, 174, 183–7, 196, 203, 205, 210, 226–9
transcendence, 5–7, 9–10, 13, 33, 37, 167, 179, 192, 194, 232; *see also* immanent causation
Tully, J., 18, 118, 203–4, 214, 216, 218, 221, 228, 229(n.5)
Turner, D., 213–4

United Nations, 81, 86, 230(n.9)
universals, 11, 32, 38–9, 48, 59(n.7), 64–6, 68–9, 84–8, 91–2, 97(n.7), 102–3, 105, 108, 110, 123–7, 138, 150, 182, 193, 229, 233
untimely, 26, 213; *see also* futures

virtual
  relationship with the actual, 15–17, 22, 103–6, 110–11, 115–18
  reality of, 107–8, 125–6
  idea, 104–6, 114, 116, 126
vitalism, 108
void, 23, 34–5, 78, 93, 116; *see also* lack

Watson, I., 18, 200, 204
Webber, J., 224–5
whiteness, 63–9, 73, 82, 121, 124;
  see also blackness
will to power, 132–4, 140–1, 144, 147–9
Wilson, V., 18, 204, 230(n.6)
Women's Business, 92

Working Group of Indigenous Peoples (WGIP), 86

Young, R., 18, 62, 72, 73, 74, 95, 176

Žižek, S., 53, 99(n.14), 183

EUP JOURNALS ONLINE
Deleuze Studies

Now three issues per year

Editor
Ian Buchanan, *Cardiff University*
Executive Editor
David Savat, *University of Western Australia*
Reviews Editor
John Marks, *University of Nottingham*
Co-editors
Claire Colebrook, Penn State
Tom Conley, Harvard University
Gary Genosko, Lakehead University
Christian Kerslake, Middlesex University
Gregg Lambert, Syracuse University

Deleuze Studies is the first paper based journal to focus exclusively on the work of Gilles Deleuze. Published triannually, and edited by a team of highly respected Deleuze scholars, *Deleuze Studies* is a forum for new work on the writings of Gilles Deleuze.

Deleuze Studies is a bold journal that challenges orthodoxies, encourages debate, invites controversy, seeks new applications, proposes new interpretations, and above all make new connections between scholars and ideas in the field. The journal publishes a wide variety of scholarly work on Gilles Deleuze, including articles that focus directly on his work, but also critical reviews of the field, as well as new translations and annotated bibliographies. It does not limit itself to any one field: it is neither a philosophy journal, nor a literature journal, nor a cultural studies journal, but all three and more.

A 2010 subscription will include a free supplementary issue of the journal, *Deleuze and Political Activism*, guest-edited by Marcelo Svirsky.

ISSN 1750-2241   eISSN 1755-1684   Three issues per year

Register to receive Table of Contents Alerts at www.eupjournals.com